Designing and Managing the Supply Chain

Concepts, Strategies, and Case Studies

David Simchi-Levi
Northwestern University, Evanston, Illinois

Philip Kaminsky
University of California, Berkeley

Edith Simchi-Levi
LogicTools, Inc., Northbrook, Illinois

Boston   Burr Ridge, IL   Dubuque, IA   Madison, WI   New York   San Francisco   St. Louis
Bangkok   Bogotá   Caracas   Lisbon   London   Madrid
Mexico City   Milan   New Delhi   Seoul   Singapore   Sydney   Taipei   Toronto

McGraw-Hill Higher Education

A Division of The **McGraw-Hill** *Companies*

This book is printed on acid-free paper.

5 6 7 8 9 0 FGR/FGR   0 9 8 7 6 5 4 3 2 1

ISBN 0-256-26168-7

Vice president/Editor-in-Chief: *Michael W. Junior*
Publisher: *Jeffrey J. Shelstad*
Senior sponsoring editor: *Scott Isenberg*
Editorial coordinator: *Nicolle Schieffer*
Senior marketing manager: *Colleen J. Suljic*
Project manager: *Kimberly Moranda*
Manager, new book production: *Melonie Salvati*
Designer: *Suzanne Montazer*
Supplement coordinator: *Rose M. Range*
New media: *Charles Pelto*
Compositor: *Techsetters, Inc.*
Typeface: *10/12 Palatino*
Printer: *Quebecor Printing Book Group/Fairfield*

Library of Congress Cataloging-in-Publication Data

Simchi-Levi, David.
    Designing and managing the supply chain / David Simchi-Levi,
Philip Kaminsky, Edith Simchi-Levi.
      p.   cm.
    Includes bibliographical references and index.
    ISBN 0-07-028594-2
    1. Physical distribution of goods—Management.   2. Marketing
channels—Management.   3. Business logistics.   4. Industrial
procurement.   I. Kaminsky, Philip.   II. Simchi-Levi, Edith.
III. Title.
HF5415.7.S425   2000
658.5—dc21   99-31791

http://www.mhhe.com

To our children, Sara and Yuval, who have the patience and humor to survive our work together

D.S.L., E.S.L.

To my family, for their support and encouragement

P.K.

THE IRWIN/MCGRAW-HILL SERIES
Operations and Decision Sciences

OPERATIONS MANAGEMENT

Bowersox and Closs, **Logistical Management: The Integrated Supply Chain Process**, *First Edition*

Chase, Aquilano, and Jacobs, **Production and Operations Management**, *Eighth Edition*

Chu, Hottenstein, and Greenlaw, **PROSIM for Windows**, *Third Edition*

Cohen and Apte, **Manufacturing Automation**, *First Edition*

Davis, Aquilano, and Chase, **Fundamentals of Operations Management**, *Third Edition*

Dobler and Burt, **Purchasing and Supply Management**, *Sixth Edition*

Flaherty, **Global Operations Management**, *First Edition*

Fitzsimmons and Fitzsimmons, **Service Management: Operations, Strategy, Information Technology**, *Second Edition*

Gray and Larson, **Project Management: The Managerial Process**, *First Edition*

Hill, **Manufacturing Strategy: Text & Cases**, *Third Edition*

Hopp and Spearman, **Factory Physics**, *Second Edition*

Lambert and Stock, **Strategic Logistics Management**, *Third Edition*

Leenders and Fearon, **Purchasing and Supply Chain Management**, *Eleventh Edition*

Melnyk and Denzler, **Operations Management**, *Second Edition*

Moses, Seshadri, and Yakir, **HOM Operations Management Software for Windows**, *First Edition*

Nahmias, **Production and Operations Analysis**, *Third Edition*

Nicholas, **Competitive Manufacturing Management**, *First Edition*

Pinedo and Chao, **Operations Scheduling**, *First Edition*

Sanderson and Uzumeri, **Managing Product Families**, *First Edition*

Schroeder, **Operations Management: Contemporary Concepts and Cases**, *First Edition*

Schonberger and Knod, **Operations Management: Customer-Focused Principles**, *Sixth Edition*

Simchi-Levi, Kaminsky, Simchi-Levi, **Designing and Managing the Supply Chain: Concepts, Strategies, and Case Studies**, *First Edition*

Sterman, **Business Dynamics: Systems Thinking and Modeling for a Complex World**, *First Edition*

Stevenson, **Production/Operations Management**, *Sixth Edition*

Vollmann, Berry, and Whybark, **Manufacturing Planning & Control Systems**, *Fourth Edition*

Zipkin, **Foundations of Inventory Management**, *First Edition*

QUANTITATIVE METHODS AND MANAGEMENT SCIENCE

Bodily, Carraway, Frey, Pfeifer, **Quantitative Business Analysis: Casebook**, *First Edition*

Bodily, Carraway, Frey, Pfeifer, **Quantitative Business Analysis: Text and Cases**, *First Edition*

Bonini, Hausman, and Bierman, **Quantitative Analysis for Business Decisions**, *Ninth Edition*

Hesse, **Managerial Spreadsheet Modeling and Analysis**, *First Edition*

Hillier, Hillier, Lieberman, **Introduction to Management Science: A Modeling and Case Studies Approach with Spreadsheets**, *First Edition*

About the Authors

David Simchi-Levi is Professor of Industrial Engineering and Management Science at Northwestern University. Prior to joining the faculty at Northwestern, he taught at Columbia University. Professor Simchi-Levi received his Ph.D. in operations research from Tel-Aviv University and has won awards for his work in supply chain, logistics, and transportation. He is the co-author, with Julien Bramel, of *The Logic of Logistics*, published by Springer-Verlag, and the founder and chairman of LogicTools, Inc., a company that provides decision support software for supply chain and logistics management.

Philip Kaminsky is Assistant Professor of Industrial Engineering at the University of California at Berkeley. He received his Ph.D. in Industrial Engineering from Northwestern University. Prior to his graduate studies, he worked for the production division of Merck & Co., Inc. He has consulted in the areas of supply chain and production management.

Edith Simchi-Levi is President of LogicTools, Inc. She received her B.S. in Mathematics and Computer Science from Tel-Aviv University. She has extensive experience in software development and numerous consulting projects in logistics and supply chain management.

Foreword

In the last few years we have seen an explosion of publications on supply chain management; numerous books have been published and many articles have appeared in academic, trade, and popular magazines. These publications are either too technical—and therefore inaccessible to practitioners and students—or they lack the breadth and depth that the topic deserves. Certainly, it is difficult to find a book appropriate for teaching supply chain management to business or engineering students. *Designing and Managing the Supply Chain* solves this problem!

The book is an important contribution and major milestone for the supply chain community. It is the first book that covers a comprehensive breadth of supply chain topics in depth, and addresses the major challenges in this area. It was written by experts from academia and industry who have been researching, consulting, and developing software for supply chain management for many years.

This book includes many classic and new case studies, numerous examples as well as in-depth analysis of some of the technical issues involved in inventory management, network design, and strategic partnering, to name a few. It is therefore an ideal textbook for classes on supply chain management at the undergraduate, Master's, and M.B.A. levels. Since each chapter is self-contained, instructors can pick the chapters they want to use, depending on the length of the class and its requirements. The book comes with two computerized games. The Computerized Beer Game provides an excellent instructional tool that engages students in managing a supply chain and provides a starting point for discussing the value of information in the supply chain, strategic partnering, centralized decision making, etc. The Risk Pool Game allows students to gain insight on an important concept in supply chain management, called risk pooling. The authors have been most creative in using games to motivate and expose students to challenging subjects.

Finally, since many companies view supply chain management as the core of their business strategy, this book will also be of interest to managers involved in any of the processes that make up the supply chain.

I want to compliment the authors for having written such an outstanding textbook for the supply chain community.

Hau L. Lee
Kleiner Perkins, Mayfield, Sequoia Capital Professor
Director, Stanford Global Supply Chain Forum
Stanford University

Preface

This book grew out of a number of supply chain management courses and Executive Education programs we have taught at Northwestern University over the past several years, as well as numerous consulting projects and supply chain decision-support systems we have developed at Logic-Tools. The courses, taught in the Master of Management in Manufacturing (M.M.M.) program, a joint M.B.A. program between the Kellogg School of Business and McCormick School of Engineering at Northwestern University, and in Executive Education programs sponsored by Kellogg, have spawned many innovative and effective supply chain education concepts. The focus in these programs has been on presenting, in an easily accessible manner, recently developed state-of-the-art models and solution methods important in the design, control, and operation of supply chains. The consulting projects and decision-support systems developed by LogicTools have focused on applying these advanced techniques to solve specific problems faced by our clients.

Interest in supply chain management, both in industry and in academia, has grown rapidly over the past several years. A number of major forces have contributed to this trend. First, in recent years it has become clear that many companies have reduced manufacturing costs as much as practically possible. Many of these companies are discovering the magnitude of savings that can be achieved by planning and managing their supply chain more effectively. Indeed, a striking example is Wal-Mart's success, which is partly attributed to implementing a new logistics strategy called cross-docking. At the same time, information and communication systems have been widely implemented, and provide access to comprehensive data from all components of the supply chain. Finally, deregulation of the transportation industry has led to the development of a variety of transportation modes and reduced transportation costs, while significantly increasing the complexity of logistics systems.

It is therefore not surprising that many companies are involved in the analysis of their supply chains. In most cases, however, this analysis is performed based on experience and intuition; very few analytical models or design tools have been used in this process. In contrast, in the last two decades the academic community has developed various models and tools for supply chain management. Unfortunately, the first generation of this technology was not robust or flexible enough to allow industry to use it effectively. This, however, has changed over the last few years during which improved analysis and insight, and effective models and decision-support systems, have been developed, but these are not necessarily familiar to industry. Indeed, to our knowledge there is no published work that discusses these problems, models, concepts, and tools at an appropriate level.

In this book, we intend to fill this gap by providing state-of-the-art models, concepts, and solution methods important in the design, control, operation, and management of supply chain systems. In particular, we have attempted to convey both the intuition behind many key supply chain concepts and to provide simple techniques that can be used to analyze various aspects of the supply chain.

The emphasis is on a format that will be accessible to executives and practitioners, as well as students interested in careers in related industries. In addition, it will introduce readers to information systems and decision-support tools that can aid in the design, analysis, and control of supply chains.

The book is written to serve as:

- A textbook for M.B.A.-level logistics and supply chain management courses.
- A textbook for B.S. and M.S. industrial engineering courses on logistics and supply chain management.
- A reference for teachers, consultants, and practitioners involved in any one of the processes that make up the supply chain.

Of course, supply chain management is a very broad area, and it would be impossible for a single book to cover all of the relevant areas in depth. Indeed, there is considerable disagreement in academia and industry about exactly what these relevant areas are. Nevertheless, we have attempted to provide a broad introduction to many critical facets of supply chain management. Although many essential supply chain management issues are interrelated, we have strived wherever possible to make each chapter as self-contained as possible, so that the reader can refer directly to chapters covering topics of interest. The discussion ranges from basic topics of inventory management, logistics network design, distribution systems, and customer value to more advanced topics of strategic alliances, the value of information in the supply chain, information technology and decisions support systems, and international issues in supply chain management. Each chapter utilizes numerous case studies and examples, and mathematical and techical sections can be skipped without loss of continuity.

In addition, the book includes two software packages, the **Computerized Beer Game** and the **Risk Pool Game**, which help to illustrate many of the concepts we discuss in the book. Indeed, in teaching executives and M.B.A. students we have found that these games help students better understand issues and concepts such as the bullwhip effect, the value of information in the supply chain, and the impact of lead times, centralized decision making, and risk pooling on supply chain operations.

Parts of this book are based on work we have done either together or with others. Chapters 1 and 2 borrow extensively from *The Logic of Logistics*, written by Julien Bramel and David Simchi-Levi and published by Springer in 1997. This, of course, is done by permission of the copyright owner. The Computerized Beer Game is discussed in an article by Philip Kaminsky and David Simchi-Levi which appeared in *Supply Chain and Technology Management*, edited by Hau Lee and Shu Ming Ng and published by The Production and Operations Management Society. Some of the material on the bullwhip effect appears in an article by Chen, Drezner, Ryan, and Simchi-Levi in *Quantitative Models for Supply Chain Management*, edited by Sridhar Tayur, Ram Ganeshan, and Michael Magazine, and published by Kluwer Academic Publishers.

Acknowledgments

It is our pleasure to acknowledge all those who helped us with this manuscript. First, we would like to thank Dr. Myron Feinstein, former director of supply chain strategy development at Unilever, New York City, who read through and commented on various chapters. Similarly, we are indebted to the reviewers, Professors Michael Ball (University of Maryland), Wendell Gilland (University of North Carolina, Chapel Hill), Eric Johnson (Vanderbilt University), Douglas Morrice (The University of Texas, Austin), Michael Pangburn (Pennsylvania State University), Powell Robinson (Texas A&M University), William Tallon (Northern Illinois University), and Rachel Yang (University of Illinois, Urbana-Champaign). Their comments were invaluable in improving the organization and presentation of the book. We are also grateful to Deniz Caglar, a Ph.D. candidate at Northwestern University, for his comments on earlier drafts of the book. In addition, we thank Dr. Kathleen A. Stair and Ms. Ann Stuart for carefully editing and proofreading many chapters.

Finally, we wish to thank Ms. Colleen Tuscher, who assisted us in the initial stage of the project, our editor, Mr. Scott Isenberg, and his assistant, Ms. Nicolle Schieffer, of Irwin/McGraw-Hill, who encouraged us throughout and helped us complete the book. Also, thanks to Ms. Kimberly Moranda and the production staff at McGraw-Hill for their help.

David Simchi-Levi, Evanston, Illinois
Philip Kaminsky, Berkeley, California
Edith Simchi-Levi, Northbrook, Illinois

List of Cases

Brief Contents

Contents

Introduction to Supply Chain Management

1.1 What Is Supply Chain Management?

Fierce competition in today's global markets, the introduction of products with short life cycles, and the heightened expectations of customers have forced business enterprises to invest in, and focus attention on, their supply chains. This, together with continuing advances in communications and transportation technologies (e.g., mobile communication and overnight delivery) has motivated the continuous evolution of the supply chain and of the techniques to manage it.

In a typical supply chain, raw materials are procured, items are produced at one or more factories, shipped to warehouses for intermediate storage, and then shipped to retailers or customers. Consequently, to reduce cost and improve service levels, effective supply chain strategies must take into account the interactions at the various levels in the supply chain. The supply chain, which is also referred to as the *logistics network*, consists of suppliers, manufacturing centers, warehouses, distribution centers, and retail outlets, as well as raw materials, work-in-process inventory, and finished products that flow between the facilities (see Figure 1.1).

In this book, we present and explain concepts, insights, practical tools, and decision support systems important for the effective management of the supply chain. But what exactly is *supply chain management*? We define it as follows:

> Supply chain management is a set of approaches utilized to efficiently integrate suppliers, manufacturers, warehouses, and stores, so that merchandise is produced and distributed at the right quantities, to the right locations, and at the right time, in order to minimize systemwide costs while satisfying service level requirements.

FIGURE 1.1

The logistics network

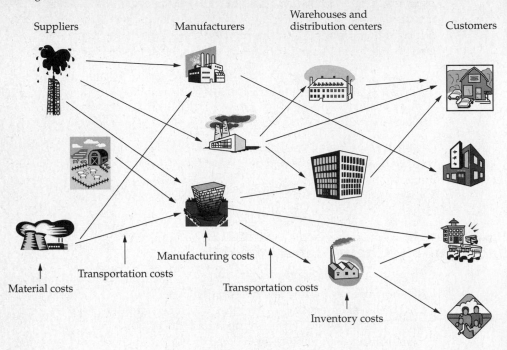

This definition leads to several observations. First, supply chain management takes into consideration every facility that has an impact on cost and plays a role in making the product conform to customer requirements; from supplier and manufacturing facilities through warehouses and distribution centers to retailers and stores. Indeed, in some supply chain analysis, it is necessary to account for the suppliers' suppliers and the customers' customers because they have an impact on supply chain performance.

Second, the objective of supply chain management is to be efficient and cost-effective across the entire system; total systemwide costs, from transportation and distribution to inventories of raw materials, work in process, and finished goods, are to be minimized. Thus, the emphasis is not on simply minimizing transportation cost or reducing inventories, but rather, on taking a *systems approach* to supply chain management.

Finally, because supply chain management revolves around efficient integration of suppliers, manufacturers, warehouses, and stores, it encompasses the firm's activities at many levels, from the strategic level through the tactical to the operational level.

Of course, a natural question is what is the difference between supply chain management and logistics management? While the answer, surprisingly, will vary depending on who is addressing this issue, we do not distinguish between logistics and supply chain management. Indeed, our definition of supply chain management is similar to the definition of *logistics management* given by the Council of Logistics Management:

> The process of planning, implementing and controlling the efficient, cost effective flow and storage of raw materials, in-process inventory, finished goods, and related information from point-of-origin to point-of-consumption for the purpose of conforming to customer requirements.

Both definitions place great emphasis on the integration of the different components in the supply chain. Indeed, it is only through supply chain integration that the firm can significantly reduce costs and improve service levels. Unfortunately, supply chain integration is difficult for two main reasons:

1. Different facilities in the supply chain may have *different, conflicting, objectives*. For instance, suppliers typically want manufacturers to commit themselves to purchasing large quantities in stable volumes with flexible delivery dates. Unfortunately, although most manufacturers would like to implement long production runs, they need to be flexible to their customers' needs and changing demands. Thus, the suppliers' goals are in direct conflict with the manufacturers' desire for flexibility. Indeed, since production decisions are typically made without precise information about customer demand, the ability of manufacturers to match supply and demand depends largely on their ability to change supply volume as information about demand arrives. Similarly, the manufacturers' objective of making large production batches typically conflicts with the objective of both warehouses and distribution centers to reduce inventory. To make matters worse, this latter objective of reducing inventory levels typically implies an increase in transportation costs.

2. The supply chain is a *dynamic system* that evolves over time. Indeed, not only do customer demand and supplier capabilities change over time, but supply chain relationships also evolve over time. For example, as customers' power increases, there is increased pressure placed on manufacturers and suppliers to produce an enormous variety of high-quality products and, ultimately, to produce customized products. Also, even when customer demand for specific products does not vary greatly, inventory and back-order levels fluctuate considerably across the supply chain. To illustrate this issue, consider Figure 1.2, which suggests that in a typical supply chain, distributor orders to the factory fluctuate far more than the underlying retailer demand.

FIGURE 1.2

Order variations in the supply chain

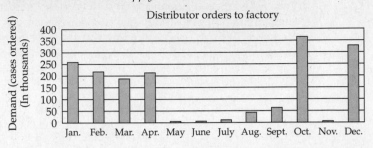

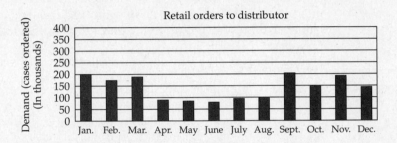

Example 1.1.1	A Korean manufacturer of electrical products such as industrial relays is facing a service level of about 70 percent; that is, only about 70 percent of all orders are delivered on time. On the other hand, inventory keeps piling up, mostly of products that are not in demand. The manufacturer's inventory turnover ratio, defined as the ratio of the annual flow to average inventory at the manufacturer's main warehouse, is about four. However, in the electronics industry, leading companies turn inventory over about nine times a year. If the Korean manufacturer can increase its inventory turns to this level, it will be able to significantly reduce inventory levels. The manufacturer is thus searching for new strategies that will increase service levels over the next three years to about 99 percent and, at the same time, significantly decrease inventory levels and cost.

Just a few years ago, most analysts would have said that these two objectives, improved service and inventory levels, cannot be achieved at the same time. Indeed, traditional inventory theory tells us that to increase service level, the firm must increase inventory and therefore cost. Surprisingly, recent developments in information and communications technologies, together with a better understanding of supply chain strategies, has lead to innovative approaches that allow the firm to improve both objectives simultaneously.

1.2 Why Supply Chain Management?

In the 1980s companies discovered new manufacturing technologies and strategies that allowed them to reduce costs and better compete in different markets. Strategies such as just-in-time manufacturing, *kanban*, lean manufacturing, total quality management, and others became very popular, and vast quantities of resources were invested in implementing these strategies. In the last few years, however, it has become clear that many companies have reduced manufacturing costs as much as is practically possible. Many of these companies are discovering that effective supply chain management is the next step they need to take in order to increase profit and market share.

Indeed, in 1997 American companies spent $862 billion, or about 10 percent of the United States gross national product (GNP), on supply related activities, see "State of Logistics Report," published by Robert V. Delaney. This figure includes the cost of movement, storage, and control of products across the supply chain, both within manufacturing plants and warehouses and between different components of the supply chain. Unfortunately, this huge investment typically includes many unnecessary cost components due to redundant stock, inefficient transportation strategies, and other wasteful practices in the supply chain. For instance, experts believe that the grocery industry can save about $30 billion, or 10 percent of its annual operating cost, by using more effective supply chain strategies [44].

To illustrate this issue, consider the following two examples:

1. It takes a typical box of cereal more than three months to get from the factory to a supermarket,
2. It takes a typical new car, on average, 15 days to travel from the factory to the dealership. This lead time should be compared with the actual travel time which is no more than four to five days.

Thus, many opportunities exist to cut costs in the supply chain. Not surprisingly, a number of companies have been able to substantially increase revenue or decrease costs through effective supply chain management.

Example 1.2.1 | Procter & Gamble estimates that it saved retail customers $65 million over the past 18 months. "According to Procter & Gamble, the essence of its approach lies in manufacturers and suppliers working closely together . . . jointly creating business plans to eliminate the source of wasteful practices across the entire supply chain" [114].

The example suggests that *strategic partnerships* between suppliers and manufacturers may have a significant impact on supply chain performance. What are the types of *business plans* and *partnerships* that can best reduce costs and improve service levels? Which one is appropriate for the particular situation at hand? What incentives and performance measures should be used to make the partnership successful? Finally, how should the benefits resulting from the strategic partnerships be shared? Should the cost savings be transferred to the customers, split between the different partners, or kept by the most powerful player?

Example 1.2.2	In two years National Semiconductor reduced distribution costs by 2.5 percent, decreased delivery time by 47 percent, and increased sales by 34 percent by closing six warehouses around the globe and air-freighting microchips to customers from a new centralized distribution center in Singapore [44].

Of course, by switching to air carriers, National Semiconductor increased transportation costs significantly. This increase was offset by a reduction in inventory costs resulting from the shift from a decentralized distribution system with a number of warehouses to a centralized system with a single warehouse. This example motivates the following question: What are the correct trade-offs between inventory and transportation costs?

Example 1.2.3	In 1979 Kmart was one of the leading companies in the retail industry, with 1,891 stores and average revenues per store of $7.25 million. At that time Wal-Mart was a small niche retailer in the South with only 229 stores and average revenues about half those of Kmart stores. In 10 years Wal-Mart had transformed itself; in 1992 it had the highest sales per square foot and the highest inventory turnover and operating profit of any discount retailer. Today Wal-Mart is the largest and highest profit retailer in the world. How did Wal-Mart do it? The starting point was a relentless focus on satisfying customer needs; Wal-Mart's goal was simply to provide customers with access to goods when and where they want them and to develop cost structures that enable competitive pricing. The key to achieving this goal was to make the way the company replenishes inventory the centerpiece of its strategy. This was done by using a logistics technique known as *cross-docking*. In this strategy, goods are continuously delivered to Wal-Mart's warehouses from where they are dispatched to stores without ever sitting in inventory. This strategy reduced Wal-Mart's cost of sales significantly and made it possible to offer everyday low prices to their customers [106].

If the cross-docking strategy works so well for Wal-Mart, shouldn't all companies use the same strategy? Clearly, different retail chains use other distribution strategies. These include strategies such as:

- *The traditional distribution strategy* in which inventory is kept at the warehouses.
- *Direct shipping* in which goods are distributed from the suppliers directly to the retail stores.

Throughout the rest of this book, we endeavor to address each of these issues in detail. We will focus not only on demonstrating why certain strategies are adopted and what the trade-offs are between different strategies, but also on explaining how specific strategies are implemented in practice.

1.3 The Complexity

The previous section described a number of supply chain management success stories. If these firms have improved supply chain performance by focusing on strategic partnering, using centralized warehousing, or employing the cross-docking strategy, what inhibits other firms from adopting the same techniques to improve their supply chain performance?

The answer seems to involve a number of major issues:

1. The supply chain is a complex network of facilities and organizations with different, conflicting objectives. This implies that finding the best supply chain strategy for a particular firm poses significant challenges. The following example illustrates a network that is fairly typical of today's global companies.

Example 1.3.1 | National Semiconductor, whose list of competitors includes Motorola Inc. and the Intel Corporation, is one of the world's largest chipmakers whose products are used in fax machines, cellular phones, computers, and cars. Currently, the company has four wafer fabrication facilities, three in the United States and one in Great Britain, and has test and assembly sites in Malaysia and Singapore. After assembly, finished products are shipped to hundreds of manufacturing facilities all over the world, including those of Compaq, Ford, IBM, and Siemens. Since the semiconductor industry is highly competitive, specifying short lead times and being able to deliver within the committed due date is critical. In 1994, 95 percent of National Semiconductor's customers received their orders within 45 days from the time the order was placed while the remaining 5 percent received their orders within 90 days. These tight lead times required the company to involve 12 different airline carriers using about 20,000 different routes. The difficulty, of course, was that no customer knew in advance if they were going to be part of the 5 percent of customers who received their order in 90 days, or the 95 percent who received their order within 45 days [44].

---

2. Matching supply and demand is a major challenge:

- Boeing Aircraft announced a write-down of $2.6 billion in October 1997 due to "raw material shortages, internal and supplier parts shortages and productivity inefficiencies. . ." [115].
- "Second quarter sales at U.S. Surgical Corporation declined 25 percent, resulting in a loss of $22 million. The sales and earnings shortfall is attributed to larger than anticipated inventories on the shelves of hospitals" [116].
- "IBM sells out New Aptiva PC; Shortage may cost millions in potential revenue" [117].

Obviously, this difficulty stems from the fact that months before demand is realized, manufacturers have to commit themselves to specific production levels. These advance commitments imply huge financial and supply risks.

3. System variations over time are also an important consideration. Even when demand is known precisely (e.g., because of contractual agreements), the planning process needs to account for demand and cost parameters varying over time due to the impact of seasonal fluctuations, trends, advertising and promotions, competitors' pricing strategies, and so forth. These time-varying demand and cost parameters make it difficult to determine the most effective supply chain management strategy; that is, the one that minimizes systemwide costs and conforms to customer requirements.

4. Many supply chain problems are new and there is no clear understanding of all of the issues involved. For instance, in high-tech industries, product life cycles are becoming shorter and shorter. In particular, many computer and printer models have life cycles of only a few months, so the manufacturer may have only one order or production opportunity. Unfortunately, since these are new products, no historical data is available that allows the manufacturer to accurately predict customer demand. At the same time, the proliferation of products in these industries makes it increasingly difficult to predict demand for a specific model. Finally, significant price declines in these industries are common, reducing the product value during its life cycle [83].

The previous examples also suggest that in some industries supply chain management is perhaps the single most important factor determining the success of the firm. Indeed, in the computer and printer industries, where most manufacturers use the same suppliers and identical technologies, companies compete on cost and service levels, the two key elements in our definition of supply chain management.

1.4 Key Issues in Supply Chain Management

In this section, we introduce some of the supply chain management issues that we discuss in much more detail throughout the remaining chapters.

These issues span a large spectrum of a firm's activities, from the strategic through the tactical to the operational level:

- The *strategic level* deals with decisions that have a long-lasting effect on the firm. This includes decisions regarding the number, location, and capacity of warehouses and manufacturing plants, and the flow of material through the logistics network.
- The *tactical level* includes decisions which are typically updated anywhere between once every quarter and once every year. These include purchasing and production decisions, inventory policies, and transportation strategies including the frequency with which customers are visited.
- The *operational level* refers to day-to-day decisions such as scheduling, lead time quotations, routing, and truck loading.

We introduce and discuss some of the key issues, questions, and trade-offs associated with different decisions below:

Distribution Network Configuration

Consider several plants producing products to serve a set of geographically dispersed retailers. The current set of warehouses is deemed inappropriate, and management wants to reorganize or redesign the distribution network. This may be due, for example, to changing demand patterns or the termination of a leasing contract for a number of existing warehouses. In addition, changing demand patterns may require a change in plant production levels, a selection of new suppliers, and a new flow pattern of goods throughout the distribution network. How should management select a set of warehouse locations and capacities, determine production levels for each product at each plant, and set transportation flows between facilities, either from plant to warehouse or warehouse to retailer, in such a way as to minimize total production, inventory, and transportation costs and satisfy service level requirements?

Inventory Control

Consider a retailer that maintains an inventory of a particular product. Since customer demand changes over time, the retailer can use only historical data to predict demand. The retailer's objective is to decide at what point to reorder a new batch of the product, and how much to order so as to minimize inventory ordering and holding costs. More fundamentally, why should the retailer hold inventory in the first place? Is it due to uncertainty in customer demand, uncertainty in the supply process, or some other reasons? If it is due to uncertainty in customer demand, is there anything that can be done to reduce it? What is the impact of the forecasting tool used to predict customer demand? Should the retailer order more than, less than, or exactly the demand forecast? And, finally, what inventory turnover ratio should be used? Does it change from industry to industry?

Distribution Strategies

Wal-Mart's recent success story highlights the importance of a particular distribution strategy referred to as *cross-docking*. As observed earlier, this is a distribution strategy in which the stores are supplied by central warehouses which act as coordinators of the supply process and as transshipment points for incoming orders from outside vendors, but which do not keep stock themselves. We refer to such warehouses as *cross-dock points*. Consider the following questions: How many cross-dock points are necessary? What are the savings achieved using a cross-docking strategy? How should a cross-docking strategy be implemented in practice? Is the cross-docking strategy better than the classical strategy in which warehouses hold inventory? Which strategy should a particular firm employ: the cross-docking strategy, the classical distribution strategy in which inventory is kept at the warehouses, or direct shipping, a strategy in which items are shipped from suppliers directly to stores?

Supply Chain Integration and Strategic Partnering

As observed earlier, integrating the supply chain is quite difficult because of its dynamics and the conflicting objectives employed by different facilities and partners. Nevertheless, the National Semiconductor, Wal-Mart, and Procter & Gamble success stories demonstrate not only that integrating the supply chain is possible, but that it can have a huge impact on the company's performance and market share. Of course, one can argue that these three examples are associated with companies that are among the biggest companies in their respective industries; these companies can implement technologies and strategies that very few others can afford. However, in today's competitive markets, most companies have no choice; they are forced to integrate their supply chain and engage in strategic partnering. This pressure stems from both their customers and their supply chain partners. How can integration be achieved successfully? Clearly, information sharing and operational planning are the keys to a successfully integrated supply chain. But what information should be shared? How should it be used? How does information affect the design and operation of the supply chain? What level of integration is needed within the organization and with external partners? Finally, what types of partnerships can be implemented, and which type should be implemented for a given situation?

Product Design

Effective design plays several critical roles in the supply chain. Most obviously, certain product designs may increase inventory holding or transportation costs relative to other designs, while other designs may facilitate a shorter manufacturing lead time. Unfortunately, product redesign is often expensive. When is it worthwhile to redesign products so as to reduce logistics costs or supply chain lead times? Is it possible to leverage product design to compensate for uncertainty in customer demand? Can one quantify the amount of savings resulting from such a strategy? What changes should be made in the supply chain to take advantage of the new product design? Finally, new concepts such as mass customization are increasingly popular. What role does supply chain management play in the successful implementation of these concepts?

Information Technology and Decision-Support Systems

Information technology is a critical enabler of effective supply chain management. Indeed, much of the current interest in supply chain management is motivated by the opportunities that appeared due to the abundance of data and the savings that can be achieved by sophisticated analysis of these data. The primary issue in supply chain management is not whether data can be received, but what data should be transferred; that is, which data are significant for supply chain management and which data can safely be ignored? How should the data be analyzed and used? What is the impact of the Internet? What is the role of electronic commerce? What infrastructure is required both internally and between supply chain partners? Finally, since information technology and decision-support systems are both available, can these technologies be viewed as the main tools used to achieve competitive advantage in the market? If they can, then what is preventing others from using the same technology?

Customer Value

Customer value is the measure of a company's contribution to its customer, based on the entire range of products, services, and intangibles that constitute the company's offerings. In recent years this measure has superseded measures such as quality and customer satisfaction. Obviously, effective supply chain management is critical if a firm wishes to fulfill customer needs and provide value. But what determines customer value in different industries? How is customer value measured? How is information technology used to enhance customer value in the supply chain? How does supply chain management contribute to customer value? How do emerging trends in customer value, such as development of relationships and experiences, affect supply chain management?

1.5   Book Objectives and Overview

For many reasons, interest in logistics and supply chain management has grown explosively in the last few years. This interest has led many companies to analyze their supply chains. In most cases, however, this has been done based on experience and intuition; very few analytical models or design tools have been used in this process. On the other hand, in the last two decades the academic community has developed various models and tools to assist with the management of the supply chain. Unfortunately, the first generation of this technology was not robust or flexible enough to be effectively utilized by industry. This, however, has changed in the last few years. Analysis and insight have improved, and effective models and decision-support systems have been developed—but these may not be familiar to industry.

This book aims to fill this gap by presenting state-of-the-art models and solution methods important in the design, control, operation, and management of supply chain systems. We intend this book to be useful both as a textbook for MBA-level logistics and supply chain courses, and as a reference for teachers, consultants, and managers involved in any one of the processes that make up the supply chain.

Each chapter includes case studies and numerous examples. In addition, each chapter is mostly self-contained, and mathematical and technical sections can be skipped without loss of continuity. Therefore, we believe the book is accessible to anyone with an interest in some of the many aspects of supply chain management. For example, transportation managers deciding which modes of transportation to use, inventory control managers wanting to ensure smooth production with as little inventory as possible, purchasing/supply managers designing contracts with their company's suppliers and clients, and logistics managers in charge of their company's supply chains can all benefit from the contents of this book.

The book includes chapters covering the following topics.

- Network configuration and site location.
- Inventory management.
- The value of information.
- Distribution strategies.
- Strategic alliances.
- International supply chain management.
- Supply chain management and product design.
- Customer value.
- Information technology.
- Decision-support systems.

In addition, two software packages, the **Computerized Beer Game** and the **Risk Pool Game**, are included with the book. The Computerized Beer Game is an advanced version of a traditional supply chain management role-playing simulation, first developed at MIT. In addition to replicating the traditional board-based game, the Computerized Beer Game has many options and features that enable the reader to explore a variety of simple and advanced supply chain management concepts which cannot be easily taught using the traditional game. This includes the value of information sharing, the impact of long and short lead times, and the difference between centralized and decentralized decision making on supply chain performance. This game complements much of what we discuss in the text; in particular, it helps to clarify many of the points raised in Chapter 4.

Similarly, the Risk Pool Game was developed to illustrate important issues in inventory management and, in particular, an important concept in supply chain management referred to as *risk pooling*, a concept that we discuss in Chapter 3. In the game, the player simultaneously manages both a supply chain with a single warehouse, and a supply chain without any warehouse. In the latter case, the player delivers finished goods directly from the suppliers to the retail outlets. Throughout the game, the software records the profits of both supply chains, so that the player can compare the performance of the centralized and decentralized systems.

CHAPTER
2

Logistics Network Configuration

CASE: THE BIS CORPORATION

The Bis Corporation is a company that produces and distributes soft drinks. Currently, two manufacturing plants located in Atlanta and Denver serve about 120,000 accounts—that is, retailers or stores—all over the United States. The current distribution system requires that all products be shipped to the three existing warehouses in Chicago, Dallas, and Sacramento prior to delivery to the retail accounts. The company was established in 1964 as a family venture and grew in the 1970s and 1980s at a fairly steady rate. Bis is now owned by 12 shareholders and run by a newly appointed CEO.

The marginal revenue in the soft drink industry is about 20 percent, and the value of each SKU (stock keeping unit) is $1,000 for all products. Despite high profitability, the new CEO is concerned that the distribution network is not the most efficient one. In a recent shareholder meeting, he pointed out that the current distribution strategy used by Bis was designed about 15 years ago and was never modified. It consists of the following steps:

- Produce and store at the manufacturing plants.
- Pick, load, and ship to a warehouse/distribution center.
- Unload and store at the warehouse.
- Pick, load, and deliver to stores.

Thus, the shareholders decided to look for outside help in modifying their logistics network. Your company was able to get the engagement, after six months of continuous work by the marketing division. The commitment you made when you received the engagement was to improve the effectiveness and to align the cost of service with account profitability. In your original proposal you mentioned that

Source: Bis is a fictional company. The material in this case is loosely based on our experience with several companies.

15

"this will be accomplished by reengineering the sales and distribution functions." It seems that the concept of reengineering the entire distribution network, together with your commitment not only to the design but also to the implementation of the new distribution strategy, is what made your proposal attractive to Bis shareholders.

Since this is a huge project, you recognize that you can do a number of things rather quickly. In particular, in the first phase, which you have just completed, you identified about 10,000 accounts that should receive deliveries directly from the manufacturing plants. This was based on:

- Dock receiving capabilities
- Storage capabilities
- Receiving methodologies
- Merchandising requirements
- Order-generation capabilities
- Delivery time window constraints
- Current pricing
- Promotional activity patterns

It is now time to redesign the distribution network. For this purpose, you have grouped the accounts into 250 zones and the different products into five product families.

The data collected include the following:

1. Demand in 1997 by SKU per product family for each customer zone.
2. Annual production capacity (in SKUs) at each manufacturing plant.
3. Maximum capacity (SKUs) for each warehouse, new and existing (35,000).
4. Transportation costs per product family per mile for distributing products from the manufacturing plants and from the warehouses.
5. Setup cost for establishing a warehouse.

Customer service is of particular concern to Bis because there are a number of competing products in the markets. No specific dollar figure can be attached to a specific level of service; however, the CEO insists that to remain competitive, delivery time should be no more than 48 hours. This implies that the distance between a warehouse and a customer zone should not be more than 900 miles.

The Bis Corporation has just finished a comprehensive market study that shows significant volume growth in its markets. This growth is estimated to be uniform across the different zones, but it varies from product to product. The estimated yearly growth for 1998 and 1999 is given in the following table.

Estimated Yearly Growth

Family	1	2	3	4	5
Multiplier	1.07	1.03	1.06	1.05	1.06

The variable production cost at the two manufacturing facilities varies by product and by manufacturing plant. The CEO and company shareholders oppose building a new manufacturing plant because of the costs and risks involved. They are willing, however, to expand production capacities at the existing plants as needed. They estimate that increasing production capacity for a family would cost about $2,000 for every 100 SKUs.

The Bis Corporation would like to address the following issues:

1. Does the model developed truly represent Bis's logistics network? How can the Bis Corporation validate the model? What is the impact of aggregating customers and products on the model accuracy?
2. How many distribution centers should be established?
3. Where should they be located?
4. How should the plant's output of each product be allocated between warehouses?
5. Should production capacity be expanded? When and where?

At the end of the chapter, we will suggest one way to analyze the case.

By the end of this chapter, you should be able to understand the following issues:

- How a company can develop a model representing its logistics network.
- How a company can validate this model.
- How aggregating customers and products affects the accuracy of the model.
- How a company knows how many distribution centers to establish.
- How a company knows where to locate these distribution centers.
- How a company allocates the output of each product in its plants among its distribution centers.
- How a company knows whether, when, and where to expand its production capacity.

2.1 Introduction

The logistics network (see Chapter 1) consists of suppliers, warehouses, distribution centers, and retail outlets as well as raw materials, work-in-process inventory, and finished products that flow between the facilities. In this chapter, we present some of the issues involved in the design and configuration of the logistics network.

Network configuration may involve issues relating to plant, warehouse, and retailer location. As explained in Chapter 1, these are strategic decisions because they have a long-lasting effect on the firm. In the discussion below, we concentrate on the following key strategic decisions:

1. Determining the appropriate number of warehouses.
2. Determining the location of each warehouse.
3. Determining the size of each warehouse.
4. Allocating space for products in each warehouse.
5. Determining which products customers will receive from each warehouse.

We therefore assume that plant and retailer locations will not be changed. The objective is to design or reconfigure the logistics network so as to minimize annual systemwide costs, including production and purchasing costs, inventory holding costs, facility costs (storage, handling, and fixed costs), and transportation costs, subject to a variety of *service level* requirements. Note that one other key decision, the selection of transportation *mode* (e.g., truck, rail) is a tactical decision discussed in Chapter 3.

In this setting, the trade-offs are clear. Increasing the number of warehouses typically yields:

- An improvement in service level due to the reduction in average travel time to the customers.
- An increase in inventory costs due to increased safety stocks required to protect each warehouse against uncertainties in customer demands.
- An increase in overhead and setup costs.
- A reduction in outbound transportation costs: transportation costs from the warehouses to the customers.
- An increase in inbound transportation costs: transportation costs from the suppliers and/or manufacturers to the warehouses.

In essence, the firm must balance the costs of opening new warehouses with the advantages of being *close* to the customer. Thus, warehouse location decisions are crucial determinants of whether the supply chain is an efficient channel for the distribution of products.

We describe below some of the issues related to data collection and the calculation of costs required for the optimization models. Some of the information provided is based on logistics textbooks such as [7], [53], and [100].

Figure 2.1 and Figure 2.2 present two typical screens of a Decision Support System (DSS) that the user would see at different stages of optimization. One represents the network prior to optimization and the second represents the optimized network.

FIGURE 2.1

The DSS screen representing data prior to optimization

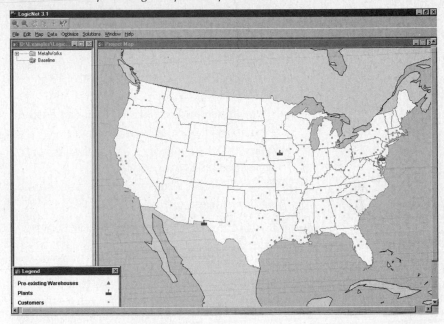

FIGURE 2.2

The DSS screen representing the optimized logistics network

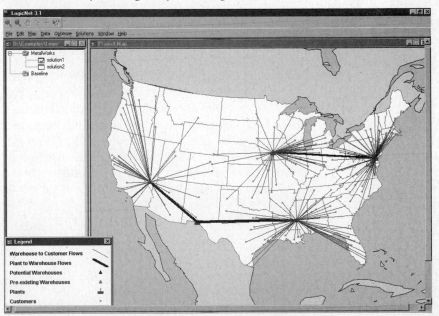

2.2 Data Collection

A typical network configuration problem involves large amounts of data, including information on:

1. Location of customers, retailers, existing warehouses and distribution centers, manufacturing facilities, and suppliers.
2. All products, including volumes, special transport modes (e.g., refrigerated).
3. Annual demand for each product by customer location.
4. Transportation rates by mode.
5. Warehousing costs, including labor, inventory carrying charges, and fixed operating costs.
6. Shipment sizes and frequencies for customer delivery.
7. Order processing costs.
8. Customer service requirements and goals.

2.2.1 Data Aggregation

A quick look at the above list suggests that the amount of data involved in any optimization model for this problem is overwhelming. For instance, a typical soft drink distribution system has between 10,000 to 120,000 accounts (customers). Similarly, in a retail logistics network, such as Wal-Mart or J. C. Penney, the number of different products that flow through the network is in the thousands or even hundreds of thousands.

For that reason, an essential first step is data aggregation. This is carried out using the following criteria:

1. Customers located in close proximity to each other are aggregated using a grid network or other clustering technique. All customers within a single cell or a single cluster are replaced by a single customer located at the center of the cell or cluster. This cell or cluster is referred to as a customer zone. A very effective technique that is commonly used is to aggregate customers according to the five-digit or three-digit zip code. Observe that if customers are classified according to their service levels or frequency of delivery, they will be aggregated together by classes. That is, all customers within the same class are aggregated independently of the other classes.

2. Items are aggregated into a reasonable number of product groups, based on

   - *Distribution pattern.* All products picked up at the same source and destined to the same customers are aggregated together.
   - *Product type.* In many cases, different products might simply be variations in product models or style or might differ only in the type of packaging. These products are typically aggregated together.

An important consideration, of course, is the impact on the model's effectiveness caused by replacing the original detailed data with the aggregated data. We address this issue in two ways.

1. Even if the technology exists to solve the logistics network design problem with the original data, it may still be useful to aggregate data because our ability to forecast customer demand at the account and product levels is usually poor. Because of the reduction in variability achieved through aggregation, forecast demand is significantly more accurate at the aggregated level.

| Example 2.2.1 | To illustrate the impact of aggregation on variability, consider an example in which two customers (e.g., retail outlets) are aggregated. Table 2.1 provides data on demand generated by these customers over the last seven years. |

TABLE 2.1   Historical Data for the Two Customers

Year	1992	1993	1994	1995	1996	1997	1998
Customer 1	22,346	28,549	19,567	25,457	31,986	21,897	19,854
Customer 2	17,835	21,765	19,875	24,346	22,876	14,653	24,987
Total	40,181	50,314	39,442	49,803	54,862	36,550	44,841

Assuming that these data correctly represent the distribution of next year's demand for each customer, Table 2.2 provides a summary of average annual demand, the standard deviation of annual demand and the coefficient of variation for each customer and for the aggregated one. For a discussion on the difference between the standard deviation and the coefficient of variation, see Chapter 3.

TABLE 2.2   Summary of Historical Data

Statistics	Average Annual Demand	Standard Deviation Annual Demand	Coefficient of Variation
Customer 1	24,237	4,658	0.192
Customer 2	20,905	3,427	0.173
Total	45,142	6,757	0.150

Note that the average annual demand for the aggregated customer is the sum of the average demand generated by each customer. However, the variability faced by the aggregated customer, measured using either the standard deviation or the coefficient of variation, is smaller than the combined variabilities faced by the two existing customers.

---

2. Various researchers report that aggregating data into about 150 to 200 points usually results in no more than a 1 percent error in the estimation of total transportation costs; see [7] and [49].

In practice, the following guidelines are typically used when aggregating the data:

- Aggregate demand points for 150 to 200 zones. If customers are classified into classes according to their service levels or frequency of delivery, each class will have 150–200 aggregated points.
- Make sure each zone has approximately an equal amount of total demand. This implies that the zones may be of different geographic sizes.
- Place the aggregated points at the center of the zone.
- Aggregate the products into 20 to 50 product groups.

Figure 2.3 presents information about 3,220 customers all located in North America while Figure 2.4 shows the same data after aggregation using a three-digit zip code resulting in 217 aggregated points.

FIGURE 2.3

The DSS screen representing data prior to aggregation

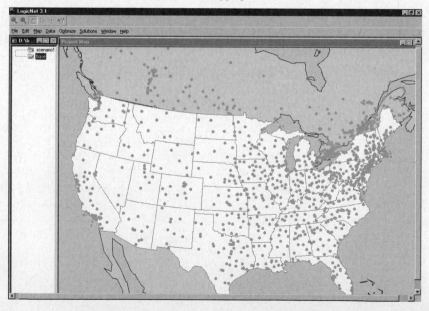

FIGURE 2.4

The DSS screen representing data after aggregation

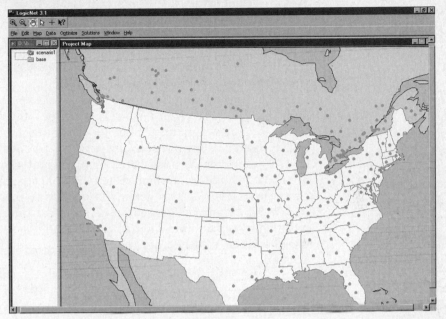

2.2.2   Transportation Rates

The next step in constructing an effective distribution network design model is to estimate transportation costs. An important characteristic of most transportation rates, including truck, rail and others, is that the rates are almost linear with distance but not with volume. We distinguish here between transportation costs associated with an *internal* and an *external* fleet.

Estimating transportation costs for company-owned trucks is typically quite simple. It involves annual costs per truck, annual mileage per truck, annual amount delivered, and the truck's effective capacity. All this information can be used to easily calculate cost per mile per SKU.

Incorporating transportation rates for an external fleet into the model is more complex. We distinguish here between two modes of transportation: truckload, referred to as TL, and less than truckload, referred to as LTL.

In the United States, TL carriers subdivide the country into zones. Almost every state is a single zone, except for certain big states, such as Florida or New York, which are partitioned into two zones. The carriers then provide their clients with zone-to-zone table costs. This database provides the cost per mile per truckload between any two zones. For example, to calculate TL cost from Chicago, Illinois, to Boston, Massachusetts, one needs to get the cost per mile for this pair and multiply it by the distance from Chicago to Boston. An important property of the TL cost structure is that it is not symmetric; that is, it is typically more expensive to ship a fully loaded truck from Illinois to New York than from New York to Illinois (why?).

In the LTL industry, the rates typically belong to one of three basic types of freight rates: *class*, *exception*, and *commodity*. The class rates are standard rates that can be found for almost all products or commodities shipped. They are found with the help of a *classification tariff* which gives each shipment a *rating* or a *class*. For instance, the railroad classification includes 31 classes ranging from 400 to 13 which are obtained from the widely used *Uniform Freight Classification*. The National Motor Freight Classification, on the other hand, includes only 23 classes ranging from 500 to 35. In all cases, the higher the rating or class, the greater the relative charge for transporting the commodity. There are many factors involved in determining a product's specific class. These include product density, ease or difficulty of handling and transporting, and liability for damage. Once the rating is established, it is necessary to identify the *rate basis number*. This number is the approximate distance between the load's origin and destination. With the commodity rating or class and the rate basis number, the specific rate per hundred pounds (hundred weight, or cwt) can be obtained from a carrier tariff table (i.e., a freight rate table).

The two other freight rates, namely *exception* and *commodity*, are specialized rates used to provide either less expensive rates (exception), or commodity-specific rates (commodity). For an excellent discussion, see [53] and [88]. Most carriers provide a database file with all of their transportation rates; these databases are typically incorporated into decision-support systems.

The profileration of LTL carrier rates and the highly fragmented nature of the trucking industry has created the need for sophisticated rating engines. An example of such a rating engine, which is widely used, is Southern Motor Carrier's Complete Zip Auditing and Rating (CZAR) engine. This engine can work with various carrier tariff tables as well as CZAR-Lite. Unlike an individual carrier's tariff, CZAR-Lite offers a market-based price list derived from studies of LTL pricing on a regional, interregional, and national basis. This provides shippers with a fair pricing system and prevents any individual carrier's operational and marketing bias from overtly influencing the shipper choice. Consequently, CZAR-Lite rates are often used as a base for negotiating LTL contracts between shippers, carriers, and third-party logistics providers.

2.2.3   *Mileage Estimation*

As explained in the previous subsection, the cost of transporting products from a specific source to a specific destination is a function of the distance between these two points. Thus, we need a tool that allows us to estimate distances. We can estimate distances using either street network or straight-line distances. Specifically, suppose we want to estimate the distance between two points, a and b. For this purpose, we need to obtain Lon_a and Lat_a, the longitude and latitude of point a (similarly for point b). Then, the straight-line distance in miles from a to b, D_{ab} is calculated as follows:

$$D_{ab} = 69\sqrt{(lon_a - lon_b)^2 + (lat_a - lat_b)^2}$$

The value 69 is approximately the number of miles per *degree* of latitude in the continental United States because longitude and latitude are given in degrees. This equation is accurate for short distances only; it does not take into account the curvature of the earth. To measure fairly long distances and correct for the earth's curvature, we use the approximation suggested by the United States Geological Survey, see [67]:

$$D_{ab} = 2(69)\sin^{-1}\sqrt{\sin\left(\frac{lat_a - lat_b}{2}\right)^2 + \cos(lat_a) \times \cos(lat_b) \times \sin\left(\frac{lon_a - lon_b}{2}\right)^2}$$

These equations result in very accurate distance calculations; in both cases, however, the equations underestimate the actual road distance. To correct for this, we multiply D_{ab} by a *circuity* factor, ρ. Typically, in a metropolitan area $\rho = 1.3$ while $\rho = 1.14$ for the continental United States.

Example 2.2.2   Consider a manufacturer shipping a single fully loaded truck from Chicago, Illinois, to Boston, Massachusetts. The manufacturer is using a TL carrier whose rate is 105 cents per mile per truckload. To calculate transportation cost for this shipment, we need geographic data. Table 2.3 provides information about the longitude and latitude of each city.

TABLE 2.3   Geographic Information

City	Longtitude	Latitude
Chicago	−87.65	41.85
Boston	−71.06	42.36

Note: The degrees in the table are in decimal representation so that 87.65 is 87° 39′ in a degrees/minutes representation, typical of paper maps. Longitude represents east-west position; any position west of the meridian has a negative value. Latitude represents north-south position; any location south of the equator has a negative value.

Application of the above equation leads to a straight-line distance from Chicago to Boston equal to 855 miles. Multiplying this number by the circuity factor, 1.14 in this case, leads to an estimate of the actual road distance equal to 974 miles. This number should be compared with the actual road distance, which is 965 miles. Thus, based on our estimate of the road distance, the transportation cost in this case is $1,023.

Applications in which exact distances are more appropriate can typically be obtained from advanced geographic information systems (GIS), as discussed in Chapter 11. However, this approach typically slows down the operation of decision-support systems dramatically, and the approximation technique described above usually provides enough accuracy for many applications.

2.2.4 Warehouse Costs

Warehousing and distribution center costs include three main components:

1. *Handling costs.* These include labor and utility costs which are proportional to annual flow through the warehouse.
2. *Fixed costs.* These capture all cost components that are not proportional to the amount of material that flows through the warehouse. The fixed cost is typically proportional to warehouse size (capacity) but in a nonlinear way (see Figure 2.5). As the figure shows, this cost is fixed in certain ranges of the warehouse size.

FIGURE 2.5

Warehouse fixed costs as a function of the warehouse capacity

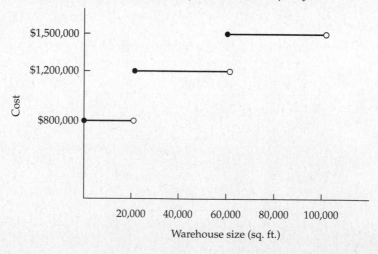

3. *Storage costs*. These represent inventory holding costs, which are proportional to *average* inventory levels (see Chapter 3).

Thus, estimating the warehouse handling costs is fairly easy while estimating the other two cost values is quite difficult. To see this difference, suppose that during the entire year 1,000 units of product are required by a particular customer. These 1,000 units are not required to flow through the warehouse *at the same time*, so the average inventory level will likely be significantly lower than 1,000 units. Thus, when constructing the data for the DSS, we need to convert these annual flows into actual inventory amounts over time. Similarly, annual flow and average inventory associated with this product tell us nothing about how much space is needed for the product in the warehouse. This is true because the amount of space that the warehouse needs is proportional to peak inventory, not annual flow or average inventory.

An effective way to overcome this difficulty is to utilize the *inventory turnover ratio*. This is defined as follows:

$$\text{Inventory turnover ratio} = \frac{\text{Annual sales}}{\text{Average inventory level}}$$

Specifically, in our case the inventory turnover ratio is the ratio of the total annual flow through the warehouse to the average inventory level. Thus, if the ratio is λ, then the average inventory level is total annual flow divided by λ. Finally, multiplying the average inventory level by the inventory holding cost gives the annual storage costs.

Finally, to calculate the fixed cost, we need to estimate the warehouse capacity. This is done in the next subsection.

2.2.5   *Warehouse Capacities*

Another important input to the distribution network design model is the actual warehouse capacity. The question is how to estimate the actual space required, given the specific annual flow of material through the warehouse. Again, the inventory turnover ratio suggests an appropriate approach. As before, annual flow through a warehouse divided by the inventory turnover ratio allows us to calculate the average inventory level. Assuming a regular shipment and delivery schedule, such as that given in Figure 2.6, it follows that the required storage space is approximately *twice* that amount. In practice, of course, every pallet stored in the warehouse requires an empty space to allow for access and handling, thus, considering this space as well as space for aisles, picking, sorting, and processing facilities, and AGVs (automatic guided vehicles), we typically multiply the required storage space by a factor (> 1). This factor depends on the specific application and allows us to assess the amount of space available in the warehouse more accurately. A typical factor used in practice is three. This

FIGURE 2.6

Inventory level as a function of time

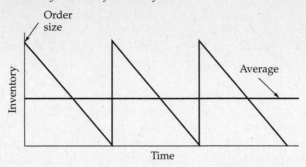

factor would be used in the following way. Consider a situation where the annual flow through the warehouse is 1,000 units and the inventory turnover ratio is 10.0. This implies that the average inventory level is about 100 units and, hence, if each unit takes 10 square feet of floor space, the required space for the products is 2,000 square feet. Therefore, the total space required for the warehouse is about 6,000 square feet.

2.2.6   *Potential Warehouse Locations*

It is also important to effectively identify potential locations for new warehouses. Typically, these locations must satisfy a variety of conditions:

- Geographical and infrastructure conditions.
- Natural resources and labor availability.
- Local industry and tax regulations.
- Public interest.

As a result, only a limited number of locations would meet all the requirements. These are the potential location sites for the new facilities.

2.2.7   *Service Level Requirements*

There are various ways to define service levels in this context. For example, we might specify a maximum distance between each customer and the warehouse serving it. This ensures that a warehouse will be able to serve its customers within a reasonable time. Sometimes we must recognize that for some customers, such as those in rural or isolated areas, it is harder to satisfy the same level of service that most other customers receive. In this case, it is often helpful to define the service level as the proportion of customers whose distance to their assigned warehouse is no more than a given distance. For instance, we might require that 95 percent of the customers be situated within 200 miles of the warehouses serving them.

2.2.8   Future Demand

As observed in Chapter 1, decisions at the strategic level, which include distribution network design, have a long-lasting effect on the firm. In particular, decisions regarding the number, location, and size of warehouses have an impact on the firm for at least the next three to five years. This implies that changes in customer demand over the next few years should be taken into account when designing the network. This is most commonly addressed using a scenario-based approach incorporating net present value calculations. For example, various possible scenarios representing a variety of possible future demand patterns over the planning horizon can be generated. These scenarios can then be directly incorporated into the model to determine the best distribution strategy.

2.3   Model and Data Validation

The previous section documents the difficulties in collecting, tabulating, and cleaning the data for a network configuration model. Once this is done, how do we ensure that the data and model accurately reflect the network design problem?

The process used to address this issue is known as model and data validation. This is typically done by reconstructing the existing network configuration using the model and collected data, and comparing the output of the model to existing data.

The importance of validation cannot be overstated. Valuable output of the model configured to duplicate current operating conditions includes all costs—warehousing, inventory, production, and transportation—generated under the current network configuration. These data can be compared to the company's accounting information. This is often the best way to identify errors in the data, problematic assumptions, modeling flaws, and so forth. In one project, for example, the transportation costs calculated during the validation process were consistently underestimating the costs suggested by the accounting data. After a careful review of the distribution practices, the consultants concluded that the effective truck capacity was only about 30 percent of the truck's physical capacity; that is, trucks were being sent out with very little load. Thus, the validation process not only helped calibrate some of the parameters used in the model but also suggested potential improvements in the utilization of the existing network.

It is often also helpful to make local or small changes in the network configuration to see how the system estimates their impact on costs and service levels. Specifically, this step involves positing a variety of what-if questions. This includes estimating the impact of closing an existing warehouse on system performance. Or, to give another example, it allows the user to change the flow of material through the existing network and see the changes in the costs. Often, managers have good intuition about what the effect of these small-scale changes on the system should be, so they can more easily identify errors in the model. Intuition about the effect of radical redesign of the entire system is often much less reliable.

Validation is critical for determining the validity of the model and data, but the process has other benefits. In particular, it helps the user make the connection between the current operations, which were modeled during the validation process, and possible improvements after optimization.

2.4 Solution Techniques

Once the data are collected, tabulated, and verified, the next step is to optimize the configuration of the logistics network. In practice, two techniques are employed:

1. Mathematical optimization techniques that include:

   • Exact algorithms that are guaranteed to find optimal solutions, that is, least-cost solutions,
   • Heuristic algorithms that find *good* solutions, not necessarily optimal solutions.

2. Simulation models that provide a mechanism to evaluate specified design alternatives created by the designer.

2.4.1 *Heuristics and the Need for Exact Algorithms*

We will start our discussion by considering mathematical optimization techniques. In order to understand the effectiveness of heuristic algorithms and the need for exact algorithms, consider the following example developed by Geoffrion and Van Roy in [41].

Example 2.4.1 | Consider the following distribution system:

• Single product.
• Two plants, referred to as plant $p1$ and plant $p2$.
• Plant $p2$ has an annual capacity of 60,000 units.

- The two plants have the same production costs.
- Two existing warehouses, referred to as warehouse $w1$ and warehouse $w2$, have identical warehouse handling costs.
- Three markets areas, $c1$, $c2$, and $c3$, with demands of 50,000, 100,000 and 50,000, respectively,
- Table 2.4 provides distribution cost per unit. For instance, distributing one unit from plant $p1$ to warehouse $w2$ costs \$5.

TABLE 2.4   Distribution costs per unit

Facility Warehouse	$p1$	$p2$	$c1$	$c2$	$c3$
$w1$	0	4	3	4	5
$w2$	5	2	2	1	2

Our objective is to find a distribution strategy that specifies the flow of products from the suppliers through the warehouses to the market areas without violating plant $p1$ production capacity constraint, that satisfies market area demands, and that minimizes total distribution costs. Observe that this problem is significantly easier to solve than the logistics network configuration problem discussed earlier. Here we assume that facility location is not an issue, and we merely attempt to find an effective distribution strategy.

For this purpose, consider the following two intuitive heuristics:

Heuristic 1. For each market we choose the cheapest warehouse to source demand. Thus, $c1$, $c2$, and $c3$ would be supplied by $w2$. Then, for this warehouse choose the cheapest plant; that is, distribute 60,000 units from $p2$ and the remaining 140,000 from $p1$. The total cost is:

$$2 \times 50,000 + 1 \times 100,000 + 2 \times 50,000$$
$$+ 2 \times 60,000 + 5 \times 140,000 = 1,120,000$$

Heuristic 2. For each market area, choose the warehouse where the total delivery costs to and from the warehouse are the lowest; that is, consider inbound and outbound distribution costs. Thus, for market area $c1$, consider the paths $p1 \rightarrow w1 \rightarrow c1$, $p1 \rightarrow w2 \rightarrow c1$, $p2 \rightarrow w1 \rightarrow c1$, $p2 \rightarrow w2 \rightarrow c1$. Among all these alternatives, the cheapest is $p1 \rightarrow w1 \rightarrow c1$, so choose $w1$ for $c1$. Using a similar analysis, we choose $w2$ for $c2$ and $w2$ for $c3$.

This implies that warehouse $w1$ delivers a total of 50,000 units while warehouse $w2$ delivers a total of 150,000 units. The best inbound flow pattern is to supply 50,000 from plant $p1$ to warehouse $w1$, supply 60,000 units from plant $p2$ to warehouse $w2$, and supply 90,000 from plant $p1$ to warehouse $w2$. The total cost for this strategy is \$920,000

Unfortunately, the two heuristics described earlier do not produce the best, or least-cost, strategy. To find the best distribution strategy, consider the following

Optimization model. Indeed, the distribution problem described earlier can be framed as the following linear programming problem.[1]

For this purpose, let:

- $x(p1, w1)$, $x(p1, w2)$, $x(p2, w1)$ and $x(p2, w2)$ be the flows from the plants to the warehouses.
- $x(w1, c1)$, $x(w1, c2)$, $x(w1, c3)$ be the flows from warehouse $w1$ to customer zones $c1$, $c2$, and $c3$.
- $x(w2, c1)$, $x(w2, c2)$, $x(w2, c3)$ be the flows from warehouse $w2$ to customer zones $c1$, $c2$, and $c3$.

The linear programming problem we need to solve is:

$$\text{Minimize } \{0x(p1, w1) + 5x(p1, w2) + 4x(p2, w1)$$
$$+ 2x(p2, w2) + 3x(w1, c1) + 4x(w1, c2)$$
$$+ 5x(w1, c3) + 2x(w2, c1) + 2x(w2, c3)\}$$

Subject to the following constraints:

$$x(p2, w1) + x(p2, w2) \leq 60,000$$
$$x(p1, w1) + x(p2, w1) = x(w1, c1) + x(w1, c2) + x(w1, c3)$$
$$x(p1, w2) + x(p2, w2) = x(w2, c1) + x(w2, c2) + x(w2, c3)$$
$$x(w1, c1) + x(w2, c1) = 50,000$$
$$x(w1, c2) + x(w2, c2) = 100,000$$
$$x(w1, c3) + x(w2, c3) = 50,000$$

All flows are greater than or equal to zero.

One can easily construct an Excel model for this problem and use the Excel linear programming solver to find the optimal strategy. For more information on how to construct the Excel model, see [58]. This strategy is described in Table 2.5.

TABLE 2.5   Optimal Distribution Strategy

Facility Warehouse	$p1$	$p2$	$c1$	$c2$	$c3$
$w1$	140,000	0	50,000	40,000	50,000
$w2$	0	60,000	0	60,000	0

The total cost for the optimal strategy is $740,000.

---

[1]This part of the section requires a basic knowledge of linear programming. It can be skipped without loss of continuity.

This example clearly illustrates the value of optimization-based techniques. *These tools can determine strategies that will significantly reduce the total system cost.*

Of course, the logistics network configuration model that we would like to analyze and solve is typically more complex than the simple example described above. One key difference is the need to establish optimal locations for warehouses, distribution centers, and cross-dock facilities. Unfortunately, these decisions render linear programming inappropriate and require the use of a technique called *integer programming*. This is true because linear programming deals with continuous variables while a decision on whether or not to open a warehouse at a specific city is a binary variable—0 if we do not open a warehouse in that location and 1 otherwise.

Thus, the logistics network configuration model is an integer programming model. Unfortunately, integer programming models are significantly more difficult to solve. The interested reader is referred to [14] for a discussion on exact algorithms for the logistics network configuration problem.

2.4.2 Simulation Models and Optimization Techniques

The mathematical optimization techniques described earlier have some important limitations. They deal with static models—typically by considering annual, or average, demand—and they do not take into account changes over time. Simulation-based tools take into account the dynamics of the system and are capable of characterizing system performance for a *given design*. Thus, it is up to the user to provide the simulation model with a number of design alternatives.

This implies that simulation models allow the user to perform a microlevel analysis. Indeed, the simulation model may include, see [46]:

1. Individual ordering pattern.
2. Specific inventory policies.
3. Inventory movements inside the warehouse.

Unfortunately, simulation models only model a prespecified logistics network design. In other words, given a particular configuration of warehouses, retailers, and so forth, a simulation model can be used to help estimate the costs associated with operating that configuration. If a different configuration is considered (e.g., a few of the customers are to be served by a different warehouse), the model has to be rerun. As you will see in more detail in Chapter 11, simulation is not an optimization tool. It is useful in characterizing the performance of a particular configuration, but not in determining an effective configuration from a large set of potential configurations.

In addition, a detailed simulation model that incorporates information about individual customer ordering patterns, specific inventory and production policies, daily distribution strategies, and so on may require enormous computational time to achieve a desired level of accuracy in system performance. This implies that typically one can consider *very few* alternatives using a simulation tool.

Thus, if system dynamics is not a key issue, a static model is appropriate and mathematical optimization techniques can be applied. In our experience, this type of model accounts for almost all the network configuration models used in practice. When detailed system dynamics is an important issue, it makes sense to utilize the following two-stage approach, suggested by Hax and Candea [46], which takes advantage of the strengths of both simulation- and optimization-based approaches:

1. Use an optimization model to generate a number of least-cost solutions at the macrolevel, taking into account the most important cost components.
2. Use a simulation model to evaluate the solutions generated in the first phase.

2.5 Key Features of a Network Configuration DSS

One of the key requirements of any decision-support system for network design is flexibility. In this context, we define *flexibility* as the ability of the system to incorporate a large set of preexisting network characteristics. Indeed, depending on the particular application, a whole spectrum of design options may be appropriate. At one end of this spectrum is the complete reoptimization of the existing network. This means that each warehouse can be either opened or closed and all transportation flows can be redirected. At the other end of the spectrum, it may be necessary to incorporate the following features in the optimization model:

1. *Customer-specific service level requirements.*
2. *Existing warehouses.* In most cases, warehouses already exist and their leases have not yet expired. Therefore, the model should not permit the closing of the warehouse.
3. *Expansion of existing warehouses.* Existing warehouses may be expandable.
4. *Specific flow patterns.* In a variety of situations, specific flow patterns (e.g., from a particular warehouse to a set of customers) should not be changed, or perhaps more likely, a certain manufacturing location does not or cannot produce certain SKUs.
5. *Warehouse-to-warehouse flow.* In some cases, material may flow from one warehouse to another warehouse.
6. *Bill of materials.* In some cases, final assembly is done at the warehouse and this needs to be captured by the model. For this

purpose, the user needs to provide information on the components used to assemble finished goods.

It is not enough for the decision-support system to incorporate all of the features described above. It also must have the capability to deal with all these issues with little or no reduction in its *effectiveness*. The latter requirement is directly related to the so-called *robustness* of the system. This stipulates that the relative quality of the solution generated by the system (i.e., cost and service level) should be independent of the specific environment, the variability of the data, or the particular setting. If a particular decision-support system is not robust, it is difficult to determine how effective it will be for a particular problem.

It is also essential that the system running time be reasonable. Of course, the term *reasonable* depends on the particular problem at hand. The running time in seconds of one popular DSS, running on a Pentium-200 personal computer, is listed in Table 2.6. The table provides running time for variety of problems. For each instance, the table provides the number of aggregated customers (Num Customers), the number of products (Num Products), the number of suppliers (Num Suppliers), the number of potential locations for warehouses (Num Potential) and the number of existing warehouses (Num Exist). In addition, the table provides the range of values (Min-Max) of the number of new warehouses considered by the DSS. This implies that the number of warehouses considered by the DSS was no less than the Min value and no more than the Max value. In each case, the model includes a service level requirement, defined as a limit on the distance between a customer and a warehouse serving it. This value is provided in the Distance column. The decision-support system found solutions guaranteed to be within 1.0 percent and 0.5 percent of the optimal solution, and the running times to get each of the solutions is listed. All of the problems listed were based on real-world data for a number of companies in the United States.

TABLE 2.6   Running Times (Seconds)

Num Customers*	Num Products	Num Suppliers	Num Potential	Num Exist	Min-Max	Distance	Running Time 1.0%	Running Time 0.5%
333	1	2	307	2	3-3	1300	12	12
333	1	2	307	2	3-7	1300	140	223
333	1	2	307	2	3-10	1300	184	209
2448	12	4	73	0	3-32	**	126	300
2066	23	23	52	0	3-25	700	393	500

*After aggregation.
**No service level requirement.

2.6   Solving the Bis Corporation Distribution Problem

We now go back to the Bis Corporation case described at the beginning of the chapter. An important issue in the analysis is an effective way to predict the impact of the estimated increase in demand on the network design. One way of doing that is to design the network based on the current demand and then evaluate the impact of future demand on the total cost; that is, fix the number and location of warehouses based on current (1997) demands and calculate total cost for 1997, 1998, and 1999. Compare this, for instance, to designing the logistics network based on, say, 1998 demands.

Specifically, consider the following three options.

Option I: Find optimal network design based on 1997 demands.
Option II: Find optimal network design based on 1998 demands.
Option III: Find optimal network design based on 1999 demands.

Consider Option I. In this case, we need to calculate total cost for 1998 and 1999, assuming that the network configuration does not change. We fix the network configuration according to this design option and evaluate the impact of the increase in demand on total cost. By calculating net present value of total logistics costs for 1997, 1998, and 1999, we get the total cost associated with this design option. Note that during this process, we are able to address capacity issues. For instance, the analysis of 1998 demand data will allow us to evaluate whether there is enough production capacity or whether production capacity needs to be increased to satisfy customer demands.

The same analysis is also applied to the other two design options, and the three net present values are used in making the final decision.

SUMMARY

In this chapter, we examined issues important in the design of the logistics network. One question often raised is the efficiency of demand aggregation. Since information is available on individual retailer demands, it is not clear why the analysis combines groups of customers and treats them as a single aggregate customer. As we have seen, there are two main reasons for aggregating demand data. The first is the size of the model that results from the input data. Indeed, the time it takes to solve a network design problem grows exponentially as the number of customers increases. Even if optimization time is not an issue, aggregating demand is important because it improves the accuracy of forecast demand. This is true because our ability to forecast customer demand at the account and product levels is usually poor. By contrast, because of the reduction in variability achieved through aggregation, forecast demand is significantly more accurate at the aggregated level.

A second issue often raised in practice is the need for a decision-support system to optimize the logistics network. The question is whether a sophisticated tool is required or spreadsheets alone are sufficient. The chapter argues that a thorough logistics network analysis should consider complex transportation cost structures, warehouse sizes, manufacturing limitations, inventory turnover ratios, inventory cost, and service levels. These issues require the use of optimization-based decision-support systems that can solve large-scale problems efficiently. For a detailed discussion, see Chapter 11.

Inventory Management and Risk Pooling

CASE: JAM ELECTRONICS: SERVICE LEVEL CRISIS

JAM Electronics is a Korean manufacturer of products such as industrial relays. The company has five manufacturing facilities in different countries in the Far East with headquarters in Seoul, South Korea.

JAM USA is a subsidiary of JAM Electronics and was established in the United States in 1978. The U.S. subsidiary provides distribution and service functions in this country. It has a central warehouse in Chicago that serves two types of customers: distributors and original equipment manufacturers (OEMs). Distributors typically keep inventory of JAM's products and supply them to their clients as needed. OEMs use JAM's products to produce different types of items such as automatic garage door openers.

JAM Electronics produces about 2,500 different products, all of them manufactured in the Far East. Finished products are stored in a central warehouse in Korea and are shipped from there to different countries. In particular, items sold in the United States are transported by ship to the warehouse in Chicago.

In recent years, JAM USA has seen a significant increase in competition and huge pressure from its clients and distributors to improve service levels and reduce costs. Unfortunately, as Al Rub, the inventory manager, points out, "the service level right now is at an all-time low. Only about 70 percent of all orders are delivered on time. On the other hand, inventory keeps piling up, mostly of products that are not in demand."

In a recent meeting with Chan Moon, the president of JAM USA; Ken Hall, vice president and general manager; and Li Chan, a representative of the Korean headquarters, Al pointed out several reasons for the low service level.

1. *Difficulty forecasting customer demand.* Indeed, changes in the economy, customer behavior, and other factors have a major impact on demand, and these are quite difficult to predict.

Source: JAM Electronics is a fictional company. The material in this case is loosely based on our experience with several companies.

2. *Long lead time in the supply chain.* A typical order placed by the warehouse in Illinois will arrive in about six to seven weeks. There are two primary reasons for the long lead time. First, there is a week of processing time in the central distribution center in Korea; second, the ocean transit time is very long.

3. *The large number of SKUs handled by JAM USA.* As pointed out earlier, JAM USA distributes about 2,500 different products, ranging from small relays to large programmable controllers, to its customers.

4. *The low priority given the U.S. subsidiary by headquarters in Seoul.* An order that arrives at the Korean headquarter from Japanese or Korean clients typically receives a higher priority over an order received from the United States. Thus, the lead time to the United States is occasionally much longer than seven weeks.

To illustrate the difficulty in forecasting customer demand, Al provided a graph that showed monthly demand information for item xxx-1534, a relay product used in the manufacture of refrigerators (see Figure 3.1). As the graph demonstrates, variability in customer demand is very high; demand changes from month to month and it is difficult to predict what customer demand is going to be even when sophisticated forecasting techniques are used.

Ken, the general manager, was very critical of Al's analysis. He pointed out that if long lead time is an issue then JAM USA needs to reduce it, perhaps by using air carriers, which would probably reduce lead time to about two weeks. Ken, however, was unsure of the impact of this change on the overall supply chain. He pointed out that "transportation costs are certainly going to increase, but where are the savings?"

The meeting ended with a decision to establish a task force headed by Ken to address the service level crisis.

As Al left the meeting, he could not help but think that many companies must be facing similar problems—high demand variability, long lead times, unreliable supply processes, and a large number of SKUs. What is the competition doing to cope with these problems?

FIGURE 3.1

Monthly demand for item xxx-1534

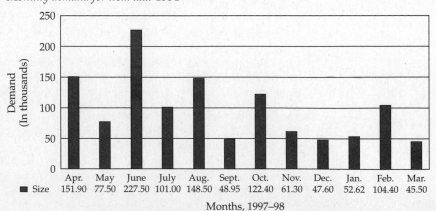

	Apr.	May	June	July	Aug.	Sept.	Oct.	Nov.	Dec.	Jan.	Feb.	Mar.
■ Size	151.90	77.50	227.50	101.00	148.50	48.95	122.40	61.30	47.60	52.62	104.40	45.50

Months, 1997–98

By the end of this chapter, you should be able to understand the following issues:

- How a firm can cope with huge variability in customer demand.
- What the relationship is between service and inventory levels.
- What the impact of lead time and lead time variability has on inventory levels.
- What an effective inventory management policy is.

3.1 Introduction

The importance of inventory management and the need for the coordination of inventory decisions and transportation policies has been evident for a long time. Unfortunately, managing inventory in complex supply chains is typically quite difficult and may have a significant impact on the customer service level and supply chain systemwide cost.

As we discussed in Chapter 1, a typical supply chain consists of suppliers and manufacturers, who convert raw materials into finished products, and distribution centers and warehouses, from which finished products are distributed to customers. This implies that inventory appears in the supply chain in several forms:

- Raw material inventory.
- Work-in-process (WIP) inventory.
- Finished product inventory.

Each of these needs its own inventory control mechanism. The difficulty in determining these mechanisms is that efficient production, distribution, and inventory control strategies that reduce systemwide costs and improve service levels must take into account the interactions of the various levels in the supply chain. Although determining these inventory control mechanisms may be challenging, the benefits can be enormous:

| Example 3.1.1 | General Motors (GM) has one of the largest production and distribution networks in the world. In 1984 GM's distribution network consisted of 20,000 supplier plants, 133 parts plants, 31 assembly plants, and 11,000 dealers. Freight transportation costs were about $4.1 billion with 60 percent for material shipments. In addition, GM inventory was valued at $7.4 billion, of which 70 percent was WIP and the rest was finished vehicles. GM has implemented a decision tool capable of reducing the combined corporate cost of inventory and transportation. Indeed, by adjusting shipment sizes (i.e., inventory policy) and routes (i.e., transportation strategy), costs could be reduced by about 26 percent annually [10]. |

Of course, the key question is: Why hold inventory at all? Some of the reasons include:

1. To protect the firm from unexpected changes in customer demand. Customer demand has always been hard to predict, and uncertainty in customer demand has increased in the last few years owing to:

- The short life cycle of an increasing number of products. This implies that historical data about customer demand may not be available or may be quite limited (see Chapter 1).
- The presence of many competing products in the marketplace. This proliferation of products makes it increasingly difficult to predict demand for a specific model. Indeed, while it is relatively easy to forecast demand across product groups—that is, to forecast demand for all products competing in the same market—it is much more difficult to estimate demand for individual products. We discuss this in more detail in Chapter 8.

2. The presence in many situations of a significant uncertainty in the quantity and quality of the supply, supplier costs, and delivery times.

3. Economies of scale offered by transportation companies which encourage firms to transport large quantities of items, and therefore hold large inventories. Indeed, many of the transportation providers try to encourage large-size shipments by offering all sorts of discounts to shippers (see Chapter 2).

Unfortunately, managing inventory effectively in this environment is often difficult, as the following examples illustrate:

- In 1993, Dell Computer's stock plunged after the company predicted a loss. Dell acknowledged that the company was sharply off in its forecast of demand, resulting in inventory write-downs [118].
- In 1993, Liz Claiborne experienced an unexpected earnings decline, as a consequence of higher-than-anticipated excess inventories [119].
- In 1994, IBM struggled with shortages in the ThinkPad line due to ineffective inventory management [120].

These examples raise two important issues in inventory management:

1. Demand forecasting.
2. Order quantity calculation.

Since demand is uncertain in most situations, forecast demand is a critical element in determining order quantity. But what is the relationship between forecast demand and the optimal order quantity? Should the order quantity be equal to, greater than, or smaller than forecast demand? And, if order quantity is different than forecast demand, by how much? These issues are discussed below.

3.2   A Single Warehouse Inventory Example

What are the key factors affecting inventory policy?

1. First and foremost is customer demand, which may be known in advance or may be random. In the latter case, forecasting tools may be used in situations in which historical data are available to estimate the average customer demand, as well as the amount of variability in customer demand (often measured as the standard deviation).
2. Replenishment lead time, which may be known at the time we place the order, or it may be uncertain.
3. The number of different products stored at the warehouse.
4. The length of the planning horizon.
5. Costs, including order cost and inventory holding cost.
   a. Typically, order cost consists of two components: the cost of the product and the transportation cost.
   b. Inventory holding cost, or inventory carrying cost, consists of:
      (1) State taxes, property taxes, and insurance on inventories.
      (2) Maintenance costs.
      (3) Obsolescence cost, which derives from the risk that an item will lose some of its value because of changes in the market.
      (4) Opportunity costs, which represent the return on investment that one would receive had money been invested in something else (e.g., the stock market) instead of inventory.
6. Service level requirement. In situations where customer demand is uncertain, it is often impossible to meet customer orders 100 percent of the time, so management needs to specify an acceptable level of service.

3.2.1   The Economic Lot Size Model

The classic *Economic Lot Size Model*, introduced by Ford W. Harris in 1915, is a simple model that illustrates the trade-offs between ordering and storage costs. Consider a warehouse facing constant demand for a *single* item. The warehouse places an order to the supplier, which is assumed to have an unlimited quantity of the product. The model assumes the following:

- Demand is constant at a rate of D items per day.
- Order quantities are fixed at Q items per order; that is, each time the warehouse places an order, it is for Q items.
- A fixed setup cost, K, is incurred every time the warehouse places an order.
- An inventory carrying cost, h, also referred to as a *holding cost*, is accrued for every unit held in inventory per day.
- The lead time, the time that elapses between the placement of an order and its receipt, is zero.
- Initial inventory is zero.
- The planning horizon is long (infinite).

Our goal is to find the optimal order policy that minimizes annual purchasing and carrying costs without shortage.

This is an extremely simplified version of a real inventory system. The assumption of a known fixed demand over a long horizon is clearly unrealistic. Replenishment of products very likely takes several days, and the requirement of a fixed order quantity is restrictive. Surprisingly, the insight derived from this model will help us to develop inventory policies that are effective for more complex realistic systems.

It is easy to see that in an optimal policy for the model described above, orders should be received at the warehouse precisely when the inventory level drops to zero. This is called the *zero inventory ordering property*, which can be observed by considering a policy in which orders are placed and received when the inventory level is not zero. Clearly, a cheaper policy would involve waiting until the inventory is zero before ordering, thus saving on holding costs.

To find the optimal ordering policy in the Economic Lot Size Model, we consider the inventory level as a function of time (see Figure 2.6 in Chapter 2). This is the so-called saw-toothed inventory pattern. We refer to the time between two successive replenishments as a *cycle* time. Thus, total inventory cost in a cycle of length T is:

$$K + \frac{hTQ}{2}$$

since the fixed cost is charged once per order, and holding cost can be viewed as the product of the per unit per time period holding cost, h, the average inventory level, $Q/2$, and the length of the cycle, T.

Since the inventory level changes from Q to 0 during a cycle of length T, and demand is constant at a rate of D units per unit time, it must be that $Q = TD$. Thus, we can divide the cost above by T, or equivalently Q/D, to get the average total cost per unit of time:

$$\frac{KD}{Q} + \frac{hQ}{2}$$

Using simple calculus, it is easy to show that the optimal order quantity that minimizes the above cost function is:

$$Q^* = \sqrt{\frac{2KD}{h}}$$

This quantity is referred to as the *economic order quantity* (EOQ).

This simple model provides two important insights:

1. An optimal policy balances between inventory holding cost per unit time and setup cost per unit time. Indeed, setup cost per unit time $= KD/Q$, while holding cost per unit time $= hQ/2$ (see Figure 3.2). Thus, as one increases the order quantity, Q, inventory holding costs per unit of time increase while setup costs per unit of time decrease. The optimal order quantity is achieved at the point in which inventory setup cost per unit of time (KD/Q) equals inventory holding cost per unit of time $(hQ/2)$. That is:

$$\frac{KD}{Q} = \frac{hQ}{2}$$

or

$$Q^* = \sqrt{\frac{2KD}{h}}$$

2. Total inventory cost is insensitive to order quantities; that is, changes in order quantities have a relatively small impact on annual setup costs and inventory holding costs. To illustrate this issue, consider a decision maker that places an order quantity Q which is a multiple b of the optimal order quantity Q^*. In other words, for a given b, the quantity ordered is $Q = bQ^*$. Thus, $b = 1$ implies that the decision maker orders the economic order quantity. If $b = 1.2$ ($b = 0.8$), the decision maker orders 20 percent more (less) than the optimal order quantity. Table 3.1 presents the impact

FIGURE 3.2

Economic lot size model: Total cost per unit time

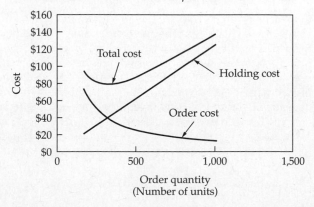

Order quantity
(Number of units)

TABLE 3.1 Sensitivity Analysis

b	0.5	0.8	0.9	1	1.1	1.2	1.5	2
Increase in cost	25.0%	2.5%	0.5%	0	0.4%	1.6%	8.0%	25.0%

of changes in b on total system cost. For example, if the decision maker orders 20 percent more than the optimal order quantity ($b = 1.2$) then the increase in total inventory cost relative to the optimal total cost is no more than 1.6 percent.

3.2.2   The Effect of Demand Uncertainty

The previous model illustrates the trade-offs between setup costs and inventory holding costs. It ignores, however, issues such as demand uncertainty and forecasting. Indeed, many companies treat the world as if it were predictable, making production and inventory decisions based on forecasts of the demand made far in advance of the selling season. Although these companies are aware of demand uncertainty when they create a forecast, they design their planning processes as if the initial forecast was an accurate representation of reality.

Unfortunately, recent technological advances have increased the level of demand uncertainty. Many products have a short life cycle. At the same time a large variety of products compete in the same market.

To illustrate the importance of incorporating demand uncertainty and forecast demand into the analysis, and to characterize the impact of demand uncertainty on the inventory policy, consider the following example.

CASE: SWIMSUIT PRODUCTION

Consider a company that designs, produces, and sells summer fashion items such as swimsuits. About six months before summer, the company must commit itself to specific production quantities for all its products. Since there is no clear indication of how the market will respond to the new designs, the company needs to use various tools to predict demand for each design, and plan production and supply accordingly. In this setting the trade-offs are clear; overestimating customer demand will result in unsold inventory while underestimating customer demand will lead to inventory stockouts and loss of potential customers.

To assist management in these decisions, the marketing department uses historical data from the last five years, current economic conditions, and other factors

Source: This case is based loosely on [35] and course material prepared at the Columbia University Graduate School of Business.

to construct a *probabilistic forecast* of the demand for swimsuits. They have identified several possible scenarios for sales in the coming season, based on such factors as possible weather patterns and competitors' behavior, and assigned each a probability, or chance. For example, the marketing department believes that a scenario that leads to 8,000 unit sales has an 11 percent chance of happening; other scenarios leading to different sales levels have different probabilities of occurring. These scenarios are illustrated in Figure 3.3. This probabilistic forecast suggests that average demand is about 13,000 units, but there is a probability that demand will be either larger than average or smaller than average.

Additional information available to the manufacturer includes:

- To start production, the manufacturer has to invest $100,000 independent of the amount produced. We refer to this cost as the *fixed production cost*.
- The *variable production cost* per unit equals $80.
- During the summer season, a swimsuit is sold at $125 per unit. This value is the *selling price*.
- Any swimsuit not sold during the summer season is sold to a discount store for $20. We refer to this value as the *salvage value*.

To identify the best production quantity, the firm needs to understand the relationship between the production quantity, customer demand, and profit.

Suppose the manufacturer produces 10,000 units while demand ends at 12,000 swimsuits. It is easily verified that profit equals revenue from summer sales minus the variable production cost minus the fixed production cost. That is:

$$\text{Profit} = 125(10{,}000) - 80(10{,}000) - 100{,}000$$
$$= 350{,}000$$

On the other hand, if the company produces 10,000 swimsuits and demand is only 8,000 units, profit equals revenue from summer sales plus salvage value minus the variable production cost minus the fixed production cost. That is:

$$\text{Profit} = 125(8{,}000) + 20(2{,}000) - 80(10{,}000) - 100{,}000$$
$$= 140{,}000$$

FIGURE 3.3

Probabilistic forecast

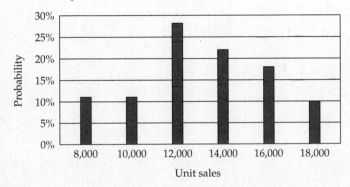

Notice that the probability that demand is 8,000 units is 11 percent while the probability that demand is 12,000 units is 27 percent. Thus, producing 10,000 swimsuits leads to a profit of $350,000 with probability of 27 percent and a profit of $140,000 with probability of 11 percent. In similar fashion, one can calculate the profit associated with each scenario given that the manufacturer produces 10,000 swimsuits. This allows us to determine the *average profit* associated with producing 10,000 units. This average profit is the total profit of all the scenarios weighted by the probability that each scenario will occur.

We would, of course, like to find the order quantity that maximizes average profit. What is the relationship between the optimal production quantity and average demand which, in this example, is 13,000 units? Should the optimal order quantity be equal to, more than, or less than the average demand?

To answer these questions, we evaluate the *marginal profit* and *marginal cost* of producing an additional swimsuit. If this swimsuit is sold during the summer season, then the marginal profit is the difference between the selling price per unit and the variable production cost per unit, which is equal to $45. If the additional swimsuit is not sold during the summer season, the marginal cost is the difference between the variable production cost and the salvage value per unit, which is equal to $60. Thus, the cost of not selling this additional swimsuit during the summer season is larger than the profit obtained from selling it during the season. Hence, the best production quantity will be less than the average demand.

Figure 3.4 plots the average profit as a function of the production quantity. It shows that the optimal production quantity, or the quantity that maximizes average profit, is about 12,000. It also indicates that producing 9,000 units or producing 16,000 units will lead to about the same average profit of $294,000. If, for some reason, we had to choose between producing 9,000 units and 16,000 units, which one should we choose?

To answer this question, we need to better understand the *risk* associated with certain decisions. For this purpose, we construct a frequency histogram (see Figure 3.5) that provides information about potential profit for the two given production quantities, 9,000 units and 16,000 units. For instance, consider profit when the

FIGURE 3.4

Average profit as a function of production quantity

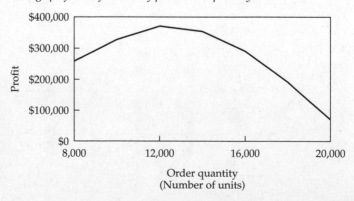

FIGURE 3.5

A frequency histogram of profit

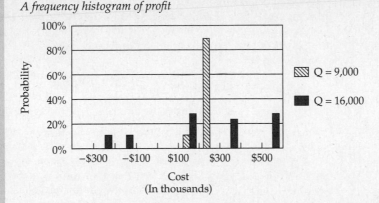

production quantity is 16,000 units. The graph shows that the distribution of profit is not symmetrical. Losses of $220,000 happen about 11 percent of the time while profits of at least $410,000 happen 50 percent of the time. On the other hand, a frequency histogram of the profit when the production quantity is 9,000 units shows that the distribution has only two possible outcomes. Profit is either $200,000 with probability of about 11 percent, or $305,000 with probability of about 89 percent. Thus, while producing 16,000 units has the same average profit as producing 9,000 units, the possible *risk* on the one hand, and possible *reward* on the other hand, increases as we increase the production size.

To summarize:

- The optimal order quantity is not necessarily equal to forecast, or average, demand. Indeed, the optimal quantity depends on the relationship between marginal profit achieved from selling an additional unit and marginal cost.

- As the order quantity increases, average profit typically increases until the production quantity reaches a certain value, after which the average profit starts decreasing.

- As we increase the production quantity, the risk—that is, the probability of large losses—always increases. At the same time, the probability of large gains also increases. This is the risk/reward trade-off.

The Effect of Initial Inventory

Suppose now that the swimsuit under consideration is a model produced last year, and that the manufacturer has an initial inventory of 5,000 units. Assuming that demand for this model follows the same pattern of scenarios as before, should the manufacturer start production, and if so, how many swimsuits should be produced?

If the manufacturer does not produce any additional swimsuits, no more than 5,000 units can be sold and no additional fixed cost will be incurred. However, if the manufacturer decides to produce, a fixed production cost is charged independent of the amount produced.

To address this issue, consider Figure 3.6, in which the solid line represents average profit excluding fixed production cost while the dotted curve represents average profit including the fixed production cost. Notice that the dotted curve is identical to the curve in Figure 3.4 while the solid line is above the dotted line for every production quantity; the difference between the two lines is the fixed production cost.

Notice also that if nothing is produced, average profit can be obtained from the solid line in Figure 3.6 and is equal to:

$$200,000 \text{ (from the figure)} + 5,000 \times 80 = 775,000$$

where the last component is the variable production cost already included in the $200,000.

On the other hand, if the manufacturer decides to produce, it is clear that production should increase inventory from 5,000 units to 12,000 units. Thus, average profit in this case is obtained from the dotted line and is equal to:

$$375,000 \text{ (from the figure)} + 5,000 \times 80$$

Since the average profit associated with increasing inventory to 12,000 units is larger than the average profit associated with not producing anything, the optimal policy is to produce.

Consider now the case in which initial inventory is 10,000 units. Following the same analysis used before, it is easy to see that there is no need to produce anything because the average profit associated with an initial inventory of 10,000 is larger than what we would achieve if we produce to increase inventory to 12,000 units. This is true because if we do not produce, we do not pay any fixed cost; if we produce, we need to pay a fixed cost independent of the amount produced.

Thus, if we produce, the most we can make on average is a profit of $375,000. This is the same average profit that we will have if our initial inventory is about 8,500 units and we decide not to produce anything. Hence, if our initial inventory is below 8,500 units, we produce to raise the inventory level to 12,000 units. On the other hand, if initial inventory is at least 8,500 units, we should not produce anything.

FIGURE 3.6

Profit and the impact of initial inventory

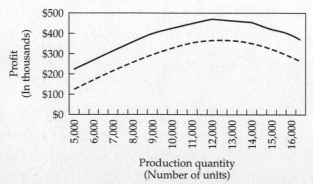

The swimsuit analysis motivates a powerful inventory policy used in practice to manage inventory: Whenever the inventory level is below a certain value, say s, we order (or produce) to increase the inventory to level S. Such a policy is referred as an (s, S) policy or a *min max* policy. We typically refer to s as the *reorder point* and to S as the *order-up-to-level*; in the swimsuit production example, the reorder point is 8,500 units and the order-up-to-level is 12,000 units. The difference between these two levels is driven by fixed costs associated with ordering, manufacturing, or transportation.

3.2.3   Multiple Order Opportunities

The model described and analyzed above assumes that the decision maker can make only a single ordering decision for the entire horizon. This may be the case for fashion items such as swimsuits or ski jackets, where the selling season is short and there is no second opportunity to reorder products based on realized customer demand, but in many practical situations, the decision maker may order products repeatedly at any time during the year.

Consider, for instance, a distributor of TV sets. The distributor faces random demand for the product and receives the supply from the manufacturer. Of course, the manufacturer cannot instantaneously satisfy orders placed by the distributor—there is a fixed lead time for delivery whenever the distributor places an order. Since demand is random and the manufacturer has a fixed delivery lead time, the distributor needs to hold inventory, even if no fixed setup cost is charged for ordering the products. At least three reasons explain why the distributor holds inventory:

1. To satisfy demand occurring during lead time. Since orders aren't met immediately, inventory must be on hand to meet customer demand during the period between the time the distributor orders and when the order arrives.
2. To protect against uncertainty in demand.
3. To balance annual inventory holding costs and annual fixed order costs. We have seen that more frequent orders lead to lower inventory levels and thus lower inventory holding costs, but they also lead to higher annual fixed order costs.

While these issues are intuitively clear, the specific inventory policy that the distributor should apply is not simple. To manage its inventory effectively, the distributor needs to decide when and how many TV sets to order.

3.2.4   No Fixed Order Costs

To answer these questions, we make the following additional assumptions.

- Daily demand is random and follows a normal distribution. In other words, we assume that the probabilistic forecast of daily demand follows the famous bell-shaped curve. Note that we can completely describe normal demand by its average and standard deviation.

- Every time the distributor orders TV sets from the manufacturer, the distributor pays an amount proportional to the quantity ordered. There is no fixed order cost.
- Inventory holding cost is charged per item per unit time.
- If a customer order arrives when there is no inventory on hand to fill the order (i.e., when the distributor is stocked out), the order is lost.
- The distributor specifies a required *service level*. The service level is the probability of not stocking out during lead time. For example, the distributor might want to ensure that the proportion of lead times in which demand is met out of stock is 95 percent. Thus, the required service level is 95 percent in this case.

To characterize the inventory policy that the distributor should use, we need the following information:

AVG = Average daily demand faced by the distributor
STD = Standard deviation of daily demand faced by the distributor
L = Replenishment lead time from the supplier to the distributor in days
h = Cost of holding one unit of the product for one day at the distributor
α = service level. This implies that the probability of stocking out is $1 - \alpha$.

In addition, we need to define the concept of *inventory position*. The inventory position at any point in time is the actual inventory at the warehouse plus items ordered by the distributor that have not yet arrived.

To describe the policy that the distributor should use, recall our previous definitions of s and S, the reorder point, and order-up-to-level. An effective inventory policy in this case is where $s = S$, so that the reorder point and the order-up-to-level are identical. Hence, whenever the inventory position level drops below level S, the distributor should order to raise its inventory position to level S.

The order-up-to-level, S, consists of two components. The first is the average inventory during lead time, which is the product of average daily demand and the lead time. This ensures that there will be enough inventory to last until the next order arrives. Thus, the average demand during lead time is exactly:

$$L \times AVG$$

The second component represents the *safety stock*, which is the amount of inventory that the distributor needs to keep at the warehouse and in the pipeline to protect against deviations from average demand during lead time. This quantity is calculated as follows:

$$z \times STD \times \sqrt{L}$$

where z is a constant associated with the service level. Thus, the order-up-to-level is equal to:

$$L \times AVG + z \times STD \times \sqrt{L}$$

The constant z is chosen from statistical tables to ensure that the probability of stockouts during lead time is exactly $1 - \alpha$. This implies that the order-up-to-level must satisfy:

$$Prob\{\text{Demand during lead time} \geq L \times AVG + z \times STD \times \sqrt{L}\} = 1 - \alpha$$

Table 3.2 provides a list of z values for different values of the service level, α.

TABLE 3.2   Service Level and z Value

Service Level	90%	91%	92%	93%	94%	95%	96%	97%	98%	99%	99.9%
z	1.29	1.34	1.41	1.48	1.56	1.65	1.75	1.88	2.05	2.33	3.08

Example 3.2.1	Suppose the distributor of the TV sets is trying to set inventory policies at the warehouse for one of the TV models. Table 3.3 provides data on the number of TV sets sold in each of the last 12 months. Every time the warehouse places an order to the manufacturer, replenishment time (i.e., lead time) is about two weeks. The distributor would like to ensure that service level is about 97 percent. Assuming there is no fixed ordering cost, what is the order-up-to-level that the distributor should use?

Table 3.3 implies that average monthly demand is 191.17 and the standard deviation of monthly demand is 66.53.

Since lead time is two weeks, we transform the average and the standard deviation to weekly values as follows:

$$\text{Average weekly demand} = \frac{\text{Average monthly demand}}{4.3}$$

TABLE 3.3   Historical Data

Month	Sept.	Oct.	Nov.	Dec.	Jan.	Feb.	Mar.	Apr.	May	June	July	Aug.
Sales	200	152	100	221	287	176	151	198	246	309	98	156

while

$$\text{Standard deviation of weekly demand} = \frac{\text{Monthly standard deviation}}{\sqrt{4.3}}$$

These data are provided in Table 3.4. This allows us to calculate average demand during lead time and safety stock using a constant $z = 1.9$ (or, more precisely 1.88) taken from Table 3.2 based on a 97 percent service level. The reorder point is simply the sum of the average demand during lead time plus the safety stock. All these data are presented in Table 3.4. Finally, in the last column the reorder point, or in this case the order-up-to-level, is expressed in terms of weeks of supply. As you can see, the distributor needs to keep about four weeks' worth of inventory at the warehouse and in the pipeline.

TABLE 3.4   Inventory Analysis

Parameter	Average Weekly Demand	Standard Deviation Weekly Demand	Average Demand During Lead Time	Safety Stock	Reorder Point	Weeks of Supply
Value	44.58	32.08	89.16	86.20	176	3.95

3.2.5   Fixed Order Costs

Suppose that in addition to the variable ordering cost the distributor pays a fixed cost, K, every time an order is placed. What inventory policy should now be used? In this case, the inventory policy that should be used is an (s, S) policy where the reorder point and order quantity are different, not the same as in the previous example. Recall that in the single-period case, the difference is due to the fixed cost associated with ordering or manufacturing. This is also the case here. Indeed, the reorder point, s, that should be used by the distributor is identical to the reorder point obtained in the previous case, that is:

$$s = L \times AVG + z \times STD \times \sqrt{L}$$

The value of the order-up-to-level, S, is calculated following the intuition developed in the Economic Lot Size Model. Recall from this model that the order quantity, Q, is calculated as follows:

$$Q = \sqrt{\frac{2K \times AVG}{h}}$$

If there was no variability in customer demand, the distributor would have ordered Q items whenever inventory is at the level $L \times AVG$ since it takes

L days to receive the order. However, there is variability in demand, so the distributor also needs to keep safety stock. The amount needed is:

$$z \times STD \times \sqrt{L}$$

where z is selected as before to achieve the required service level. Therefore, the order-up-to-level is:

$$S = \max\{Q, L \times AVG\} + z \times STD \times \sqrt{L}$$

where max means take the maximum of the terms Q and $L \times AVG$.

Figure 3.7 illustrates the inventory level over time when this type of policy is implemented.

FIGURE 3.7

(s, S) policy with multiple order opportunities

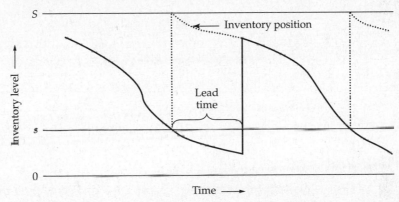

Example 3.2.2

We continue with the previous example and assume that whenever our distributor places an order for TV sets, there is a fixed ordering cost of $4,500, which is independent of the order size. The cost of a TV set to the distributor is $250 and annual inventory holding cost is about 18 percent of the product cost. Thus, weekly inventory holding cost per TV set is:

$$\frac{0.18 \times 250}{52} = 0.87$$

or 87 cents. This implies that the order quantity, Q, should be calculated as:

$$Q = \sqrt{\frac{2 \times 4,500 \times 44.58}{0.87}} = 679$$

and hence the order-up-to-level is:

$$\text{Safety stock} + Q = 86 + 679 = 765$$

That is, the distributor should place an order to raise the inventory position to 765 TV sets whenever the inventory level is below or at 176 units.

3.2.6   Variable Lead Times

In many cases, the assumption that the delivery lead time to the warehouse is fixed and known in advance does not necessarily hold. Indeed, in many practical situations the lead time to the warehouse must be assumed to be normally distributed with average lead time denoted by *AVGL* and standard deviation denoted by *STDL*. In this case, the reorder point, *s*, is calculated as follows:

$$s = AVG \times AVGL + z\sqrt{AVGL \times STD^2 + AVG^2 \times STDL^2}$$

where $AVG \times AVGL$ represents average demand during lead time while

$$\sqrt{AVGL \times STD^2 + AVG^2 \times STDL^2}$$

is the standard deviation of demand during lead time. Thus, the amount of safety stock that has to be kept is equal to:

$$z\sqrt{AVGL \times STD^2 + AVG^2 \times STDL^2}$$

As before, the order-up-to-level is the sum of safety stock plus the maximum between *Q* and average demand during lead time, that is:

$$S = \max\{Q, AVGL \times AVG\} + z\sqrt{AVGL \times STD^2 + AVG^2 \times STDL^2}$$

Finally, the constant *z* is chosen from Table 3.2.

3.3   Risk Pooling

Consider the following distribution problem faced by ACME, a company that produces and distributes electronic equipment in the Northeast of the United States. The current distribution system partitions the Northeast into two markets, each of which has a single warehouse. One warehouse is located in Paramus, New Jersey, and the second is located in Newton, Massachusetts. Customers, typically retailers, receive items directly from the warehouses; in the current distribution system, each customer is assigned to a single market and receives deliveries from the corresponding warehouse.

The warehouses receive items from a manufacturing facility in Chicago. Lead time for delivery to each of the warehouses is about one week and the manufacturing facility has sufficient production capacity to satisfy any warehouse order. The current distribution strategy provides a 97 percent service level; that is, the inventory policy employed by each warehouse is designed so that the probability of a stockout is 3 percent. Of course, unfilled orders are lost to the competition and thus cannot be satisfied by future deliveries.

Since the original distribution system was designed over seven years ago, the company's newly appointed CEO has decided to review the current logistics and distribution system. ACME handles about 1,500 different products in its supply chain and serves about 10,000 accounts in the Northeast.

ACME is considering the following alternative strategy: Replace the two warehouses with a single warehouse located between Paramus and Newton that will serve all customer orders. We will refer to this proposed system as the centralized distribution system. The CEO insists that the same service level, 97 percent, be maintained regardless of the logistics strategy employed.

Obviously, the current distribution system with two warehouses has an important advantage over the single warehouse system because each warehouse is close to a particular subset of customers, decreasing delivery time. However, the proposed change also has an important advantage; it allows ACME to achieve either the same service level of 97 percent with much lower inventory or a higher service level with the same amount of total inventory.

Intuitively this is explained as follows. With random demand, it is very likely that a higher-than-average demand at one retailer will be offset by a lower-than-average demand at another. As the number of retailers served by a warehouse goes up, this likelihood also goes up.

How much can ACME reduce inventory if the company decides to switch to the centralized system but maintain the same 97 percent service level?

To answer that question, we need to perform a more rigorous analysis of the inventory policy that ACME should use in both the current system and the centralized system. We will explain this analysis for two specific products, Product A and Product B, although the analysis must be conducted for all products.

For both products, an order from the factory costs $60 per order and holding inventory costs are $0.27 per unit per week. In the current distribution system, the cost of transporting a product from a warehouse to a customer is, on average, $1.05 per product. It is estimated that in the centralized distribution system, the transportation cost from the central warehouse is, on average, $1.10 per product. For this analysis, we assume that delivery lead time is not significantly different in the two systems.

Tables 3.5 and 3.6 provide historical data for Products A and B, respectively. The tables include weekly demand information for each product for the last eight weeks in each market area. Observe that Product B is a slow-moving product—the demand for Product B is fairly small relative to the demand for Product A.

Table 3.7 provides a summary of average weekly demand and the standard deviation of weekly demand for each product. It also presents the *coefficient of variation* of demand faced by each warehouse. This is defined as follows:

$$\text{Coefficient of variation} = \frac{\text{Standard deviation}}{\text{Average demand}}$$

TABLE 3.5   Historical Data for Product A

Week	1	2	3	4	5	6	7	8
Massachusetts	33	45	37	38	55	30	18	58
New Jersey	46	35	41	40	26	48	18	55
Total	79	80	78	78	81	78	36	113

TABLE 3.6   Historical Data for Product B

Week	1	2	3	4	5	6	7	8
Massachusetts	0	2	3	0	0	1	3	0
New Jersey	2	4	0	0	3	1	0	0
Total	2	6	3	0	3	2	3	0

TABLE 3.7   Summary of Historical Data

Statistics	Product	Average Demand	Standard Deviation Demand	Coefficient of Variation
Massachusetts	A	39.3	13.2	0.34
Massachusetts	B	1.125	1.36	1.21
New Jersey	A	38.6	12.0	0.31
New Jersey	B	1.25	1.58	1.26
Total	A	77.9	20.71	0.27
Total	B	2.375	1.9	0.81

It is important at this point to understand the difference between the standard deviation and the coefficient of variation, both of which provide a measure of variability of customer demand. Indeed, while the standard deviation measures the absolute variability of customer demands, the coefficient of variation measures variability relative to average demand. For instance, in the case of the two products analyzed here, we observe that Product A has a much larger standard deviation while Product B has a significantly larger coefficient of variation. This distinction between the two products plays an important role in the final analysis.

Finally, note that for each product the average demand faced by the warehouse in the centralized distribution system is the sum of the average demand faced by each of the existing warehouses. However, the variability faced by the central warehouse, measured either by the standard deviation or the coefficient of variation, is much smaller than the combined variabilities faced by the two existing warehouses. This has a major impact on inventory levels in the current and proposed systems. These levels, calculated as we have described in previous sections, are shown in Table 3.8.

Notice that the average inventory for Product A at the warehouse in Paramus, New Jersey, is about

$$\text{Safety stock} + \frac{Q}{2} = 88$$

Similarly, average inventory at the Newton, Massachusetts, warehouse for the same product is about 91 units, while average inventory in the centralized warehouse is about 132 units. Thus, average inventory for Product A is reduced by about 26 percent when ACME shifts from the current system to the new, centralized system—a significant reduction in average inventory.

The average inventory for Product B is 15 at the warehouse in Paramus, 15 at the warehouse in Newton, and 20 at the centralized warehouse. In this case, ACME is going to achieve a reduction of about 33 percent in average inventory level.

The previous example illustrates risk pooling, an important concept in supply chain management. Risk pooling suggests that demand variability is reduced if one aggregates demand across locations because, as we aggregate demand across different locations, it becomes more likely that high demand from one customer will be offset by low demand from another. This reduction in variability allows us to reduce safety stock and therefore reduce average inventory. For example, in the centralized distribution system described above, the warehouse serves all customers, which leads to a reduction in variability measured by either the standard deviation or the coefficient of variation.

We summarize the three critical points we have made about risk pooling.

TABLE 3.8   Inventory Levels

	Product	Average Demand during Lead Time	Safety Stock	Reorder Point	Q	Order-up-to-Level
Massachusetts	A	39.3	25.08	65	132	158
Massachusetts	B	1.125	2.58	4	25	26
New Jersey	A	38.6	22.80	62	131	154
New Jersey	B	1.25	3	5	24	27
Central	A	77.9	39.35	118	186	226
Central	B	2.375	3.61	6	33	37

1. Centralizing inventory reduces both safety stock and average inventory in the system. Intuitively this is explained as follows. In a centralized distribution system, whenever demand from one market area is higher than average while demand in another market area is lower than average, items in the warehouse that were originally allocated for one market can be reallocated to the other. The process of reallocating inventory is not possible in a decentralized distribution system where different warehouses serve different markets.

2. The higher the coefficient of variation, the greater the benefit obtained from centralized systems; that is, the greater the benefit from risk pooling. This is explained as follows. Average inventory includes two components: one proportional to average weekly demand (Q) and the other proportional to the standard deviation of weekly demand (safety stock). Since reduction in average inventory is achieved mainly through a reduction in safety stock, the higher the coefficient of variation the larger the impact of safety stock on inventory reduction.

3. The benefits from risk pooling depend on the behavior of demand from one market relative to demand from another. We say that demand from two markets is *positively correlated* if it is very likely that whenever demand from one market is greater then average, demand from the other market is also greater than average. Similarly, when demand from one market is smaller than average, so is demand from the other. Intuitively, the benefit from risk pooling decreases as the correlation between demand from the two markets becomes more positive.

In Chapter 8, we provide a different example of risk pooling. In that case, risk pooling is applied by *aggregating demand across products*, rather than across customers as we do here.

3.4 Centralized versus Decentralized Systems

The analysis in the previous section raises an important practical issue: What are the trade-offs that we need to consider in comparing centralized distribution systems with decentralized distribution systems?

Safety stock. Clearly, safety stock decreases as a firm moves from a decentralized to a centralized system. The amount of decrease depends on a number of parameters including the coefficient of variation and the correlation between the demand from the different markets.

Service level. When the centralized and decentralized systems have the same total safety stock, the service level provided by the centralized system is higher. As before, the magnitude of the increase in service level depends on the coefficient of variation and the correlation between the demand from the different markets.

Overhead costs. Typically, these costs are much greater in a decentralized system because there are fewer economies of scale.

Customer lead time. Since the warehouses are much closer to the customers in a decentralized system, response time is much lower (see Chapter 2).

Transportation costs. The impact on transportation costs depends on the specifics of the situation. On one hand, as we increase the number of warehouses, outbound transportation costs—the costs incurred for delivering the items from the warehouses to the customers—decrease because warehouses are much closer to the market areas. On the other hand, inbound transportation costs—the costs of shipping the products from the supply and manufacturing facilities to the warehouses—increase. Thus, the net impact on total transportation cost is not immediately clear.

3.5   Managing Inventory in the Supply Chain

The inventory models and examples considered so far assume a single facility (e.g., a warehouse or a retail outlet) managing its inventory in order to minimize its own cost as much as possible. In a typical supply chain, the main objective is to reduce systemwide cost; thus it is important to consider the interaction of the various facilities and the impact this interaction has on the inventory policy that should be employed by each facility.

For this purpose, consider a retail distribution system with a single warehouse serving a number of retailers. We make two important, but reasonable, assumptions:

1. Inventory decisions are made by a single decision maker whose objective is to minimize systemwide cost.
2. The decision maker has access to inventory information at each of the retailers and at the warehouse.

Under these assumptions, an inventory policy based on the so-called *echelon inventory* is an effective way to manage the system. More importantly, and as we will see, this policy can be extended in a natural way to manage more complex supply chains.

To understand this policy, it is necessary to introduce the concept of echelon inventory. In a distribution system, each stage or level (i.e., the warehouse or the retailers) is often referred to as an echelon. Thus, the echelon inventory at any stage or level of the system is equal to the inventory on hand at the echelon, plus all *downstream inventory*. For example, the echelon inventory at the warehouse is equal to the inventory at the warehouse, plus all of the inventory in transit to and in stock at the retailers. Similarly, the *echelon inventory position* at the warehouse is the echelon inventory at the warehouse, plus those items ordered by the warehouse that have not yet arrived (see Figure 3.8).

This suggests the following effective approach to managing the single warehouse multi-retailer system. First, the individual retailers are managed as described in Section 3.2.3, using the appropriate (s, S) inventory policy. Second, the warehouse ordering decisions are based on the echelon inventory position at the warehouse. Specifically, the reorder point, s, and order-up-to-level, S, are calculated for each retailer using the approach described in Section 3.2.3. Whenever the inventory position at a retailer falls below the reorder point, s, an order is placed to raise its inventory position to S. Similarly, a reorder point, s, and an order-up-to-level, S, are calculated for the warehouse. In this case, however, the warehouse policy controls its echelon inventory position; that is, whenever the echelon inventory position for the warehouse is below s, an order is placed to raise its echelon inventory position to S.

How should the reorder point associated with the warehouse echelon inventory position be calculated? In this case, the reorder point is:

$$s = L^e \times AVG + z \times STD\sqrt{L^e}$$

where

$L^e = $ *echelon lead time*, defined as the lead time between the retailers and the warehouse *plus* the lead time between the warehouse and its supplier

$AVG = $ average demand across all retailers (i.e., the average of the aggregate demand)

$STD = $ standard deviation of (aggregate) demand across all retailers

FIGURE 3.8

The warehouse echelon inventory

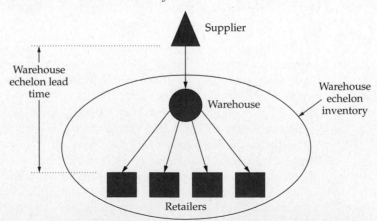

Example 3.5.1	Consider the TV distributor from Example 3.2.1, where we determined the inventory policy for the warehouse. Now suppose that the warehouse supplies a group of retailers. The historical demand data provided in Table 3.3 is the aggregate demand data for the retailers. Finally, the two weeks' lead time is the echelon lead time—the time it takes an order placed by the warehouse to reach a customer. Thus, the distributor needs to ensure that a total of 176 units of inventory, or about four weeks' supply, is somewhere in the system, either in the pipeline to the warehouse, at the warehouse, in transit to the retailers, or at the retailers.

What about the retailers? In this case, we need to perform exactly the same calculations, but this time utilizing the specific demand faced by each retailer and the associated lead time from the warehouse to that retailer.

Suppose, for example, that the average weekly demand at a specific retailer is 11.6, with a standard deviation of 4.5. Furthermore, suppose that it takes one week for items to get from the warehouse to the retailer. Using the same approach as before to achieve a 97 percent service level, we find that the reorder level, s, for the retailer is 20. Thus, an order is placed whenever the retailer inventory position is 20. Obviously, if other retailers face different demand or lead times, they will have different reorder levels.

Finally, it is important to point out that this technique can be extended to more complex supply chains—supply chains with additional levels—provided that the supply chains are under centralized control and that inventory information from each of the echelons is available to the decision maker.

3.6 Practical Issues

In a recent survey,[1] materials and inventory managers were asked to identify effective inventory reduction strategies. The top five strategies in this survey are:

1. Periodic inventory review policy. In this strategy, inventory is reviewed at a fixed time interval and every time it is reviewed, a decision is made on the order size. The periodic inventory review policy makes it possible to identify slow-moving and obsolete products and allows management to continuously reduce inventory levels.

2. Tight management of usage rates, lead times, and safety stock. This allows the firm to make sure inventory is kept at the appropriate level. Such an inventory control process allows the firm to identify, for example, situations in which usage rates decrease for a few months. If no

---

[1] *Inventory Reduction Report*, no. 98-4 (April 1998) pp. 12–14.

appropriate action is taken, this decrease in usage rates implies an increase in inventory levels over the same period of time.

3. ABC approach. In this strategy, items are classified into three categories. Class A items include all high-value products, which typically account for about 80 percent of annual ($) sales and represent about 20 percent of inventory SKUs. Class B items include products which account for about 15 percent of annual sales while Class C products represent low-value items, products whose value is no more than 5 percent of sales. Because Class A items account for the major part of the business, a high-frequency periodic review policy (e.g., a weekly review) is appropriate in this case. Similarly, a periodic review policy is applied to control Class B products, although the frequency of review is not as high as that for Class A products. Finally, depending on product value, the firm either keeps no inventory of expensive Class C products, or keeps a high inventory of inexpensive Class C products.

4. Reduce safety stock levels. This can perhaps be accomplished by focusing on lead time reduction.

5. Quantitative approaches. These approaches are similar to those described in this chapter which focus on the right balance between inventory holding and ordering costs.

Observe that the focus in the survey was not on reducing cost but on reducing inventory levels. Indeed, in the last few years we have seen a significant effort by industry to increase the *inventory turnover ratio* defined as follows:

$$\textit{Inventory turnover ratio} = \frac{\text{annual sales}}{\text{average inventory level}}$$

This definition implies that an increase in inventory turnover leads to a decrease in average inventory levels. For instance, retailing powerhouse Wal-Mart has the highest inventory turnover ratio of any discount retailer. This suggests that Wal-Mart has a higher level of liquidity, smaller risk of obsolescence, and reduced investment in inventory. Of course, a low inventory level in itself is not always appropriate since it increases the risk of lost sales.

Thus, the question is, what is the appropriate inventory turns that the firm should use in practice? A recent survey of industry practices suggests that the answer does change from year to year and depends, in particular, on the specific industry.[2] Indeed, the survey reports a significant increase in inventory turnover ratios in 1997; about 51.6 percent of the manufacturers participating in the survey increased their turnover. Table 3.9 provides some examples of inventory turnover in different manufacturing companies, by industry, in 1997.

---

[2]*Inventory Reduction Report*, no. 98-3 (March 1998) pp. 10–12.

TABLE 3.9 Inventory Turnover Ratio for Different Manufacturers

Industry	Upper Quartile	Median	Lower Quartile
Electronic components & accessories	9.8	5.7	3.7
Electronic Computers	9.4	5.3	3.5
Household audio & video equipment	6.2	3.4	2.3
Household electrical appliances	8.0	5.0	3.8
Industrial chemicals	10.3	6.6	4.4
Dairy products	34.4	19.3	9.2
Publishing and printing	9.8	2.4	1.3

Source: Based on a survey conducted by Robert Morris Associates.

SUMMARY

Matching supply and demand in the supply chain is a critical challenge. To reduce cost and provide the required service level, it is important to take into account inventory holding and set-up costs, lead time, and forecast demand. Unfortunately, the so-called *first rule* of inventory management states that *forecast demand is always wrong*. Thus, a single number, forecast demand, is not enough when determining an effective inventory policy. Indeed, the inventory management strategies described in this chapter also take into account information about demand variability.

The *second rule* of inventory management is that *aggregate demand information is always more accurate than disaggregate data*. That is, aggregate demand data has much smaller variability. This is exactly the basis for the risk pooling concept that enables lower inventory level without affecting service level.

CHAPTER

4

The Value of Information

CASE: BARILLA SPA (A)

Giorgio Maggiali was becoming increasingly frustrated. As director of logistics for the world's largest pasta producer, Barilla SpA (Societa per Aziont translates as "Society for Stockholders" and is interpreted as "Inc."), Maggiali was acutely aware of the growing burden that demand fluctuations imposed on the company's manufacturing and distribution system. Since his appointment in 1988 as Director of Logistics, he had been trying to make headway on an innovative idea proposed by Brando Vitali, who had served as Barilla's director of logistics before Maggiali. The idea, which Vitali called Just-In-Time Distribution (JITD), was modeled after the popular "Just-In-Time" manufacturing concept. In essence, Vitali proposed that, rather than follow the traditional practice of delivering product to Barilla's distributors on the basis of whatever orders those distributors placed with the company, Barilla's own logistics organization would instead specify the "appropriate" delivery quantities—those that would more effectively meet the end consumer's needs yet also would distribute the workload on Barilla's manufacturing and logistics systems more evenly.

For two years Maggiali, a strong supporter of Vitali's proposal, had tried to implement the idea, but now, in the spring of 1990, little progress had been made. It seemed that Barilla's customers were simply unwilling to give up their authority to place orders as they pleased; some were even reluctant to provide the detailed sales data upon which Barilla could make delivery decisions and improve its demand forecasts. Perhaps more disconcerting was the internal resistance from Barilla's own sales and marketing organizations, which saw the concept as infeasible or dangerous, or both. Perhaps it was time to discard the idea as simply unworkable. If not, how might Maggiali increase the chances that the idea would be accepted?

Source: Copyright © 1994 by the President and Fellows of Harvard College. This case was written by Janice H. Hammond of Harvard Business School.

Company Background

Barilla was founded in 1875 when Pietro Barilla opened a small shop in Parma, Italy, on Via Vittorio Emanuele. Adjoining the shop was the small "laboratory" Pietro used to make the pasta and bread products he sold in his store. Pietro's son Ricardo led the company through a significant period of growth and, in the 1940s, passed the company to his own sons, Pietro and Gianni. Over time Barilla evolved from its modest beginnings into a large, vertically integrated corporation with flour mills, pasta plants, and bakery-product factories located throughout Italy.

In a crowded field of more than 2,000 Italian pasta manufacturers, Pietro and Gianni Barilla differentiated their company with a high-quality product supported by innovative marketing programs. Barilla revolutionized the Italian pasta industry's marketing practices by creating a strong brand name and image for its pasta, selling pasta in a sealed cardboard box with a recognizable color pattern rather than in bulk, and investing in large-scale advertising programs. In 1968, to support the double-digit sales growth the company had experienced during the 1960s, Pietro and Gianni Barilla began construction of a 125 million square meter state-of-the art pasta plant in Pedrignano, a rural town 5 km outside Parma.

The cost of this massive facility—the largest and most technologically advanced pasta plant in the world—drove the Barillas deeply into debt. In 1971 the brothers sold the company to the U.S. multinational firm, W. R. Grace, Inc. Grace brought additional capital investment and professional management practices to the company and launched an important new Mulino Bianco ("White Mill") line of bakery products. Throughout the 1970s, facing difficult economic conditions and new Italian legislation that both capped retail pasta prices and increased the cost-of-living allowances for employees, Grace struggled to make its Barilla acquisition pay off. In 1979, Grace sold the company back to Pietro Barilla, who by then had secured the necessary funds to purchase it.

The capital investments and organizational changes that Grace had brought to Barilla, combined with improving market conditions, helped Pietro Barilla launch a successful return to the company. During the 1980s, Barilla enjoyed an annual growth rate of over 21 percent (see Table 4.1). Growth was realized through the expansion of existing businesses, both in Italy and other European countries, as well as through acquisition of new, related businesses.

By 1990 Barilla had become the largest pasta manufacturer in the world, making 35 percent of the pasta sold in Italy and 22 percent of the pasta sold in Europe. Barilla's share in Italy comprised its three brands: The traditional Barilla brand represented 32 percent of the market; the remaining 3 percent of market share was divided between its Voiello brand (a traditional Neapolitan pasta competing in the high-priced segment of the semolina pasta market) and its Braibanti brand (a high-quality, traditional Parmesan pasta made from eggs and semolina). About half of Barilla's pasta was sold in northern Italy and half in the south, where Barilla held a smaller share of the market than in the north but where the market was larger. In addition, Barilla held a 29 percent share of the Italian bakery products market.

In 1990 Barilla was organized into seven divisions: three pasta divisions (Barina, Voiello, and Braibanti), the Bakery Products Division (manufacturing medium to long shelf-life bakery products), the Fresh Bread Division (manufacturing very short shelf-life bakery products), the Catering Division (distributing cakes and

TABLE 4.1   Barilla Sales, 1960–1991

Year	Barilla Sales (lire in billions*)	Italian Wholesale Price Index
1960	15	10.8
1970	47	41.5
1980	344	57.5
1981	456	67.6
1982	609	76.9
1983	728	84.4
1984	1,034	93.2
1985	1,204	100.0
1986	1,381	99.0
1987	1,634	102.0
1988	1,775	106.5
1989	2,068	121.7
1990[†]	2,390	126.0

*In 1990, 1,198 lire = US $1.00.
[†]1990 figures are estimates.
Source: Based on company documents and
International Financial Statistics Yearbook,
International Monetary Fund

frozen croissants to bars and pastry shops), and the International Division. Barilla's corporate headquarters were located adjacent to the Pedrignano pasta plant.

Industry Background

The origins of pasta are unknown. Some believe it originated in China and was first brought to Italy by Marco Polo in the 13th century. Others claim that pasta's origins were rooted in Italy, citing as proof a bas-relief on a third-century tomb located near Rome that depicts a pasta roller and cutter. "Regardless of its origins," Barilla marketing literature pronounced, "since time immemorial, Italians have adored pasta." Per capita pasta consumption in Italy averaged nearly 18 kilos per year, greatly exceeding that of other western European countries (see Table 4.2). There was limited seasonality in pasta demand—for example, special pasta types were used for pasta salads in the summer while egg pasta and lasagna were very popular for Easter meals.

In the late 1980s the Italian pasta market as a whole was relatively flat, growing less than 1 percent per year. By 1990 the Italian pasta market was estimated at 3.5 trillion lire. Semolina pasta and fresh pasta were the only growth segments of the Italian pasta market. In contrast, the export market was experiencing record growth; pasta exports from Italy to other European countries were expected to rise as much as 20 percent to 25 percent per year in the early 1990s. Barilla's management estimated that two-thirds of this increase would be attributed to the new

---

TABLE 4.2   **Per Capita Consumption of Pasta and Bakery Products, in Kilograms, 1990**

Country	Bread	Breakfast Cereals	Pasta	Biscuits
Belgium	85.5	1.0	1.7	5.2
Denmark	29.9	3.7	1.6	5.5
France	68.8	0.6	5.9	6.5
Germany (West)	61.3	0.7	5.2	3.1
Greece	70.0		6.2	8.0
Ireland	58.4	7.7		17.9
Italy	130.9	0.2	17.8	5.9
Netherlands	60.5	1.0	1.4	2.8
Portugal	70.0		5.7	4.6
Spain	87.3	0.3	2.8	5.2
United Kingdom	43.6	7.0	3.6	13.0
Average	70.3	2.5	5.2	7.1

Adapted from *European Marketing Data and Statistics* 1992, Euromonitor Plc 1992, p. 323.

flow of exported pasta to eastern European countries seeking low-priced basic food products. Barilla managers viewed the eastern European market as an excellent export opportunity, with the potential to encompass a full range of pasta products.

Plant Network

Barilla owned and operated an extensive network of plants located throughout Italy (see Table 4.3 and Figure 4.1), including large flour mills, pasta plants, and fresh bread plants, as well as plants producing specialty products such as panettone (Christmas cake) and croissants. Barilla maintained state-of-the-art research and development (R&D) facilities and a pilot production plant in Pedrignano for developing and testing new products and production processes.

Pasta Manufacturing.   The pasta-making process is similar to the process by which paper is made. In Barilla plants, flour and water (and for some products, eggs and/or spinach meal) were mixed to form dough, which was then rolled into a long, thin continuous sheet by sequential pairs of rollers set at increasingly closer tolerances. After being rolled to the desired thickness, the dough sheet was forced through a bronze extruding die screen; the die's design gave the pasta its distinctive shape. After passing through the extruder, Barilla workers cut the pasta to a specified length. The cut pieces were then hung over dowels (or placed onto trays) and moved slowly through a long tunnel kiln that snaked across the factory floor. The temperature and humidity in the kiln were precisely specified for each size and shape of pasta and had to be tightly controlled to ensure a high-quality product. To keep changeover costs low and product quality high, Barilla followed

TABLE 4.3   Barilla Plant Locations and Products
             Manufactured, 1989

Index	Plant Location	Products
1	Bribanti	Pasta
2	Cagliari	Pasta
3	Foggia	Pasta
4	Matera	Pasta
5	Pedrignano	Pasta, noodles, biscuits
6	Viale Barilla	Tortellini, noodles, fresh pasta
7	Caserta	Pasta, rusks, breadsticks
8	Grissin Bon	Breadsticks
9	Rubbiano	Rusks, breadsticks
10	Milano	Panettone, cakes, croissants
11	Pomezia	Croissants
12	Mantova	Biscuits, cakes
13	Melfi	Snacks
14	Ascoli	Snacks, sliced loafs
15	Rodolfi	Sauces
16	Altamura	Flour mill
17	Castelplanio	Flour mill
18	Ferrara	Flour mill
19	Matera	Flour mill
20	Termoli	Flour mill
21	Milano	Fresh bread
22	Milano	Fresh bread
23	Altopascio	Fresh bread
24	Padova	Fresh bread
25	Torino	Fresh bread

a carefully chosen production sequence that minimized the incremental changes in kiln temperature and humidity between pasta shapes. After completing the four-hour drying process, the pasta was weighed and packaged.

At Barilla, raw ingredients were transformed into packaged pasta on fully automated 120-meter-long production lines. In the Pedrignano plant, the largest and most technologically advanced of Barilla's plants, 11 lines produced 9,000 quintals (900,000 kilos) of pasta each day. Barilla employees used bicycles to travel within this enormous facility.

Barilla's pasta plants were specialized by the type of pasta produced in the plant. The primary distinctions were based on the consumption of the pasta—for example, whether it was made with or without eggs or spinach, and whether it was sold as dry or fresh pasta. All of Barilla's pasta was made with flour ground from *grano duro* (high protein "hard" wheat), the highest-quality flour for making traditional pasta products. Semolina, for example, is a finely ground durum wheat flour. Barilla used flours made from *grano tenero* (tender wheat), such as farina, for more delicate products like egg pasta and bakery products. Barilla's flour mills ground flour from both types of wheat.

FIGURE 4.1

Map of Barilla plant locations and products manufactured

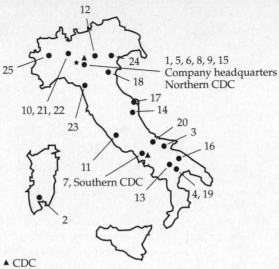

▲ CDC
★ Company headquarters
● Refers to Table 4.3 index

Even within the same family of pasta products, individual products were assigned to plants based on the size and shape of the pasta. "Short" pasta products, such as macaroni or fusilli, and "long" products, such as spaghetti or capellini, were made in separate facilities because of the different sizes of equipment required.

Channels of Distribution

Barilla divided its entire product line into two general categories:

- "Fresh" products, including fresh pasta products, which had 21-day shelf lives, and fresh bread, which had a one-day shelf life.
- "Dry" products including dry pasta, and longer shelf-life bakery products such as cookies, biscuits, flour, bread sticks, and dry toasts. Dry products represented about 75 percent of Barilla's sales and had either "long" shelf lives of 18 to 24 months (e.g., pasta and dried toasts) or "medium" shelf lives of 10 to 12 weeks (e.g., cookies). In total, Barilla's "dry" products were offered in some 800 different packaged shop keeping units (SKUs). Pasta was made in 200 different shapes and sizes and was offered in more than 470 different packaged SKUs. The most popular pasta products were offered in a variety of packaging options; for example, at any one time Barilla's #5 spaghetti might be offered in a 5-kg package, a 2-kg package, a 1-kg package with a northern Italian motif, a 2-kg package with a southern Italian motif, a 0.5-kg "northern-motif" package, a 0.5-kg "southern-motif" package, a display pallet, and a special promotional package with a free bottle of Barilla pasta sauce.

Most Barilla products were shipped from the plants in which they were made to one of two Barilla central distribution centers (CDCs): the Northern CDC in Pedrignano or the Southern CDC on the outskirts of Naples. See Figure 4.2. (Certain products, such as fresh bread, did not flow through the CDCs.). Other fresh products were moved quickly through the distribution system; fresh product inventory was typically held only three days in each of the CDCs. In contrast, each CDC held about a month's worth of dry product inventory.

Barilla maintained separate distribution systems for its fresh and dry products because of their differences in perishability and retail service requirements. Fresh products were purchased from the two CDCs by independent agents (*concessionari*) who then channeled the products through 70 regional warehouses located throughout Italy. Nearly two-thirds of Barilla's dry products were destined for supermarkets; these products were shipped first to one of Barilla's CDCs, where they were purchased by distributors. The distributors in turn shipped the product to supermarkets. Brando Vitali's JITD proposal focused solely on dry products sold through distributors. The remainder of the dry products was distributed through 18 small Barilla-owned warehouses, mostly to small shops.

Barilla products were distributed through three types of retail outlets: small independent grocers, supermarket chains, and independent supermarkets. In sum, Barilla estimated that its products were offered in 100,000 retail outlets in Italy alone.

FIGURE 4.2

Barilla distribution patterns

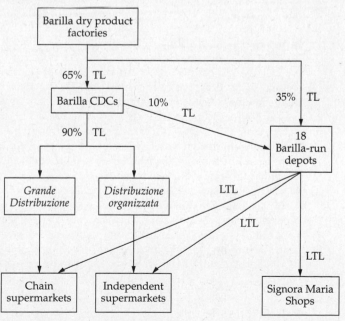

TL = Delivery in truckload quantities.
LTL = Delivery in less-than-truckload quantities.

Note: Shipping percentages are based on product weight.

1. Small independent shops. Small shops were more prevalent in Italy than in other western European countries. Through the late 1980s the Italian government had supported small grocers (often referred to as "Signora Maria" shops) by restricting the number of licenses provided to operate large supermarkets. However, in the early 1990s the number of supermarkets began to grow as governmental restrictions abated.

Approximately 35 percent of Barilla's dry products (30 percent in the north of Italy and 40 percent in the south) were distributed from Barilla's internally owned regional warehouses to small independent shops, which typically held over two weeks of inventory at the store level. Small shop owners purchased products through brokers who dealt with Barilla purchasing and distribution personnel.

2. Supermarkets. The remaining dry products were distributed through outside distributors to supermarkets—70 percent to supermarket chains and 30 percent to independent supermarkets. A supermarket typically held from 10 to 12 days of dry product inventory within the stores, and on average carried a total of 4,800 dry product SKUs. Although Barilla offered many pasta products in multiple types of packages, most retailers would carry a product in only one (and at most two) packaging options.

Dry products destined for a supermarket chain were distributed through the chain's own distribution organization, known as a *Grande Distribuzione* ("grand distributors") or GDs; those destined for independent supermarkets were channeled through a different set of distributors known as *Distribuzione Organizzata* ("organized distributors") or DOs. A DO acted as a central buying organization for a large number of independent supermarkets. Most DOs had regional operations, and the retailers they served usually got their products from only a single DO.

Due to regional preferences and differences in retail requirements, a typical distributor might distribute 130 of Barilla's 800 dry product SKUs. Most distributors handled products coming from about 200 different suppliers; of these, Barilla typically would be the largest in terms of the physical volume of products purchased. Distributors typically carried from 7,000 to 10,000 SKUs in total. However, their strategies varied. For example, one of Barilla's largest DOs, Cortese, carried only 100 of Barilla's dry products and carried a total of only 5,000 SKUs.

Both GDs and DOs purchased products from the Barilla CDCs, maintained inventory in their own warehouses, and then filled supermarket orders from their warehouse inventory. A distributor's warehouse typically held a two weeks' supply of Barilla dry products in inventory.

Many supermarkets placed daily orders with distributors; the store manager would walk up and down the store aisles and note each product that needed to be replenished and the number of boxes required (more sophisticated retailers used handheld computers to record order quantities as they checked the shelves). The order would then be transmitted to the store's distributor; orders were typically received at the store 24 to 48 hours after receipt of the order at the distribution center.

Sales and Marketing

Barilla enjoyed a strong brand image in Italy. Its marketing and sales strategy was based upon a combination of advertising and promotions.

Advertising.   Barilla brands were heavily advertised. Advertising copy differentiated Barilla pasta from basic commodity "noodles" by positioning the brand as the highest quality, most sophisticated pasta product available. One ad campaign was built on the phrase: "Barilla: a great collection of premium Italian pasta." The "collection" dimension was illustrated by showing individual uncooked pasta shapes against a black background, as though they were jewels, evoking a sense of luxury and sophistication. Unlike other pasta manufacturers, Barilla avoided images of traditional Italian folklore, preferring modern, sophisticated settings in major Italian cities.

Advertising themes were supported by sponsorships of well-known athletes and celebrities. For example, Barilla engaged tennis stars Steffi Graf to promote Barilla products in Germany and Stefan Edberg in the Scandinavian countries. Luminaries such as actor Paul Newman were also used to promote Barilla products. In addition, Barilla advertising focused on developing and strengthening loyal relationships with Italian families by using messages such as "Where there is Barilla, there is a home."

Trade Promotions.   Barilla's sales strategy relied on the use of trade promotions to push its products into the grocery distribution network. A Barilla sales executive explained the logic of the promotion-based strategy:

> We sell to a very old-fashioned distribution system. The buyers expect frequent trade promotions, which they then pass along to their own customers. So a store will know right away if another store is buying Barilla pasta at a discount. You have to understand how important pasta is in Italy. Everyone knows the price of pasta. If a store is selling pasta at a discount one week, consumers notice the reduced price immediately.

Barilla divided each year into 10 or 12 "canvass" periods, typically four to five weeks in length, each corresponding to a promotional program. During any canvass period, a Barilla distributor could buy as many products as desired to meet current and future needs. Incentives for Barilla sales representatives were based on achieving the sales targets set for each canvass period. Different product categories were offered during different canvass periods, with the discount depending on the margin structure of the category. Typical promotional discounts were 1.4 percent for semolina pasta, 4 percent for egg pasta, 4 percent for biscuits, 8 percent for sauces, and 10 percent for breadsticks.

Barilla also offered volume discounts. For example, Barilla paid for transportation, thus providing incentives of 2 percent to 3 percent for orders in full truckload quantities. In addition, a sales representative might offer a buyer a 1,000 lire per carton discount (representing a 4 percent discount) if the buyer purchased a minimum of three truckloads of Barilla egg pasta.

Sales Representatives.   Barilla sales representatives serving DOs spent an estimated 90 percent of their time working at the store level. In the store, sales reps helped merchandise Barilla products and set up in-store promotions; took note of competitive information, including competitors' prices, stockouts, and new product introductions; and discussed Barilla products and ordering strategies with store management. In addition, each sales rep spent a half day in a regularly scheduled weekly meeting with the distributor's buyer, helping the distributor place its weekly order, explaining promotions and discounts, and settling problems such as returns and deletions associated with the last delivery. Each rep carried a portable computer for inputting distributor orders. The rep also would spend a few hours a week at the CDC, discussing new products and prices, covering problems concerning the previous week's deliveries, and settling disputes about different discounts and deal structures.

In contrast, a very small sales force served the GDs. The GD sales force rarely visited GD warehouses and usually sent their orders to Barilla via fax.

Distribution

Distributor Ordering Procedures.   Most distributors—GDs and DOs alike—checked their inventory levels and placed orders with Barilla once a week. Barilla products would then be shipped to the distributor over the course of the week that started 8 days after the order was placed and ended 14 days after the order was placed—the average lead time was 10 days. For example, a large distributor that ordered every Tuesday might order several truckloads to be delivered from the following Wednesday through the following Tuesday (see below). Distributors' sales volumes varied; small distributors might order only one truckload a week whereas the largest warranted deliveries of as many as five truckloads a week.

Most distributors used simple periodic review inventory systems. For example, a distributor might review inventory levels of Barilla products each Tuesday; the distributor would then place orders for those products whose levels fell below the reorder level. Nearly all of the distributors had computer-supported ordering systems but few had forecasting systems or sophisticated analytical tools for determining order quantities.

Impetus for the JITD Program.   As the 1980s progressed, Barilla increasingly felt the effects of fluctuating demand. Orders for Barilla dry products often swung wildly from week to week (see Figure 4.3). Such extreme demand variability strained Barilla's manufacturing and logistics operations. For example, the specific sequence of pasta production necessitated by the tight heat and humidity specifications in the tunnel kiln made it difficult to quickly produce a particular pasta that had been sold out owing to unexpectedly high demand. On the other hand, holding sufficient finished goods inventories to meet distributors' order requirements was extremely expensive when weekly demand fluctuated so widely and was so unpredictable.

Some manufacturing and logistics personnel favored asking distributors or retailers to carry additional inventory to check the fluctuation in distributors' orders, noting that with their current inventory levels, many distributors' service levels to the retailers were unacceptable (see Figure 4.4 for sample distributor inventory levels and stockout rates). Others felt that the distributors and retailers were already carrying too much inventory. In the late 1980s a Barilla logistics manager discussed retail inventory pressure:

> Our customers are changing. And do you know why they are changing? As I see it, they are realizing they do not have enough room in their stores and warehouses to carry the very large inventories manufacturers would like

FIGURE 4.3

Weekly demand for Barilla dry products from Cortese's Northeast Distribution Center to the Pedrignano CDC, 1989

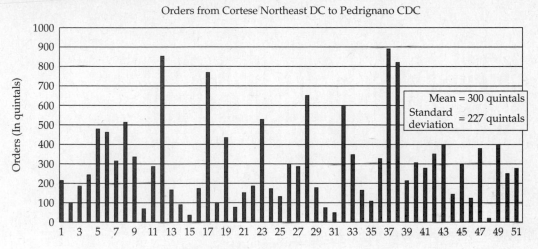

Orders from Cortese Northeast DC to Pedrignano CDC

Mean = 300 quintals
Standard deviation = 227 quintals

them to. Think of shelf space in retail outlets. You cannot easily increase it. Yet manufacturers are continuously introducing new products, and they want retailers to display each product on the fronts of their shelves! That would be impossible even if supermarkets were made from rubber![1]

Distributors felt similar pressure to increase the inventory of items they already stocked and to add items they currently did not carry.

In 1987 Brando Vitali, then Barilla's director of logistics, had expressed strong feelings about finding an alternative approach to order fulfillment. At that time, he noted, "Both manufacturers and retailers are suffering from thinning margins; we must find a way to take costs out of our distribution channel without compromising service." Vitali was seen as a visionary whose ideas stretched beyond the day-to-day details of a logistics organization. He envisioned an approach that would radically change the way in which the logistics organization managed product delivery. In early 1988 Vitali explained his plan:

I envision a simple approach: rather than send product to the distributors according to their internal planning processes, we should look at all of the distributors' shipment data and send only what is needed at the stores—no more, no less. The way we operate now it's nearly impossible to anticipate demand swings, so we end up having to hold a lot of inventory and do a lot of scrambling in our manufacturing and distribution operations to meet distributor demand. And even so, the distributors don't seem to do such a great job servicing their retailers. Look at the stockouts (see Figure 4.4) these DOs have experienced in the last year. And that's despite their holding a couple of weeks of inventory.

_____
[1]Claudia Ferrozzi, *The Pedrignano Warehouse* (Milan: GEA, 1988).

FIGURE 4.4

Sample stockout and inventory levels, Cortese's Northeast Distribution Center, 1989

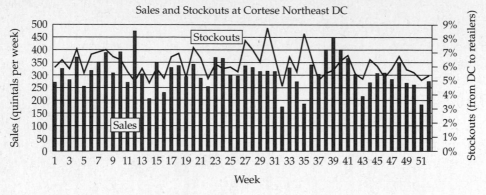

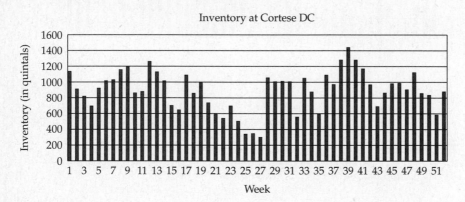

In my opinion, we could improve operations for ourselves and our customers if we were responsible for creating the delivery schedules. We'd be able to ship product only as it is needed, rather than building enormous stocks in both of our facilities. We could try to reduce our own distribution costs, inventory levels, and ultimately our manufacturing costs if we didn't have to respond to the volatile demand patterns of the distributors.

We have always had the mentality that orders were an unchangeable input into our process and therefore that one of the most important capabilities we needed to achieve was flexibility to respond to those inputs. But in reality, demand from the end consumer is the input and I think that we should be able to manage the input filter that produces the orders.

How would this work? Every day each distributor would provide us data on what Barilla products it had shipped out of its warehouse to retailers during the previous day, as well as the current stock level for each Barilla SKU. Then we could look at all of the data and make replenishment decisions based on our own forecasts. It would be similar to using point-of-sale data from retailers—

we would just be responding to see-through information one step behind the retailer. Ideally, we would use actual retail sell-through data, but that's hard to come by given the structure of our distribution channel and the fact that most grocers in Italy aren't equipped yet with the necessary bar-code scanners and computer linkages.

Of course, it's not quite as simple as that. We need to improve our own forecasting systems so we can make better use of the data that we receive. We'll also need to develop a set of decision rules that we can use to determine what to send after we've made a new forecast.

Vitali's proposal, "Just-in-Time Distribution," met with significant resistance within Barilla. The sales and marketing organizations were particularly vocal in their opposition to the plan. A number of sales representatives felt their responsibilities would be diminished if such a program were put in place. A range of concerns was expressed from the bottom to the top of the sales organization. The following remarks were heard from Barilla sales and marketing personnel:

- "Our sales levels would flatten if we put this program in place."
- "We run the risk of not being able to adjust our shipments sufficiently quickly to changes in selling patterns or increased promotions."
- "It seems to me that a pretty good part of the distribution organization is not yet ready to handle such a sophisticated relationship."
- "If space is freed up in our distributors' warehouses when inventories of our own product decrease, we run the risk of giving our competitors more distributor shelf space. The distributors would then push our competitors' product more than our own, since once something is bought it must be sold."
- "We increase the risk of having our customers' stock out of our product if we have disruption in our supply process. What if we have a strike or some other disturbance?"
- "We wouldn't be able to run trade promotions with JITD. How can we get the trade to push Barilla product to retailers if we don't offer some sort of incentive?"
- "It's not clear that costs would even be reduced. If a DO decreases its stock, we at Barilla may have to increase our own inventory of those products for which we cannot change production schedules due to our lack of manufacturing flexibility."

Vitali countered the concerns of the sales organization:

I think JITD should be considered a selling tool, rather than a threat to sales. We're offering the customer additional service at no extra cost. In addition, the program will improve Barilla's visibility with the trade and make distributors more dependent on us—it should improve the relationships between Barilla and the distributors rather than harm them. And what's more, the information regarding the supply at the distributors' warehouses provides us with objective data that would permit us to improve our own planning procedures.

Giorgio Maggiali, head of materials management for Barilla's fresh products group, was appointed director of logistics in late 1988 when Vitali was promoted to head one of the company's new divisions. Maggiali was a hands-on manager, known for his orientation to action. Shortly after his appointment, Maggiali appointed a recent college graduate, Vincenzo Battistini, to help him develop and implement the JITD program.

Maggiali recounted his frustrations in implementing the JITD program:

> In 1988 we developed the basic ideas for the approach we wanted to use and tried to convince several of our distributors to sign on. They weren't even interested in talking about it; the manager of one of our largest distributors pretty much summed up a lot of the responses we had when he cut off a conversation saying, "Managing stock is my job; I don't need you to see my warehouse or my figures. I could improve my inventory and service levels myself if you would deliver my orders more quickly. I'll make you a proposal— I'll place the order and you deliver within 36 hours." He didn't understand that we just can't respond to wildly changing orders without more notice than that. Another distributor expressed concerns about becoming too closely linked to Barilla. "We would be giving Barilla the power to push product into our warehouses just so Barilla can reduce its costs." Still another asked, "What makes you think that you could manage my inventories any better than I can?"

> We were finally able to convince a couple of our distributors to have in-depth discussions about the JITD proposal. Our first discussion was with Marconi, a large, fairly old-fashioned GD. First Battistini and I visited Marconi's logistics department and presented our plan. We made it clear that we planned to provide them with such good service that they could both decrease their inventories and improve their fill rate to their stores. The logistics group thought it sounded great, and was interested in conducting an experimental run of the program. But as soon as Marconi's buyers heard about it, all hell broke loose. First the buyers started to voice their own concerns; then, after talking to their Barilla sales reps, they started to repeat some of our own sales department's objections as well. Marconi finally agreed to sell us the data we wanted, but otherwise things would continue as before with Marconi making decisions about replenishment quantities and timing. This clearly wasn't the type of relationship we were looking for, so we talked to other distributors, but they weren't much more responsive.

> We need to regroup now and decide where to go with JITD. Is this type of program feasible in our environment? If so, what kind of customer should we target? And how do we convince them to sign up?

The Barilla case raises two important issues:

- Variations in distributors' order patterns have caused severe operational inefficiencies and cost penalties for Barilla. The extreme variability in orders that Barilla receives is surprising considering the distribution of demand for pasta in Italy. Indeed, while variability in aggregate demand for pasta is quite small, orders placed by the distributors have a huge variability.
- In the proposed JITD strategy, Barilla will be in charge of the channel between the CDCs and the distributors and decide on the timing and size of shipments to its distributors. Thus, unlike

traditional supply chains in which distributors place orders and manufacturers try to satisfy these orders as much as possible, in JITD "Barilla's own logistics organization would specify the appropriate delivery quantities—those that would more effectively meet the end consumer's needs yet would also more evenly distribute the workload on Barilla's manufacturing and logistics systems." In the last few years, such a strategy has been referred to as *vendor managed inventory (VMI)*.

By the end of this chapter, you should be able to answer the following questions:

- What are the reasons for the increase in variability in Barilla's supply chain?
- How can the firm cope with the increase in variability?
- What is the impact of transferring demand information across the supply chain?
- Can the VMI strategy solve the operational problems faced by Barilla?
- How can the supply chain meet conflicting goals of different partners and facilities?

4.1 Introduction

We live in the "Information Age." Databases, electronic data interchange (EDI), decision-support systems, the Internet, and intranets are just a few of the technologies dominating the business page of the daily newspaper. In Chapter 10, we examine these technologies in detail and look at the issues surrounding their implementation. In this chapter, we consider the value of using any type of information technology; we deal specifically with the potential availability of more and more information throughout the supply chain and the implications this availability has on effective design and management of the integrated supply chain.

The implications of this abundance of available information are enormous. The supply chain pundits and consultants like to use the phrase, *In modern supply chains, information replaces inventory.* We don't dispute this idea, but its meaning is vague. After all, at some point the customer needs products, not just information! Nevertheless, information changes the way supply chains can and should be effectively managed, and these changes may lead to, among other things, lower inventories. Indeed, our objective in this chapter is to characterize how information affects the design and operation of the supply chain. We show that by effectively harnessing the information now available, one can design and operate the supply chain much more efficiently and effectively than ever before.

It should be apparent to the reader that having accurate information about inventory levels, orders, production, and delivery status throughout the supply chain should not make the managers of a supply chain less effective than if this information were not available. After all, they could choose to ignore it. As we will see, however, this information provides a tremendous opportunity to improve the way the supply chain is designed and managed. Unfortunately, using this information effectively does make the design and management of the supply chain more complex because many more issues must be considered.

We argue here that this abundant information:

- Helps reduce variability in the supply chain.
- Helps suppliers make better forecasts, accounting for promotions and market changes.
- Enables the coordination of manufacturing and distribution systems and strategies.
- Enables retailers to better serve their customers by offering tools for locating desired items.
- Enables retailers to react and adapt to supply problems more rapidly.
- Enables lead time reductions.

The chapter is based on the seminal work in [61] and [62] as well as the recent work in [30] and [22]. In the next section, we follow the review article [23].

4.2 The Bullwhip Effect

In recent years many suppliers and retailers have observed that while customer demand for specific products does not vary much, inventory and back-order levels fluctuate considerably across their supply chain. For instance, in examining the demand for Pampers disposal diapers, executives at Procter & Gamble noticed an interesting phenomenon. As expected, retail sales of the product were fairly uniform; there is no particular day or month in which the demand is significantly higher or lower than any other. However, the executives noticed that distributors' orders placed to the factory fluctuated much more than retail sales. In addition, P&G's orders to its suppliers fluctuated even more. This increase in variability as we travel up in the supply chain is referred to as the *bullwhip effect*.

Figure 4.5 illustrates a simple four-stage supply chain: a single retailer, a single wholesaler, a single distributor, and a single factory. The retailer observes customer demand and places orders to the wholesaler. The wholesaler receives products from the distributor who places orders

FIGURE 4.5

The supply chain

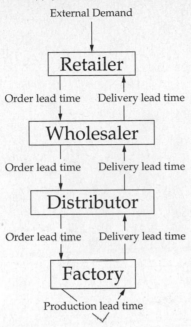

to the factory. Figure 4.6 provides a graphical representation of orders, as a function of time, placed by different facilities. The figure clearly shows the increase in variability across the supply chain.

To understand the impact of the increase in variability on the supply chain, consider the second stage in our example, the wholesaler. The wholesaler receives orders from the retailer and places orders to his supplier, the distributor. To determine these order quantities, the wholesaler must forecast the retailer's demand. If the wholesaler does not have access to the customer's demand data, he must use orders placed by the retailer to perform his forecasting.

Since variability in orders placed by the retailer is significantly higher than variability in customer demand, as Figure 4.6 shows, the wholesaler is forced to carry more safety stock than the retailer or else to maintain higher capacity than the retailer in order to meet the same service level as the retailer.

This analysis can be carried over to the distributor as well as the factory, resulting in even higher inventory levels and therefore higher costs at these facilities.

Consider, for example, a simple widget supply chain. A single factory, WidgetMakers Inc., supplies a single retailer, the WidgetStore. Average annual widget demand at the WidgetStore is 5,200 units, and shipments

FIGURE 4.6

The increase in variability in the supply chain

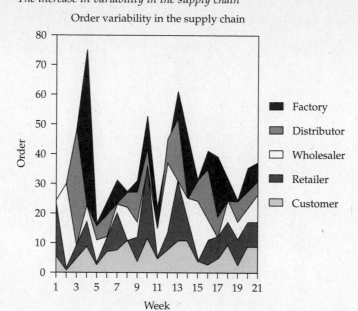

Order variability in the supply chain

are made from WidgetMakers to the store each week. If the variability in orders placed by the WidgetStore is low, so that the shipment every week is about 100 units, WidgetMakers' production capacity and weekly shipping capacity need be only about 100 units. If weekly variability is very high, so that during certain weeks WidgetMakers must make and ship 400 units and some weeks no units at all, it is easy to see that production and shipping capacity must be much higher and that some weeks this capacity will be idle. Alternatively, WidgetMakers could build up inventory during weeks with low demand and supply these items during weeks with high demand, thus increasing inventory holding costs.

Thus, it is important to identify techniques and tools that will allow us to control the bullwhip effect; that is, to control the increase in variability in the supply chain. For this purpose, we need to first understand the main factors contributing to the increase in variability in the supply chain.

1. *Demand forecasting.* Traditional inventory management techniques, (see Chapter 3) practiced at each level in the supply chain lead to the bullwhip effect. To explain the connection between forecasting and the bullwhip effect we need to revisit inventory control strategies in supply chains. As discussed in Chapter 3, an attractive policy used in practice by each stage of the supply chain is the *min-max inventory policy*. Here, whenever the inventory position at a facility is less than a given number, referred to as the *reorder point*, the facility raises its inventory level up to a given target level, called the *order-up-to-level*.

The reorder point is typically set equal to the average demand during lead time plus a multiple of the standard deviation of demand during lead time. The latter quantity is referred to as *safety stock.* Typically, managers use *standard forecast smoothing techniques* to estimate average demand and demand variability. An important characteristic of all forecasting techniques is that as more data are observed, the more we modify the estimates of the mean and the standard deviation (or variability) in customer demands. Since safety stock, as well as the order-up-to-level, strongly depends on these estimates, the user is forced to change order quantities, thus increasing variability.

2. *Lead time.* It is easy to see that the increase in variability is magnified with increasing lead time. For this purpose, recall from Chapter 3 that to calculate safety stock levels and reorder points, we in effect multiply estimates of the average and standard deviation of the daily customer demands by the lead time. Thus, with longer lead times, a small change in the estimate of demand variability implies a significant change in safety stock, reorder level, and thus in order quantities. This of course leads to an increase in variability.

3. *Batch ordering.* The impact of batch ordering is quite simple to understand. If the retailer uses batch ordering, as happens when using a min-max inventory policy, then the wholesaler will observe a large order, followed by several periods of no orders, followed by another large order, and so on. Thus, the wholesaler sees a distorted and highly variable pattern of orders.

It is useful to remind the reader that firms use batch ordering for a number of reasons. First, as pointed out in Chapter 3, a firm that is faced with fixed ordering costs needs to apply the min-max inventory policy, which leads to batch ordering. Second, as transportation costs become more significant, retailers may order quantities that allow them to take advantage of transportation discounts (e.g., full truckload quantities). This may lead to some weeks with large orders, and some with no orders at all. Finally, the quarterly or yearly sales quotas or incentives observed in many businesses can also result in unusually large orders observed on a periodic basis.

4. *Price fluctuation.* Price fluctuation can also lead to the bullwhip effect. If prices fluctuate, retailers often attempt to *stock up* when prices are lower. This is accentuated by the prevailing practice in many industries of offering promotions and discounts at certain times or for certain quantities.

5. *Inflated orders.* Inflated orders placed by retailers during shortage periods tend to magnify the bullwhip effect. Such orders are common when retailers and distributors suspect that a product will be in short supply, and therefore anticipate receiving supply proportional to the amount ordered. When the period of shortage is over, the retailer goes back to its standard orders, leading to all kinds of distortions and variations in demand estimates.

4.2.1 *Quantifying the Bullwhip Effect*[2]

So far, we have discussed factors contributing to the increase in variability in the supply chain. To better understand and control the bullwhip effect, we also would find it useful to *quantify* the bullwhip effect; that is, quantify the increase in variability that occurs at every stage of the supply chain. This would be useful not only to demonstrate the magnitude of the increase in variability, but also to show the relationship between the forecasting technique, the lead time, and the increase in variability.

To quantify the increase in variability for a simple supply chain, consider a two-stage supply chain with a retailer who observes customer demand and places an order to a manufacturer. Suppose that the retailer faces a fixed lead time, L, so that an order placed by the retailer at the end of period t is received at the start of period $t + L$. Also, suppose the retailer follows a simple order-up-to-inventory policy in which the retailer places an order to bring its inventory level up to a target level in every period.

As discussed in Chapter 3, the order-up-to-point is calculated as:

$$L \times AVG + z \times STD \times \sqrt{L}$$

where AVG and STD are the average and standard deviation of daily (or weekly) customer demand. The constant z is chosen from statistical tables to ensure that the probability of stockouts during lead time is equal to the specified level of service.

To implement this inventory policy, the retailer must estimate the average and standard deviation of demand based on its observed customer demand. Thus, in practice, the order-up-to-point may change from day to day according to changes in the current estimate of the average and the standard deviation.

Specifically, the order-up-to-point in period t, y_t, is estimated from the observed demand as:

$$y_t = \hat{\mu}_t L + z\sqrt{L}S_t$$

where $\hat{\mu}_t$ and S_t are the estimated average and standard deviation of daily customer demand at time t.

Suppose the retailer uses one of the simplest forecasting techniques: the moving average. In other words, in each period the retailer estimates the mean demand as an average of the previous p observations of demand.

---

[2]This section can be skipped without loss of continuity.

The retailer estimates the standard deviation of demand in a similar manner. That is, if D_i represents customer demand in period i, then:

$$\hat{\mu}_t = \frac{\sum_{i=t-p}^{t-1} D_i}{p}$$

and

$$S_t^2 = \frac{\sum_{i=t-p}^{t-1}(D_i - \hat{\mu}_t)^2}{p-1}$$

Note that the expressions above imply that in every period the retailer calculates a new mean and standard deviation based on the p most recent observations of demand. Then, since the estimates of the mean and standard deviation change every period, the target inventory level will also change in every period.

In this case, we can quantify the increase in variability; that is, we can calculate the variability faced by the manufacturer and compare it to the variability faced by the retailer. If the variance of the customer demand seen by the retailer is $Var(D)$, then the variance of the orders placed by that retailer to the manufacturer, $Var(Q)$, relative to the variance of customer demand satisfies:

$$\frac{Var(Q)}{Var(D)} \geq 1 + \frac{2L}{p} + \frac{2L^2}{p^2}$$

Figure 4.7 shows the lower bound on the increase in variability as a function of p for various values of the lead time, L. In particular, when p is large, and L is small, the bullwhip effect due to forecasting error is negligible. The bullwhip effect is magnified as we increase the lead time and decrease p.

For instance, suppose the retailer estimates the mean demand based on the last five demand observations, that is, $p = 5$. Suppose also that an order placed by the retailer at the end of period t is received at the start of

FIGURE 4.7

A lower bound on the increase in variability given as a function of p

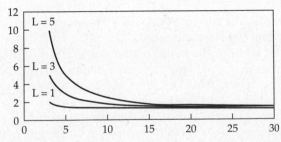

period $t + 1$. This implies that L equals 1. In this case the variance of the orders placed by the retailer to the manufacturer will be at least 40 percent larger than the variance of the customer demand seen by the retailer, that is:

$$\frac{Var(Q)}{Var(D)} \geq 1.4$$

Next consider the same retailer, but now assume, as is the case in the retail industry, that the retailer uses 10 demand observations (i.e., $p = 10$) to estimate the mean and standard deviation of demand. Then the variance of the orders placed by the retailer to the manufacturer will be at least 1.2 times the variance of the customer demand seen by the retailer. In other words, by increasing the number of observations used in the moving average, the retailer can significantly reduce the variability of the orders it places to the manufacturer.

4.2.2   The Impact of Centralized Information on the Bullwhip Effect

One of the most frequent suggestions for reducing the bullwhip effect is to centralize demand information within a supply chain; that is, to provide each stage of the supply chain with complete information on the actual customer demand. To understand why centralized demand information can reduce the bullwhip effect, note that if demand information is centralized, each stage of the supply chain can use the actual customer demand data to create more accurate forecasts, rather than relying on the orders received from the previous stage, which can vary significantly more than the actual customer demand.

In this subsection, we consider the value of sharing customer demand information within a supply chain. For this purpose, consider again the initial four-stage supply chain, described in Figure 4.5, with a single retailer, wholesaler, distributor, and factory. To determine the impact of centralized demand information on the bullwhip effect, we distinguish between two types of supply chains: one with centralized demand information and a second with decentralized demand information. These systems are described below.

Supply Chain with Centralized Demand Information
In the first type of supply chain, the *centralized supply chain*, the retailer, or the first stage in the supply chain, observes customer demand, forecasts the mean demand using a moving average with p demand observations, finds his target inventory level based on the forecast mean demand, and places an order to the wholesaler. The wholesaler, or the second stage of the supply chain, receives the order along with the retailer's forecast mean demand, uses this forecast to determine his target inventory level,

and places an order to the distributor. Similarly, the distributor, or the third stage of the supply chain, receives the order along with the retailer's forecast mean demand, uses this forecast to determine his target inventory level, and places an order to the fourth stage of the supply chain, the factory.

In this centralized supply chain, each stage of the supply chain receives the retailer's forecast mean demand and follows an order-up-to-inventory policy based on this mean demand. Therefore, in this case we have centralized the demand information, the forecasting technique, and the inventory policy.

Following the analysis above, it is not difficult to show that the variance of the orders placed by the kth stage of the supply chain, $Var(Q^k)$, relative to the variance of the customer demand, $Var(D)$, is just:

$$\frac{Var(Q^k)}{Var(D)} \geq 1 + \frac{2\sum_{i=1}^{k-1} L_i}{p} + \frac{2(\sum_{i=1}^{k-1} L_i)^2}{p^2}$$

where L_i is the lead time between stage i and stage $i + 1$. For example, if the lead time from the retailer to the wholesaler is two periods, then $L_1 = 2$. Similarly, if the lead time from the wholesaler to the distributor is two periods, then $L_2 = 2$, and if the lead time from the distributor to the factory is also two periods, then $L_3 = 2$. In this case, the total lead time from the retailer to the factory is:

$$L_1 + L_2 + L_3 = 6 \text{ periods}$$

This expression for the variance of the orders placed by the kth stage of the supply chain is very similar to the expression for the variability of the orders placed by the retailer given in the previous section, with the single stage lead time L replaced by the k stage lead time $\sum_{i=1}^{k-1} L_i$. Thus, we see that *the variance of the orders placed by a given stage of a supply chain is an increasing function of the total lead time between that stage and the retailer.* This implies that the variance of the orders becomes larger as we move up the supply chain, so that the orders placed by the second stage of the supply chain are more variable than the orders placed by the retailer (the first stage) and the orders placed by the third stage will be more variable than the orders placed by the second stage, and so on.

Decentralized Demand Information

The second type of supply chain that we consider is the *decentralized supply chain*. There the retailer does not make its forecast mean demand available to the remainder of the supply chain. Instead, the wholesaler must estimate the mean demand based on the orders received from the retailer.

Again we assume that the wholesaler uses a moving average with p observations—these are the latest p orders placed by the retailer—to forecast the mean demand. It then uses this forecast to determine the target inventory level and places an order to the supplier, the distributor. Similarly, the distributor uses a moving average with p observations of the orders placed by the wholesaler to forecast the mean and standard deviation of demand, and uses these forecasts to determine the target inventory level. The distributor's target level is used to place orders to the fourth stage of the supply chain.

It turns out that in this system the variance of the orders placed by the kth stage of the supply chain, $Var(Q^k)$, relative to the variance of the customer demand, $Var(D)$ satisfies:

$$\frac{Var(Q^k)}{Var(D)} \geq \prod_{i=1}^{k-1} \left[1 + \frac{2L_i}{p} + \frac{2L_i^2}{p^2} \right]$$

where, as before, L_i is the lead time between stage i and $i + 1$.

Note that this expression for the variance of the orders placed by the kth stage of the supply chain is very similar to the expression for the variability of orders placed by the retailer in the centralized case, but now the variance increases multiplicatively at each stage of the supply chain. Again the variance of the orders becomes larger as we move up the supply chain so that the orders placed by the wholesaler are more variable than the orders placed by the retailer.

Managerial Insights on the Value of Centralized Information

We have already seen that for either type of supply chain, centralized or decentralized, the variance of the order quantities becomes larger as we move up the supply chain so that the orders placed by the wholesaler are more variable than the orders placed by the retailer, and so on. The difference in the two types of supply chains is in terms of how much the variability grows as we move from stage to stage.

The results above indicate that the variance of the orders grows additively in the total lead time for the centralized supply chain, while the increase is multiplicative for the decentralized supply chain. In other words, a decentralized supply chain, in which only the retailer knows the customer demand, can lead to significantly higher variability than a centralized supply chain, in which customer demand information is available at each stage of the supply chain, particularly when lead times are large. We therefore conclude that *centralizing demand information can significantly reduce the bullwhip effect.*

This reduction is illustrated nicely in Figure 4.8, which shows the ratio between variability of orders placed by stage k, for $k = 3$ and $k = 5$, and variability of customers' demands for the centralized and decentralized systems when $L_i = 1$ for each i. It also shows the ratio between variability in orders placed by the retailer and variability in customers' demands ($k = 1$).

Thus, it is now clear that by sharing demand information with each stage of the supply chain, we can significantly reduce the bullwhip effect. Indeed, when demand information is centralized, each stage of the supply chain can use the actual customer demand data to estimate the average

FIGURE 4.8

Increase in variability for centralized and decentralized systems

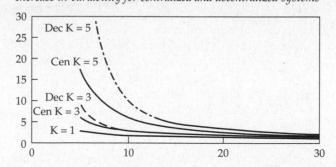

demand. On the other hand, when demand information is not shared, each stage must use the orders placed by the previous stage to estimate the average demand. As we have already seen, these orders are more variable than the actual customer demand data, and thus the forecasts created using these orders are more variable, leading to more variable orders.

Finally, it is important to point out that the bullwhip effect exists even when demand information is completely centralized and all stages of the supply chain use the same forecasting technique and inventory policy. In other words, if every stage of the supply chain follows a simple order-up-to policy and if each stage uses the same customer demand data and forecasting technique to predict the expected demand, then we will still see the bullwhip effect. However, the analysis indicates that if information is not centralized—that is, if each stage of the supply chain is not provided with customer demand information—then the increase in variability can be significantly larger. Thus, we conclude that *centralizing demand information can significantly reduce, but will not eliminate, the bullwhip effect.*

4.2.3   Methods for Coping with the Bullwhip Effect

Our ability to identify and quantify the causes of the bullwhip effect lead to a number of suggestions for reducing the bullwhip effect or for eliminating its impact. These include reducing uncertainty, reducing the variability of the customer demand process, reducing lead times, and engaging in strategic partnerships. These issues are discussed briefly below.

1. *Reducing uncertainty.* One of the most frequent suggestions for decreasing or eliminating the bullwhip effect is to reduce uncertainty throughout the supply chain by centralizing demand information; that is, by providing each stage of the supply chain with complete information on actual customer demand. The results presented in the previous subsection demonstrate that centralizing demand information can reduce the bullwhip effect.

Note, however, that even if each stage uses the same demand data, each may still employ different forecasting methods and different buying practices, both of which may contribute to the bullwhip effect. In addition, the results presented in the previous subsection indicate that even when each stage uses the same demand data, the same forecasting method, and the same ordering policy, the bullwhip effect will continue to exist.

2. *Reducing variability.* The bullwhip effect can be diminished by reducing the variability inherent in the customer demand process. For example, if we can reduce the variability of the customer demand seen by the retailer, then even if the bullwhip effect occurs, the variability of the demand seen by the wholesaler will also be reduced.

We can reduce the variability of customer demand through, for example, the use of an "everyday low pricing" (EDLP) strategy. When a retailer uses EDLP, it offers a product at a single consistent price, rather than offering a regular price with periodic price promotions. By eliminating price promotions, a retailer can eliminate many of the dramatic shifts in demand that occur along with these promotions. Therefore, everyday low pricing strategies can lead to much more stable—that is, less variable—customer demand patterns.

3. *Lead time reduction.* The results presented in the previous subsections clearly indicate that lead times serve to magnify the increase in variability due to demand forecasting. We have demonstrated the dramatic effect that increasing lead times can have on the variability at each stage of the supply chain. Therefore, lead time reduction can significantly reduce the bullwhip effect throughout a supply chain.

Observe that lead times typically include two components: order lead times (i.e., the time it takes to produce and ship the item) and information lead times (i.e., the time it takes to process an order). This distinction is important since order lead times can be reduced through the use of cross-docking while information lead time can be reduced through the use of electronic data interchange (EDI).

4. *Strategic partnerships.* The bullwhip effect can be eliminated by engaging in any of a number of strategic partnerships. These strategic partnerships change the way information is shared and inventory is managed within a supply chain, possibly eliminating the impact of the bullwhip effect. For example, in vendor managed inventory (VMI, see Chapter 6), the manufacturer manages the inventory of its product at the retailer outlet, and therefore determines for itself how much inventory to keep on hand and how much to ship to the retailer in every period. Therefore, in VMI the manufacturer does not rely on the orders placed by a retailer, thus avoiding the bullwhip effect entirely.

Other types of partnerships are also applied to reduce the bullwhip effect. The previous analysis indicates, for example, that centralizing demand information can dramatically reduce the variability seen by the upstream stages in a supply chain. Therefore, it is clear that these upstream stages would benefit from a strategic partnership that provides an incentive for the retailer to make customer demand data available to the rest of the supply chain. See Chapter 6 for a detailed discussion.

It is now appropriate to return to the Barilla case and find the solutions to the following questions:

1. How did Barilla try to sell the VMI (JITD) program to its distributors?
2. How did Barilla implement the VMI strategy?
3. Was the program successful in solving many of Barilla's operational problems?

CASE: BARILLA SPA (B)

Giorgio Maggiali described Barilla's third attempt to sell the JITD program to its distributors:

> After being rejected by Marconi, we went to Aldo, a large DO in Udine that has been a great customer of ours for years. Battistini made a presentation to the logistics group that was very well received. Aldo's top management agreed to hear our JITD presentation, but it seemed clear to me that we needed to get Rossini (Leonardo Rossini, Barilla's executive vice president of sales) involved. I talked to him and made it clear to our general manager, "Either Rossini and I go to Aldo together or this whole JITD thing is over."

Under strong pressure from general management to commit to the JITD program, Rossini agreed to go. Maggiali continued:

> Battistini and I saw this as a good opportunity for Barilla's logistics and sales organizations to work with Aldo's logistics and buying organizations. But again, we were unsuccessful in gaining buy-in for the program. Aldo said they'd consider it, but essentially said "Don't call us, we'll call you." Well it's been two years now and no one has called.
>
> We came away from the Aldo meeting realizing that despite our own convictions that we could make JITD work, the distributors just didn't believe it—in part because we didn't have any proof of its benefits. No one wanted to be the first. It became clear to us that in order to have the credibility to sell the JITD idea to our customers, we had to demonstrate that it would work. Thus we decided to turn our efforts to our own dry product depots (regional warehouses).

From July 1990 to September 1990, Barilla developed the methodology it would use to replenish distributors' inventory. In September Battistini ran a JITD experiment at its Florence depot, using a personal computer to store the necessary data and perform computations. During the first month of the program, inventory in the Florence warehouse dropped from 10.1 days to 3.6 days while its service level to retail stores increased from 98.8 percent to 99.8 percent (see Figure 4.9). Battistini experimented with the model's parameters to see how far Barilla could bring down the inventory levels in Florence. Despite the higher service levels, the staff at the Florence depot rebelled. The depot manager called Battistini: "The system is becoming too brittle; I am not letting another pallet ship from this depot until you send me some more inventory!" In response, Battistini allowed the inventory to rise to five days. He noted, "You'd think the warehouse would be half empty by now, but in fact we've been growing so much in that region that we'd already made plans to expand the warehouse. Now we've been able to accommodate the growth within the existing warehouse and avoid a substantial investment."

Battistini next targeted Barilla's Milan depot for a JITD trial. Performance improvement similar to that experienced at Florence resulted (see Figure 4.10).

FIGURE 4.9

Results of internal experiments in Florence

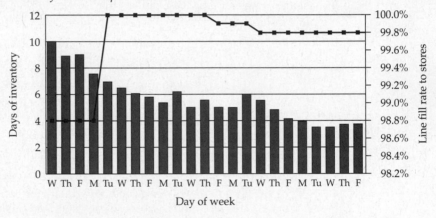

FIGURE 4.10

Results of internal experiments in Milan

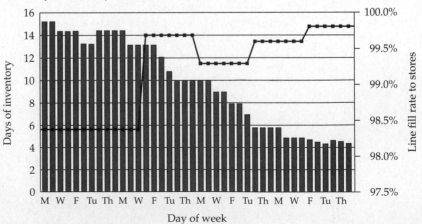

Maggiali noted, "Clearly we're delighted with our results in our depots. We're convinced that the distributors should sign up for the program. But will they find these results conclusive? What should our next steps be?"

To answer these questions, let's continue with the third and final part of the case.

CASE: BARILLA SPA (C)

In late 1990, Barilla logistics managers began to turn their JITD efforts towards the large DO, Cortese, a long-time Barilla distributor. Prior to any meetings between Barilla and Cortese management, Claudio Ferrozzi, a consultant with the Milan firm GEA, met with Cortese management to discuss the benefits of JITD. (Ferrozzi had worked on various logistics projects with Cortese during the previous five years, and had also been closely involved with the development of Barilla's JITD program.) Shortly thereafter, a meeting was arranged between Barilla and Cortese managers. Representing Barilla were Giorgio Maggiali, director of logistics; Leonardo Rossini, executive vice president of sales, and Vincenzo Battistini, the logistics manager in charge of JITD development and implementation. Nine Cortese managers attended the meeting, including the managing director, new services manager and logistics manager from Cortese headquarters, as well as logistics, purchasing, marketing and sales personnel from Cortese's distribution center (DC) in Marchese. Claudio Ferrozzi also attended the meeting.

In late 1993, Maggiali reflected on the visit:

> This time we finally had it figured out. We had both our sales director and our logistics director at the meeting, as well as top managers cutting across Cortese's functional areas, including the managing director. And Ferrozzi was there as a neutral party, known and trusted by both groups. Eventually we were able to hammer out a JITD test to be performed at the Cortese distribution center in Marchese.

Battistini described the implementation details:

> For the first six months, we simply had the Marchese DC send its shipment data to us each day. We weren't hooked up electronically yet, so they sent the information by fax. We used the data to create a database of Marchese's historical demand patterns, and then began to simulate what the shipments would have been if the JITD program had been in place. We wanted to demonstrate to Cortese management (and to some degree, to ourselves!) that we would have made good shipment decisions had the JITD program been fully implemented.
>
> At the end of the six-month period, we established an EDI link between our two computers and started the JITD system. The results were pretty dramatic—even more pronounced than in the tests in our own regional warehouses in Florence and Milan. Prior to JITD, Marchese's service level to its

retail customers had been about average in the industry—the stockout rate was typically in the 2 percent to 5 percent range, and occasionally was as high as 10 percent to 13 percent. During the first five months of the JITD program, the stockout rate was negligible—usually less than 0.25 percent and never exceeding 1 percent. Cortese was delighted with these results; management felt that the higher service levels increased retailers' loyalty to Cortese. Marchese also saw its average inventory levels drop during that period. It still built up inventory for its promotions to its customers, but overall inventories fell. (See Figure 4.11).

Cortese management soon agreed to put several more of its distribution centers on the JITD program. The results were again positive—Cortese's fill rates to its customers rose, and its inventories dropped. It was amazing to see how much we could flatten our own shipment patterns while still offering superior service to Cortese. (See Figure 4.12).

As we've approached different customers, they say "our system's different, can you accommodate it?" We've now developed the capability to simply translate those customers' various standards into our own internal standards. JITD sales comprised 75 billion lire in 1991, 137 billion in 1992, and is expected to rise to over 200 billion in 1993. We've developed a protocol that we can

FIGURE 4.11

Results of test in the Marchese Distribution Center

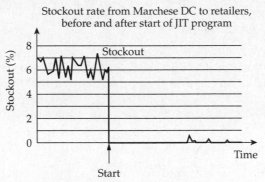

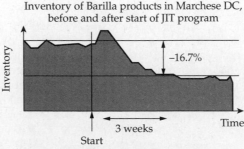

Note: "Start" indicates the beginning of operations under the JITD program.

FIGURE 4.12

Shipments from Barilla to the Marchese Distribution Center before and after start of JITD program

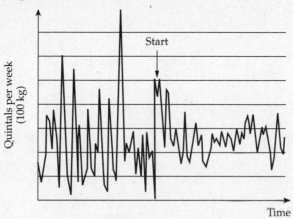

Note: "Start" indicates the beginning of operations
under the JITD program.

pretty much use to communicate with all of our customers. In addition, we have a database that identifies each of our SKUs by three different product codes: each customer's code for the product, our own product code, and the product's EAN bar code number.[3] We can then receive information from the client using either the client's code or the bar code number, and immediately translate it into our own internal format. Maintaining our own internal codes allows us to make minor changes in the product or to modify our internal coding system without having to go to all of our customers with the changes. This reduces the impact that our internal changes have on our clients.

Communication with Customers

By the end of 1993, all of Barilla's JITD customers were linked electronically to Barilla headquarters. They sent information via EDI either through a standard third-party EDI network or directly to Barilla using a modem. Each day, each distribution center participating in the program sent the following information to Barilla headquarters:

1. Customer code number to identify customer (DC).
2. Inventory level for each Barilla SKU carried by the DC.
3. The previous day's "sell-through" (i.e., all shipments of Barilla products out of the DC to customers on the previous day).

---

[3]The EAN (Euopean Article Numbering System) was the most common bar code standard in Europe. An EAN bar code contained 14 digits, compared to 12 digits in a UPC (Uniform Product Code) bar code.

4. Stockouts on the previous day for every Barilla SKU carried by the DC.

5. An advance order for any promotions that the customer planned to run in the future (e.g., an order for 80 additional cartons of Tripolini n. 18, for delivery in four weeks).

6. Preferred delivery carton size.

Using the customer code as an identifier, Barilla merged these data with the historical data file that Barilla maintained for each customer. On the basis of these data, Barilla made shipment decisions.

Barilla's Shipping Decision Rules

Battistini developed the algorithm for determining shipment quantities for the JITD program in conjunction with GEA consultants Claudio Ferrozzi and Fabrizio Tellarini. From the program's inception, Battistini had been largely responsible for the day-to-day JITD operations. He described the general approach as follows:

> We fill each truck on the basis of customer need. Our trucks have an interior height of 2.4 meters, and are filled by placing half-pallets, which are 0.9 m tall, on top of full pallets, which are 1.5 m tall. Thus, we developed a decision rule that allocates the space on the truck to customer needs in half-pallet quantities. We then make adjustments so that there are an equal number of full and half-pallets in each truck.
>
> Our first priority is to cover any emergency situations, specifically those products for which a customer has stocked out or expects to stock out before the truck arrives. After allocating space for those products, we then allocate space to products whose inventory levels are expected to be below their "target stock" level. As in the first case, we always allocate the first space to the product that falls short of the inventory goals by the largest amount. Usually by the time all products' inventories have been built up to their target levels, the truck is full. If not, we may load a couple of pallets of promotional items due at a later date or build up the inventory of those products closest to their target stock levels.
>
> We have made some adjustments to the algorithm. For example, we've modified it to allow us to minimize the number of different types of product going in the truck or to mix very heavy products (such as flour) with lighter products (such as dry toast) so the truck doesn't weigh out before it cubes out.[4] But overall, it's really a pretty simple method.
>
> For forecasting, we use a simple weighted average over the last 30 days to forecast future sales. I've tried using an exponential smoothing approach but found it too sensitive to changes. So I calculate "average" demand and standard deviation from the weighted distribution, and then calculate target safety stock as a function of average demand levels, demand uncertainty, and lead times.
>
> We make tentative shipment plans to each customer the week prior to shipment so we can determine the number of trucks to hire for the next week, but

---

[4]A truck is said to "weigh out" when it reaches its weight limitation; it is said to "cube out" when it reaches its volume (space) limitation.

since we collect all of the information daily, we continue to fine-tune our plans for the actual content of a shipment until two days prior to a truck's departure.

Now we are facing a number of different questions regarding the expansion of the program. What type of distributors should we focus on for future JITD implementations? Where will the payoff really be? Should we consider international expansion? If so, how far should we expand? Distributors in both Germany and Sweden have asked about this program. Would a JITD customer that far away be sensible?

Another set of issues concerns how we tie the JITD program into our manufacturing processes. In February 1992 we started to give production planning our weekly forecast for the following week; we then give them daily updates of that forecast. These forecasts directly feed an "automatic" short term production planning system; longer term production planning decisions are still made by our manufacturing organization.

We now return to the main theme of the chapter, using information to improve supply chain performance.

4.3   Effective Forecasts

Information leads to more effective forecasts. The more factors that predictions of future demand can take into account, the more accurate these predictions can be.

For example, consider retailer forecasts. These are typically based on an analysis of previous sales at the retailer. However, future customer demand is clearly influenced by such issues as pricing, promotions, and the release of new products. Some of these issues are controlled by the retailer, but some are controlled by the distributor, wholesaler, manufacturer, or the competitors. If this information is available to the retailer's forecasters, the forecasts will obviously be more accurate.

Similarly, distributor and manufacturer forecasts are influenced by factors under retailer control. For example, the retailer may design promotions or set pricing. Also, the retailer may introduce new products into the stores, altering demand patterns.

In addition, because a manufacturer or distributor has fewer products to consider than the retailer, he may have more information about these products. For example, sales may be closely tied to some event. If a retailer is aware of this, he can increase inventories or raise prices to take advantage of this fact.

For all of these reasons, many supply chains are moving toward cooperative forecasting systems. In these systems, sophisticated information systems enable an iterative forecasting process, in which all of the participants in the supply chain collaborate to arrive at an agreed upon forecast.

This implies that all components of the supply chain share and use the same forecasting tool, leading to a decrease in the bullwhip effect (see Chapter 10, Section 10.5.1).

Example 4.3.1	In fall 1996 Warner-Lambert, the consumer goods manufacturer, and Wal-Mart, the department store, began a pilot study of the collaborative planning, forecasting, and replenishment (CPFR) system. This software system facilitates collaboration in forecasting efforts between retailers and manufacturers. CPFR makes it easy to exchange drafts of forecasts as well as details of future sales promotions and past sales trends. The software "makes it easy for each side to review related messages and append new ones." Other companies, including Procter & Gamble, intend to adopt the CPFR system, and software companies intend to launch competing versions of this software. These systems go under the general name of *collaborative systems* [111].

4.4   Information for the Coordination of Systems

Within any supply chain are many systems, including various manufacturing, storage, transportation, and retail systems. We have seen that managing any one of these systems involves a series of complex trade-offs. For example, to efficiently run a manufacturing operation, setup and operating costs must be balanced with the costs of inventory and raw materials. Similarly, we have seen in Chapter 3 that inventory level is a delicate balance between holding costs, order setup costs, and required service level. We have also seen in Chapter 3 that there is a balance between inventory costs and transportation costs, because transportation typically involves quantity discounts of one type or another.

However, all of these systems are connected. Specifically, the outputs from one system within the supply chain are the inputs to the next system. For example, the outputs from the manufacturing operation may be the inputs to a transportation or storage system, or both. Thus, trying to find the best set of trade-offs for any one stage isn't sufficient. We need to consider the entire system and coordinate decisions.

This will be true whether or not there is a common owner for several of the systems in the supply chain. If there is, it is clearly in this owner's best interest to ensure that the overall cost is reduced, although this could lead to an increase in costs in one system if larger decreases occur elsewhere. Even if there is no common owner, however, the various systems still need some kind of coordination to operate effectively. The issue, of course, is whose best interest is it to reduce *overall* system cost and how will these savings be shared among the system owners?

To explain this, observe that when the system is not coordinated—that is, each facility in the supply chain does what is best for that facility—the result is *local optimization*. Each component of the supply chain optimizes its own operation without due respect to the impact of its policy on other components in the supply chain.

The alternative to this approach is *global optimization*, which implies that one identifies what is best for the entire system. In this case, two issues need to be addressed:

1. Who will optimize?
2. How will the savings obtained through the coordinated strategy be split between the different supply chain facilities?

We address these issues in Chapter 6 as part of a detailed discussion on strategic partnerships.

To coordinate these facets of the supply chain, information must be available. Specifically, the knowledge of production status and costs, transportation availability and quantity discounts, inventory costs, inventory levels, and various capacities and customer demand is necessary to coordinate systems, especially in cost-effective ways.

4.5   Locating Desired Products

There is more than one way to meet customer demand. Typically, for a make to stock system, we think of meeting customer demand from retail inventory if at all possible. However, there are other ways to meet customer demand.

For example, suppose you go to a retailer to buy a large appliance and it is not available. Perhaps you will go to the retailer's competitor down the street. But what if the retailer searches a database and promises to have the item delivered to your house within 24 hours. You will probably feel like you've received great customer service, even though the retailer is out of stock of the item you wanted. Thus, being able to locate and deliver goods is sometimes as effective as having them in stock. But if the goods are located at the retailer's competitor, it is not clear whether this competitor would be willing to transfer the item. We discuss these kinds of issues in detail in Chapter 6, Section 6.5, "Distributor Integration."

4.6   Lead Time Reduction

The importance of lead time reduction cannot be overstated. It typically leads to:

1. The ability to quickly fill customer orders that can't be filled from stock.
2. Reduction in the bullwhip effect.
3. More accurate forecasts due to a decreased forecast horizon.
4. Reduction in finished goods inventory levels (see Chapter 3). This is true because one can stock raw materials and packaging material (or subassembly) inventories to reduce finished goods cycle time.

For all of these reasons, many firms are actively searching for suppliers with shorter lead times, and many potential customers consider lead time a very important criterion for vendor selection.

Much of the manufacturing revolution of the past 20 years led to reduced lead times, see [47]. Similarly, in Chapter 5 we will discuss distribution network designs that reduce lead times; these designs can exist only because of the availability of information about the status of the entire supply chain. However, as discussed earlier, effective information systems (e.g., EDI) cut lead times by reducing that portion of the lead time linked to order processing, paperwork, stock picking, transportation delays, and so on. Often these can be a substantial portion of the lead time, especially if there are many different stages in the supply chain and this information is transmitted one stage at a time. Clearly, if a retailer order *rapidly* propagates up the supply chain through the tiers of suppliers as far back as is necessary to meet the order, lead time can be greatly reduced.

Similarly, transferring point-of-sale (POS) data from the retailer to its supplier can help reduce lead times significantly because the supplier can anticipate an incoming order by studying POS data. These issues are covered in depth in Chapter 6 where we discuss strategic partnering between retailers and suppliers.

4.7   Integrating the Supply Chain

As we have mentioned previously, information enables us to integrate the various stages in the supply chain. Why is this important? If the objectives at every stage of the supply chain were complementary, then there would be no need to integrate management of the supply chain. Each stage of the supply chain could be managed independently, and the overall system would run efficiently. However, as we will discuss in detail below, the managers of different stages in the supply chain have conflicting goals, and it is exactly these conflicts which necessitate the integration of the different stages in the supply chain. By carefully using the available information, we can reduce the cost of the system while accounting for these conflicting goals and objectives. This is easier to do in a centralized system, but even in a decentralized system it may be necessary to find incentives to bring about the integration of supply chain facilities.

4.7.1 Conflicting Objectives in the Supply Chain[5]

We begin with the raw material suppliers. To operate and plan efficiently, these suppliers would like to see stable volume requirements, with little variation in the mix of required materials. In addition, they prefer flexible delivery times, so that they can deliver efficiently to more than one customer. Finally, most suppliers would like to see large volume demands, so that they can take advantage of economies of scope and scale.

Manufacturing management also has its own wish list. High production costs frequently limit the number of expensive changeovers as well as quality problems which may occur at the start of production runs. Typically, manufacturing management wants to achieve high productivity through production efficiencies, leading in turn to low production costs. These goals are facilitated if the demand pattern is known far into the future and has little variability.

The materials, warehousing, and outbound logistics management also have lists of criteria. These include minimizing transportation costs by taking advantage of quantity discounts, minimizing inventory levels, and quickly replenishing stock.

Finally, to satisfy their customers, retailers need short order lead times and efficient and accurate order delivery. The customers in turn demand in-stock items, enormous variety, and low prices.

4.7.2 Designing the Supply Chain for Conflicting Goals

In the past, for some of these goals to be met, others had to be sacrificed. The supply chain was viewed as a set of trade-offs that had to be made. Typically, high inventory levels and shipping costs, and less product variety, enabled manufactures and retailers to come closer to meeting their goals. At the same time, customers' expectations were not as high as they are today. As we know, however, these expectations have increased dramatically in recent times as customers demand high variety and low cost, even as increased pressure to control inventory and transportation costs has also become prevalent. Fortunately, the large amount of information now available allows supply chains to be designed so that they come closer to meeting all of these apparently conflicting goals. In effect, some of the trade-offs that were considered several years ago to be inherent in any supply chain may not be trade-offs at all.

In the following subsections, we discuss many of these perceived trade-offs and how, through the use of advanced information technology and creative network design, they don't have to be trade-offs at all in a modern supply chain—or, at the very least, their impact can be reduced.

---

[5]This section is based on the recent work of Lee and Billington [60].

The Lot Size–Inventory Trade-Off

As we have seen, manufacturers would like to have large lot sizes. Per unit setup costs are reduced, manufacturing expertise for a particular product increases, and processes are easier to control. Unfortunately, typical demand doesn't come in large lot sizes, so large lot sizes lead to high inventory. Indeed, much of the focus of the "manufacturing revolution" of the 1980s involved switching to manufacturing systems with smaller lot sizes.

Setup time reduction, Kanban and CONWIP (constant work in progress) systems, and other "modern manufacturing practices" were typically geared toward reducing inventories and improving system responsiveness. Although traditionally viewed in a manufacturing context, this approach to manufacturing has implications across the entire supply chain. Retailers and distributors would like short delivery lead times and wide product variety to respond to the needs of their customers. These advanced manufacturing systems make it possible for manufacturers to meet these needs by enabling them to respond more rapidly to customer needs.

This is especially true if information is available to ensure that the manufacturer has as much time as possible to react to the needs of downstream supply chain members. Similarly, if distributors or retailers have the ability to observe factory status and manufacturer inventory, they can quote lead times to customers more accurately. In addition, these systems enable retailers and distributors to develop an understanding of, and confidence in, the manufacturers' ability. This confidence allows the distributors and retailers to reduce the inventory they hold in anticipation of manufacturing problems.

The Inventory–Transportation Cost Trade-Off

There is a similar trade-off between inventory and transportation costs. To see this, we need to review the nature of transportation costs, which we explored in more detail in Chapter 2. First, consider a company that operates its own fleet of trucks. Each truck has some fixed cost of operation (e.g., depreciation, driver time) and some variable cost (e.g., gas). If a truck is always full when it makes a delivery, the cost of operating the truck is spread out over the largest possible number of items. Since, in the end, the same total number of goods are always delivered (more or less equal to customer demand), carrying full truckloads minimizes transportation costs.

Similarly, if an outside firm is used for shipping, the firm typically provides quantity discounts. Also, it is usually cheaper to ship in quantities of full truckloads (TL shipping) than partial (less than) truckloads (LTL shipping). Thus, in this case too, operating full trucks minimizes transportation costs.

In many cases, however, demand is in units of far less than a single truckload. Thus, when items are delivered in full truckloads, they typically have to wait for longer periods of time before they are consumed, leading to higher inventory costs.

Unfortunately, this trade-off can't be eliminated completely. However, we can use advanced information technology to reduce this effect. For example, advanced production control systems can be used to manufacture items as late as possible to ensure full truckloads. Similarly, distribution control systems may allow a materials management manager to combine shipments of different products from warehouses to stores in order to fill trucks. This requires knowledge of orders and demand forecasts, as well as supplier delivery schedules. Cross-docking, described earlier in the chapter, also helps to control this trade-off by allowing the retailer to combine shipments from many different manufacturers onto one truck destined for a particular location.

Indeed, recent advances in decision-support systems allow the supply chain to find the appropriate balance between transportation and inventory costs by taking into account all aspects of the supply chain. Regardless of the transportation strategy selected, competition in the transportation industry will force costs down. This effect is enhanced by advanced transportation modes and carrier selection programs which ensure that the most cost-effective approach is used for each particular delivery, lowering overall transportation costs.

The Lead Time–Transportation Cost

Total lead time is made up of time devoted to processing orders, to procuring and manufacturing items, and to transporting items between the various stages of the supply chain. As we mentioned above, transportation costs are lowest when large quantities of items are transported between stages of the supply chain. However, lead times can often be reduced if items are transported immediately after they are manufactured or arrive from suppliers. Thus, there is a trade-off between holding items until enough accumulate to reduce transportation costs, and shipping them immediately to reduce lead time.

Again, this trade-off cannot be completely eliminated, but information can be used to reduce its effect. Transportation costs can be controlled as described in the previous section, reducing the need to hold items until a sufficient number accumulate. In addition, improved forecasting techniques and information systems reduce the other components of lead time, so that it may not be essential to reduce the transportation component.

The Product Variety–Inventory Trade-Off

Evidently product variety greatly increases the complexity of supply chain management. Manufacturers that make a multitude of different products with smaller lot sizes find their manufacturing costs increase and their manufacturing efficiency decreases. To maintain the same lead times as a company may have had with fewer products, smaller amounts will probably be shipped so warehouses will need to hold a larger variety of products; thus, increasing product variety increases both transportation and warehousing costs. Finally, because it is usually difficult to accurately forecast the demand for each product, because all are competing for the same customers, higher inventory levels must be maintained to ensure the same service level.

The main issue that a firm supplying a variety of products needs to address is how to match supply and demand effectively. For instance, consider a manufacturer of winter ski jackets. Typically, 12 months before the selling season the firm introduces a number of designs that it will sell in the winter. Unfortunately, it is not clear how many ski jackets to produce from each design; therefore, it is not clear how to plan production.

One way to support the required product variety efficiently is to apply the concept called *delayed differentiation*, which we will discuss in Chapter 5, Section 5.6, and Chapter 8. In a supply chain in which delayed differentiation is utilized, *generic products* are shipped as far as possible down the supply chain before variety is added. This could mean that a single product is received in the distribution center, and there it is modified or customized according to customer demand as seen by the warehouse.

Observe that by doing so, we are again using the concept of risk pooling introduced in Chapter 3. Indeed, by shipping a generic product to the warehouses, we have aggregated customer demand across all products. As we have seen, this implies a more accurate demand forecast with a much smaller variability, leading to reduced safety stock. This process of aggregating across products is similar to the process of aggregating across retailers (see Chapter 3).

Delayed differentiation is one example of *design for logistics*, a concept we will discuss in much more detail in Chapter 8.

The Cost–Customer Service Trade-off

All of these trade-offs are examples of the cost–customer service trade-off. Reducing inventories, manufacturing costs, and transportation costs typically comes at the expense of customer service. In the preceding subsections, we have seen that the level of customer service can be maintained while decreasing these costs by using information and appropriate supply chain designs. Implicitly, we have defined customer service as the ability of a retailer to meet a customer's demand from stock.

Of course, customer service could mean the ability of a retailer to meet a customer's demand quickly. We have discussed how transshipping may make this possible without increasing inventory. In addition, direct shipping from warehouses to the homes of retail customers is another way to achieve this. For example, Sears delivers a large proportion of the large appliances that it sells directly from warehouses to the end customer. This controls inventory cost at retail stores and allows warehouses to take direct advantage of risk pooling effects. For this kind of system to work, information about warehouse inventories must be available at the stores, and order information should be rapidly transmitted to the warehouse. This is just one example of a system in which available information and appropriate supply chain design lead to decreased costs and increased service. In this case, costs are lower having the inventory stored in a centralized warehouse than having a larger inventory in the store. At the same time customer service is improved because customers have a larger inventory to choose from and appliances are immediately delivered to their homes.

Finally, it is important to point out that so far we have emphasized how supply chain technology and management can be applied to increase customer service levels *defined in some traditional sense* and reduce costs. However, advanced supply chain management techniques and information systems could be used to give customers a kind of service that they have never been able to realize before, and for which suppliers could charge a premium. One such example is the concept of *mass customization* which involves delivering highly personalized goods and services to customers at reasonable prices and at high volume. Although this may not have been economically feasible in the past, improving logistics and information systems now makes this possible. The concept of mass customization is explained in more detail in Chapter 8.

SUMMARY

The bullwhip effect suggests that variability in demand increases as one moves up in the supply chain. This increase in variability causes significant operational inefficiencies (e.g., it forces every facility in the supply chain to increase inventory significantly). Indeed, in [61] the authors estimate that in certain industries, such as the pharmaceutical industry, this distorted information can cause the total inventory in the supply chain to exceed 100 days of supply. Thus, it is important to identify strategies to efficiently cope with the bullwhip effect. In this chapter, we have identified specific techniques to "counteract" the bullwhip effect, one of which is information sharing; that is, centralized demand information.

Finally, we looked at the interaction of various supply chain stages. Typically, operating a supply chain is viewed as a series of trade-offs both within and between the different stages. We concluded that information is the key enabler of integrating the different supply chain stages and discussed how information can be used to reduce the necessity of many of these trade-offs.

CHAPTER
5 Distribution Strategies

CASE: MODERN BOOK DISTRIBUTION, INC.

Richard Guy, CEO of Modern Book Distribution, Inc. (MBD) scanned the "Executive Summary" of the consulting report he had just received. Guy saw the report was filled with the latest buzzwords and hot concepts:

Establish cross-docking facilities for high-volume deliveries to large customers. . .centralize storage operations to decrease safety stock levels. . .leverage point-of-sale data to move toward a pull distribution strategy. . .

Guy was familiar with all of these phrases and concepts at a superficial level, of course—anybody who occasionally picked up *The Wall Street Journal* or *Business Week* would be. He was less sure, however, if the consultants were trying to dazzle him with fads or if the kind of radical operating changes that were being proposed in the report would help to position MBD for the future.

Founded 80 years ago, MBD had been for many years one of the largest book distributors in the country. From its seven regional warehouses, MBD services major bookstore chains and smaller independent booksellers throughout the country. The company had continuously strived to improve its service levels and operating efficiency, and it was considered the most efficient book distributor in the industry. Using advanced forecasting techniques to control inventory levels and technologically advanced warehouses to control operating expenses, MBD shipped virtually all of the orders it received within two days from its stock of nearly 500,000 books, the largest in the industry.

The bookselling industry, however, had been changing dramatically, and Guy realized that MBD would have to make changes to remain a book distributing powerhouse. In particular, two relatively new types of retailers were becoming more and more dominant in the industry: the large superstores and the online booksellers. Both of these categories of retailers presented new and unique challenges to their distributors.

Source: MBD is a fictional company. This case is loosely based on the experiences of several companies in this industry.

In the past MBD had interacted primarily with the superstores through large regional distribution centers (DCs) that the superstores maintained. In general, MBD had shipped to the DCs consolidated orders of many different titles bound ultimately for many different stores. As these superstores learned from the experiences of large retailers in other industries, they started to demand new kinds of services from their distributors. For example, some retailers had started to strongly encourage MBD to ship directly to stores, bypassing the DCs. In addition, as the industry consolidated, these huge superstores were developing more leverage with their distributors. They used this leverage to force the distributors to accept lower and lower margins.

Online booksellers presented an entirely different set of challenges to Guy and the managers at MBD. These retailers had very little inventory at hand. Instead, they took orders and relayed them to distributors like MBD, who delivered the books to the retailers for repackaging and shipment. Recently, these retailers had started moving toward a new business model—one in which the distributors handled packaging and shipment of books directly to the end customers.

Guy realized that these industry changes could provide opportunities for his company if he could figure out how to take advantage of them. Clearly, if MBD was to maintain its reputation as one of the nation's leading book distributors, it would have to start doing things differently. Furthermore, he had the consultant's report, filled with recommendations and designs for new distribution systems. Guy knew that he and his management team would have to develop an understanding of these issues in order to properly assess the consultant's suggestions. As he prepared for the next day's meeting, Guy make a list of many questions:

- Should MBD establish more regional warehouses? Should it eliminate some warehouses and become more centralized?
- Should MBD develop a system for transferring inventory between regional warehouses?
- Should MBD encourage customers to utilize direct shipping services? Should it discourage them?
- Was cross-docking really a viable strategy for book distributors?
- Should MBD encourage retailers to make point-of-sale (POS) data available? What is the value of this data?

By the end of this chapter, you should be able to answer the following questions.

- Why are large retailers asking MBD to ship directly to retail stores?
- What distribution strategies are appropriate for MBD's businesses? What questions should MBD management ask when assessing these strategies?
- How can MBD benefit from changes in the book distribution industry?
- What is a pull distribution strategy? Should MBD implement such a strategy? What would it require? What would it cost?

- What are the advantages to MBD in having fewer warehouses and a more centralized operation? More warehouses and a more decentralized operation?

5.1 Introduction

In Chapter 2, we introduced the basic concepts of network design and configuration. In this chapter, we delve more deeply into supply network design. We consider:

- Different general strategies for the operation of a centralized supply network versus a decentralized operation.
- Alternate ways to utilize warehouses and strategies to eliminate them completely.
- Different approaches to meeting customer demand.

As you will see, there is no precise recipe to determine which of the following issues are relevant to a particular distribution problem or which of the following strategies will succeed. Many companies have successfully implemented each of the strategies and concepts we discuss. Indeed, most successful supply chains have elements of many of the strategies that we will discuss below. We will point out some characteristics of systems in which these approaches have proven successful, but the appropriate supply chain design for a particular situation, product, or company can only be selected by carefully considering the specific characteristics of the situation.

Obviously, the availability of information plays an important role in the design of the supply network. In some cases, the network must be designed to make this information available. In other cases, the network must be designed to *take advantage* of information that is already available. And in many cases, an expensive network must be designed to compensate for the lack of information.

5.2 Centralized versus Decentralized Control

In a centralized system, decisions are made at a central location for the entire supply network. Typically, the objective is to minimize the total cost of the system subject to satisfying some service-level requirements. This is clearly the case when the network is owned by a single entity, but it is also true in a centralized system that includes many different organizations. In this case, the savings, or profits, need to be allocated across the network using some contractual mechanism. We have already seen that centralized control leads to global optimization. Similarly, in a decentralized system each facility identifies its most effective strategy without considering the impact on the other facilities in the supply chain. Thus, a decentralized system leads to local optimization.

It is easy to see that, theoretically, a centralized distribution network will be at least as effective as a decentralized one because the centralized decision makers can make all of the decisions that decentralized decision makers would make, but also have the option of considering the interplay of decisions made at different locations in the supply network.

In a logistics system in which each facility can access only its own information, a centralized strategy is not possible. With advances in information technologies, however, all facilities in a centralized system can have access to the same data. Indeed, in Chapter 10 we discuss the concept of *single-point-of-contact*. In this case, information can be accessed from anywhere in the supply chain and is the same no matter what mode of inquiry is used or who is seeking the information. Thus, centralized systems allow the sharing of information and, more importantly, the utilization of this information in ways that reduce the bullwhip effect (see Chapter 4) and improve forecasts. Finally, they allow the use of coordinated strategies across the entire supply chain—strategies that reduce systemwide costs and improve service levels.

Sometimes, of course, a system cannot be centralized "naturally." The retailers, manufacturers, and distributors might all have different owners and different objectives. In these cases, it is often helpful to form partnerships to approach the advantages of a centralized system. We discuss these kinds of partnerships in Chapter 6.

5.3 Distribution Strategies

We now consider the portion of the supply chain beginning with the manufacturer and supplier and continuing, in the case of retail goods, to the end customer—the retailer. Typically, three distinct outbound distribution strategies are utilized.

1. **Direct shipment.** In this strategy, items are shipped directly from the supplier to the retail stores without going through distribution centers.
2. **Warehousing.** This is the classical strategy in which warehouses keep stock and provide customers with items as required.
3. **Cross-docking.** In this strategy, items are distributed continuously from suppliers through warehouses to customers. However, the warehouses rarely keep the items for more than 10 to 15 hours.

We have already discussed traditional warehousing strategies in some depth in Chapter 3. Here we describe direct shipment and cross-docking.

5.3.1 Direct Shipment

Direct shipment strategies exist to bypass warehouses and distribution centers. Employing direct shipment, the manufacturer or supplier delivers goods directly to retail stores. The advantages of this strategy are that:

- The retailer avoids the expenses of operating a distribution center.
- Lead times are reduced.

This type of distribution strategy also has a number of important disadvantages:

- Risk-pooling effects, which we described in Chapter 3, are negated because there is no central warehouse.
- The manufacturer and distributor transportation costs increase because it must send smaller trucks to more locations.

For these reasons, direct shipment is common when the retail store requires fully loaded trucks, which implies that the warehouse does not help in reducing transportation cost. It is most often mandated by powerful retailers or used in situations where lead time is critical. Sometimes, the manufacturer is reluctant to be involved with direct shipping but may have no choice in order to keep the business. Direct shipment is also prevalent in the grocery industry, where lead times are critical because of perishable goods.

Example 5.3.1   JCPenney has successfully implemented a direct shipping strategy. JCPenney sells general merchandise through nearly a thousand stores and millions of catalogs. With 200,000 items from more than 20,000 suppliers, managing the flow of goods is a formidable task. Each individual store retains total accountability for sales, inventory, and profit and is responsible for sales forecasts and releasing orders. Orders are communicated to buyers who coordinate the shipment with distribution personnel to ensure quick response, and an internal control and tracking system is used to monitor the flow of materials. In most cases, products are shipped directly to Penney's stores.

5.3.2 Cross-Docking

Cross-docking is a strategy that Wal-Mart made famous. In this system, warehouses function as inventory coordination points rather than as inventory storage points. In typical cross-docking systems, goods arrive at warehouses from the manufacturer, are transferred to vehicles serving the retailers, and are delivered to the retailers as rapidly as possible. Goods spend very little time in storage at the warehouse—often less than 12 hours.

This system limits inventory costs and decreases lead times by decreasing storage time.

Of course, cross-docking systems require a significant start-up investment and are very difficult to manage:

1. Distribution centers, retailers, and suppliers must be linked with advanced information systems to ensure that all pickups and deliveries are made within the required time windows.

2. A fast and responsive transportation system is necessary for a cross-docking system to work.

3. Forecasts are critical, necessitating the sharing of information.

4. Cross-docking strategies are effective *only* for large distribution systems in which a large number of vehicles are delivering and picking up goods at the cross-dock facilities at any one time. In such systems, there is enough volume every day to allow shipments of fully loaded trucks from the suppliers to the warehouses. Since these systems typically include many retailers, demand is sufficient so items that arrive at the cross-docking facilities can be delivered immediately to the retail outlets in full truckload quantities.

Example 5.3.2 | The tremendous market growth of Wal-Mart over the past 15 to 20 years highlights the importance of an effective strategy that coordinates inventory replenishment and transportation policies [106]. Over this time period Wal-Mart developed into the largest and highest-profit retailer in the world. A number of major components in Wal-Mart's competitive strategy were critical to its success, but perhaps the most important has been its enthusiastic use of cross-docking. Wal-Mart delivers about 85 percent of its goods utilizing cross-docking techniques, as opposed to about 50 percent for Kmart. To facilitate cross-docking, Wal-Mart operates a private satellite communications system that sends point-of-sale (POS) data to all of its vendors, allowing them to have a clear picture of sales at all of its stores. In addition, Wal-Mart has a dedicated fleet of 2,000 trucks and, on average, stores are replenished twice a week. Cross-docking enables Wal-Mart to achieve economies of scale by purchasing full truckloads. It reduces the need for safety stocks and has cut the cost of sales by 3 percent compared to the industry average, a major factor explaining Wal-Mart's large profit margins.

Very few major retailers utilize one of these strategies exclusively. Typically, different approaches are used for different products, making it necessary to analyze the supply chain and determine the appropriate approach to use for a particular product or product family.

To evaluate these concepts we proceed with a simple question: What are the factors that influence distribution strategies? Obviously, customer demand and location, service level, and costs, including transportation and inventory costs, all play a role. It is important to note the interplay of inventory and transportation costs (see Chapter 3). Both transportation and inventory costs depend on shipment size, but in opposite ways. Increasing lot sizes reduces the delivery frequency and enables the shipper to take advantage of price breaks in shipping volume, therefore reducing transportation costs. However, large lot sizes increase inventory cost per item because items remain in inventory for a longer period of time until they are consumed.

Demand variability also has an impact on the distribution strategy. Indeed, as we observed in Chapter 3, demand variability has a huge impact on cost; the larger the variability, the more safety stock needed. Thus, stock held at the warehouses provides protection against demand variability and uncertainty, and due to *risk pooling*, the more warehouses a distributor has, the more safety stock is needed. On the other hand, if the warehouses are not used for inventory storage, as in the cross-docking strategy, or if there are no warehouses at all, as in direct shipping, more safety stock is required in the distribution system. This is true because in both cases *each store* needs to keep enough safety stock. This effect is mitigated, however, by distribution strategies that enable better demand forecasts and smaller safety stocks, and transshipment strategies, described below. Any assessment of different strategies must also consider lead time and volume requirements, as well as the capital investment involved in the various alternatives.

Table 5.1 summarizes and compares the three distribution strategies discussed in this subsection. The inventory at warehouses strategy refers to the classical distribution strategy in which inventory is kept at the warehouses. The allocation row in the table refers to the point at which the

TABLE 5.1   Distribution Strategies

Strategy → Attribute ↓	Direct Shipment	Cross-Docking	Inventory at Warehouses
Risk pooling			Take advantage
Transportation costs		Reduced inbound costs	Reduced inbound costs
Holding costs	No warehouse costs	No holding costs	
Allocation		Delayed	Delayed

allocation of different products to different retail outlets needs to be made. Clearly, in direct shipment, allocation decisions have to be made earlier than in the other two, so forecast horizons need to be longer.

5.4 Transshipment

The growth of rapid transportation options and advanced information systems has made transshipment an important option to consider when selecting supply chain strategies. By *transshipment*, we mean the shipment of items between different facilities *at the same level in the supply chain* to meet some immediate need.

Most often, transshipment is considered at the retail level. As we mentioned above, transshipment capability allows the retailer to meet customer demand from *the inventory of other retailers*. To do this, the retailer must know what other retailers have in inventory, and must have a rapid way to ship the items either to the store where the customer originally tried to make the purchase or to the customer's home. These requirements can be met only with advanced information systems, which allow a retailer to see what other retailers have in stock and facilitate rapid shipping between retailers.

It is easy to see that if the appropriate information systems exist, shipment costs are reasonable, and all of the retailers have the same owner, transshipment makes sense. In this case, the system is effectively taking advantage of the risk-pooling concept, even if no central warehouse exists, because one can view inventory in different retail outlets as part of a large, single pool.

Retailers that are independently owned and operated may want to avoid transshipment because they will be helping their competitors. In Chapter 6, we consider the issues associated with *distributor integration*, in which independent distributors cooperate in various ways, including transshipment of needed goods.

5.5 Central versus Local Facilities

Another critical decision in supply chain design involves whether to use centralized or local production and warehousing facilities. We discussed certain elements of this decision in Chapter 2. Here we summarize additional important considerations:

Safety stock. Consolidating warehouses allows the vendor to take advantage of risk pooling. In general, this means that the more centralized an operation is, the lower safety stock levels will be.

Overhead. Economies of scale suggest that operating a few large central warehouses leads to lower total overhead cost relative to operating many smaller warehouses.

Economies of scale. In many manufacturing operations, economies of scale can be realized if manufacturing is consolidated. It is often much more expensive to operate many small manufacturing facilities than to operate a few large facilities with the same total capacity.

Lead time. Lead time to market can often be reduced if a large number of warehouses are located closer to the market areas.

Service. This depends on how *service* is defined. As we indicated above, centralized warehousing enables the utilization of risk pooling, which means that more orders can be met with a lower total inventory level. On the other hand, shipping time from the warehouse to the retailer will be longer.

Transportation costs. Transportation costs are directly related to the number of warehouses used. As the number of warehouses increases, transportation costs between the production facilities and the warehouses also increase because total distance traveled is greater and, more importantly, quantity discounts are less likely to apply. However, transportation costs from the warehouses to the retailers are likely to fall because the warehouses tend to be much closer to the market areas.

Of course, it is possible that in an effective distribution strategy, some products will be stored in a central facility while others will be kept in various local warehouses. For instance, very expensive products with low customer demand may be stocked at a central warehouse while low-cost products facing high customer demand may be stocked at many local warehouses. In addition, the use of centralized or local production and warehousing facilities is not necessarily an either-or decision. There are degrees of local and centralized operation, with varying degrees of the advantages and disadvantages listed above. Finally, advanced information systems help each type of system maintain some of the advantages of the other type. For example, lead times from central warehouses and safety stock for local warehouses can be reduced.

5.6   Push versus Pull Systems

Supply chain networks are often categorized as push or pull systems. Probably, this stems from the manufacturing revolution of the 1980s, in which manufacturing systems were divided into these categories. It is important to clearly understand what we mean by push or pull distribution systems.

5.6.1 Push-Based Supply Chain

In a *push-based supply chain*, see Figure 5.1, production decisions are based on long-term forecasts [6]. Typically, the manufacturer uses orders received from the retailer's warehouses to forecast customer demand. It therefore takes much longer for a push-based supply chain to react to the changing marketplace. This can lead to:

- The inability to meet changing demand patterns.
- The obsolescence of supply chain inventory as demand for certain products disappears.

In addition, we saw in Chapter 4 that the variability of orders received from the retailers and the warehouses is much larger than the variability in customer demand; that is, the bullwhip effect. This increase in variability leads to:

- Excessive inventories due to the need for large safety stocks (see Chapter 3).
- Larger and more variable production batches.
- Unacceptable service levels.
- Product obsolescence.

Specifically, as observed in Chapter 4, the bullwhip effect leads to inefficient resource utilization, because planning and managing is much more difficult. For instance, it is not clear how a manufacturer should determine production capacity. Should it be based on peak demand, which implies that most of the time the manufacturer has expensive resources sitting idle, or should it be based on average demand, which requires extra—and expensive—capacity during periods of peak demand? Similarly, it is not clear how to plan transportation capacity—based on peak demand or average demand. Thus, in a push-based supply chain we often find increased transportation costs, high inventory levels and/or high manufacturing costs, due to the need for emergency production changeovers.

FIGURE 5.1

A push system

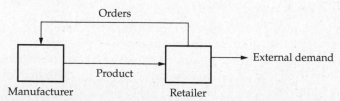

5.6.2   *Pull-Based Supply Chain*

In a *pull-based supply chain*, see Figure 5.2, production is demand driven so that it is coordinated with actual customer demand rather than a forecast [6]. For this purpose, the supply chain uses fast information flow mechanisms to transfer information about customer demand (e.g., POS data) to the manufacturing facilities. This leads to:

- A decrease in lead times achieved through the ability to better anticipate incoming orders from the retailers.
- A decrease in inventory at the retailers since inventory levels at these facilities increase with lead times (see Chapter 3).
- A decrease in variability in the system and, in particular, variability faced by manufacturers (see the discussion in Section 4.2.2) due to lead time reduction.
- Decreased inventory at the manufacturer due to the reduction in variability.

Thus, in a pull-based supply chain, we typically see a significant reduction in system inventory level, enhanced ability to manage resources, and a reduction in system costs when compared with an equivalent push-based system.

On the other hand, pull-based systems are often difficult to implement when lead times are so long that it is impractical to react to demand information. Also, in pull-based systems, it is frequently more difficult to take advantage of economies of scale in manufacturing and transportation since systems are not planned far ahead in time.

In some cases, a push-based system is appropriate for part of the supply chain while a pull-based system is appropriate for the rest of it. In Chapter 8, we discuss postponement, or delayed differentiation, in the context of supply chain management. In this strategy, the initial stages of the supply chain are operated in a push-based manner, and the final stages are operated using a pull-based strategy. This is accomplished by producing bulk products in the first stages, and then differentiating these

FIGURE 5.2

A pull system

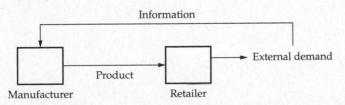

products based on customer demand. The interface between the push-based stages and the pull-based stages is known as the *push-pull boundary*, or the *postponement boundary*.

SUMMARY

In this chapter, we have discussed many of the different strategies that can be employed in an effective supply chain design. The decision between a system subject to centralized control and a decentralized system is critical. In general, a centralized system can be operated more effectively than a decentralized system, although it may be necessary to form partnerships to implement centralized control. Also, depending on the details of the supply chain, direct shipment strategies, traditional warehousing strategies, or cross-docking strategies may be the most effective way to distribute goods. Of course, each of these approaches has a unique set of requirements for it to be successful. In some cases, providing a transshipment option can also help to raise service levels and lower operating expenses.

In addition to selecting between centralized and decentralized *control*, it is also necessary to decide between centralized storage and production facilities on the one hand, or localized ones on the other. Both choices have advantages and disadvantages, and the decision made on which to select can have a profound effect on the cost and efficiency of a supply chain.

Finally, the fundamental choice between a push-based system and a pull-based system needs to be made. If possible, it is usually more effective to implement a pull-based system, and many forward-thinking firms are moving toward a pull approach if they don't already have one in place. Sometimes, a hybrid approach, in which the first stages of the supply chain are operated in a push fashion and the remaining stages are operated as a pull system, is the most appropriate.

CHAPTER 6

Strategic Alliances

CASE: AUDIO DUPLICATION SERVICES, INC. (ADS)

Audio Duplication Services is a compact disk and cassette duplication and distribution company. Its major customers, the big record companies, use ADS to duplicate and distribute CDs and cassettes. ADS stores the master tapes and, when a customer requests it, makes a certain number of copies and delivers them to its customers' customers, music stores and other points of sale such as department stores Wal-Mart and Kmart, and electronics stores such as Circuit City and Best Buy. ADS is one of six big players in the audio duplication market. ADS has about 20 percent of the $5 billion market while its two biggest competitors share another 40 percent.

Managers at ADS are currently trying to understand and react to some difficult supply chain related issues.

- Some of the big national retailers are putting pressure on ADS's customers, the record companies, to manage inventory in the following way, known as vendor managed inventory or VMI agreement. The record companies will be put in charge of deciding how much of each album, CD, and cassette title is delivered to each store, and when each delivery is made. To help with these decisions, the record companies will be provided with continuously updated point-of-sale (POS) data from each of the stores. Also, the record companies will own the inventory until it is sold, at which point payment will be transferred from the retailers to the record companies. Since ADS provides the record companies with duplication and distribution services, the record companies have asked ADS to help with the logistics of the VMI agreement.

- In the past, ADS has shipped to the distribution centers of large national retailers, and the retailers have arranged for distribution to the individual stores. Now, the retailers are providing strong incentives to ship directly to individual stores. Of course, this means higher expenses for ADS.

Source: ADS is a fictional company. The material in this case is loosely based on the authors' experience with several companies.

- In general, ADS's shipping costs are increasing. Currently, ADS has a shipping manager who arranges with different shippers to make deliveries on a shipment-by-shipment basis. Perhaps there is a better way to manage these deliveries, either by purchasing a fleet of trucks and doing the shipping in-house, or by outsourcing the entire shipping function to a third party. Maybe something between these two extremes will be best.

Of course, ADS is facing even bigger issues, such as the future of the audio duplication industry as online audio distribution technologies become more prevalent. In any event, each record company periodically reviews its contract with its audio duplication service, so management must address each of the above issues effectively for the company to remain successful.

By the end of this chapter, you should be able to answer the following questions:

- Why are major retailers moving toward VMI relationships?
- When should a company handle its logistics needs in-house, and when should external sources be used?
- What other types of business partnerships can be used to improve supply chain performance?
- Can pressures like the ones described in this case be used to a company's advantage?

6.1 Introduction

One of the paradoxes of business today is that at the same time that complex business practices (such as the ones we have discussed in the preceding chapters) are becoming essential for firms to survive and thrive, the necessary financial and managerial resources to implement these practices are becoming increasingly scarce. This is one reason why it may not always be effective to perform all of these key business functions in-house. Frequently, a company may find it effective to use other firms with special resources and technical knowledge to perform these functions.

Even if a firm has the available resources to perform a particular task, another firm in the supply chain may sometimes be better suited to perform that task simply because its relative location in the supply chain better positions it to do so. Often a combination of position in the supply chain, resources, and expertise determines the most appropriate firm in the supply chain to perform a particular function. Of course, it is not enough to *know* who in the supply chain should perform a particular function—steps must be taken so that the function is actually performed by the appropriate firm.

As with any business function, there are four basic ways for a firm to ensure that a logistics related business function is completed [66]:

1. Internal activities. A firm can perform the activity using internal resources and expertise, if they are available. As we will discuss more completely in the next section, if this activity is one of the *core strengths* of the firm, this may be the best way to perform the activity.

2. Acquisitions. If a firm doesn't have the expertise or specialized resources internally, it can acquire another firm that does. This certainly gives the acquiring firm full control over the way the particular business function is performed, but it has several possible drawbacks. For one thing, acquiring a successful company can be difficult and expensive. The culture of the acquired company may clash with that of the acquiring company, and the effectiveness of the acquired company could be lost in the assimilation process. The acquired company may have previously dealt with the acquiring company's competitors, and it could lose this business. This may hurt its overall effectiveness. For these reasons, as well as many others, an acquisition may not be appropriate.

3. Arm's-length transactions. Most business transactions are of this type. A firm needs a specific item or service, such as the delivery of a load of items, the maintenance of a vehicle, or the design and installation of logistics management software, and purchases or leases the item or service. Many times, an arm's-length transaction is the most effective and appropriate arrangement. Of course, the goals and strategies of the supplier might not match those of the buyer. In general, this kind of short-term arrangement fulfills a particular business need but doesn't lead to long-term strategic advantages.

4. Strategic alliances. These are typically multifaceted, goal-oriented, long-term partnerships between two companies in which both risks and rewards are shared. In many cases, the problems of outright acquisition can be avoided while at the same time mutual goals can lead to the commitment of many more resources than in the case of arm's-length transactions. Strategic alliances typically lead to long-term strategic benefits for both partners.

This chapter focuses on *strategic alliances* related to supply chain management. In the next section, we introduce a framework for analyzing the advantages and disadvantages of strategic alliances. In Sections 6.3, 6.4, and 6.5, the three most important types of supply chain related strategic alliances are discussed in greater detail: retailer-supplier partnerships (RSP), third-party logistics (3PL), and distributor integration (DI).

6.2   A Framework for Strategic Alliances

There are many difficult strategic issues that play a part in the selection of appropriate *strategic alliances*. In his classic book, *Partnerships for Profit*, Jordan Lewis [66] introduces an effective general framework for analyzing strategic alliances. This framework, which we briefly introduce in this section, is very helpful for considering the kinds of supply chain related strategic alliances that we address in the rest of this chapter.

To determine whether a particular strategic alliance is appropriate for your firm, consider how the alliance will help address the following issues:

Adding Value to Products.   A partnership with the appropriate firm can help add value to existing products. For example, partnerships that improve time to market, distribution times, or repair times help to increase the perceived value of a particular firm. Similarly, partnerships between companies with complementary product lines can add value to both companies' products.

Improving Market Access.   Partnerships that lead to better advertising or increased access to new market channels can be beneficial. For example, complementary consumer product manufacturers can cooperate to address the needs of major retailers, increasing sales for everyone.

Strengthening Operations.   Alliances between appropriate firms can help to improve operations by lowering system costs and cycle times. Facilities and resources can be used more efficiently and effectively. For example, companies with complementary seasonal products can effectively use warehouses and trucks year-round.

Adding Technological Strength.   Partnerships in which technology is shared can help add to the skills base of both partners. Also, the difficult transitions between old and new technologies can be facilitated by the expertise of one of the partners. For example, a supplier may need a particular enhanced information system to work with a certain customer. Partnering with a firm that already has expertise in this system makes it easier to address difficult technological issues.

Enhancing Strategic Growth.   Many new opportunities have high entry barriers. Partnerships might enable firms to pool expertise and resources to overcome these barriers and explore new opportunities.

Enhancing Organizational Skills.   Alliances provide a tremendous opportunity for organizational learning. In addition to learning from one another, partners are forced to learn more about themselves and to become more flexible so that these alliances work.

Building Financial Strength.   In addition to addressing these competitive issues, alliances can help to build financial strength. Income can be increased and administrative costs can be shared between partners or even reduced owing to the expertise of one or both of the partners. Of course, alliances also limit investment exposure by sharing risk.

Strategic alliances have their downsides. The list above is useful for determining these. Each company has its *core strengths* or competencies—specific talents that differentiate the company from its competitors and give it an advantage in the eyes of its customers. These core strengths must not be weakened by the alliance, which can happen if resources are diverted from these strengths or if technological or strategic strengths are compromised to make the partnership successful. Similarly, key differences with competitors must not be diminished. This is possible if key technology is shared or if entry barriers are reduced for the competition.

Determining these core strengths is clearly very important—unfortunately, it is also very difficult—what they are depends on the nature of the business and of the firm. Core strengths don't necessarily correspond to large investment of resources, and they may be intangible items such as management skills or brand image. To determine a firm's core strengths, consider how the firm's internal capabilities contribute to differentiating it from its competition in each of the seven key items listed above. Now, how will *strategic alliances* help or hurt in each of these areas?

The following example illustrates the advantages and disadvantages of strategic alliances. Consider how IBM, Intel, and Microsoft benefited and were hurt by the relationships described in this example.

Example 6.2.1 | Although not specifically related to logistics, the example of the IBM personal computer (PC) highlights the advantages and the disadvantages of outsourcing key business functions. When IBM decided to enter the PC market in late 1981, the company did not have the infrastructure in place to design and build a personal computer. Rather than take the time to develop these capabilities, IBM outsourced almost all the major components of the PC. For example, the microprocessor was designed and built by Intel, and the operating system was provided by a small company in Seattle called Microsoft. IBM was able to get this computer to market within 15 months of beginning its design by tapping the expertise and resources of other companies. Furthermore, within three years IBM replaced Apple Computer as the number one supplier of personal computers. By 1985 IBM's market share was more than 40 percent. However, the downside to IBM's strategy soon became clear, as competitors such as Compaq were able to enter the market by utilizing the same suppliers as IBM. Furthermore, when IBM tried to regain control of the market by introducing its PS/2 line of computers, featuring a new, proprietary design and an operating system called OS/2, other companies did not follow IBM's lead, and the original architecture remained dominant in the market. By the end of 1995 IBM's market share had fallen to less than 8 percent, behind market leader Compaq's 10 percent [21].

Although strategic alliances are becoming increasingly prevalent in all walks of business, three types are particularly significant in supply chain management. Third-party logistics (3PL), retailer supplier partnerships (RSP), and distributor integration (DI) are discussed in detail in the next three sections. As you read about these issues, try to place them in the framework described above.

6.3   Third-Party Logistics

The use of third party logistics (3PL) providers to take over some or all of a company's logistics responsibilities is becoming more prevalent. Indeed, the third party logistics industry, which essentially began in the 1980s, was a $40 billion industry in 1998; experts predict that it will grow to $50 billion by 2000 [59].

6.3.1   What is 3PL?

Third-party logistics is simply the use of an outside company to perform all or part of the firm's materials management and product distribution function. 3PL relationships are typically more complex than traditional logistics supplier relationships—they are true strategic alliances.

Although companies have used outside firms to provide particular services, such as trucking and warehousing, for many years, these relationships had two typical characteristics: they were *transaction based*, and the companies hired were often *single function* specific. Modern 3PL arrangements involve long-term commitments and often multiple function or process management. For example, Ryder Dedicated Logistics has a five-year agreement to design, manage, and operate all of Whirlpool Corporation's inbound logistics [59].

3PL providers come in all sizes and shapes, from small companies with a few million dollars in revenues to huge companies with revenues in the billions. Most of these companies can manage many stages of the supply chain.

Surprisingly, the use of third-party logistics is most prevalent among large companies. Firms like Minnesota Mining & Manufacturing Co. (3M), Eastman Kodak, Dow Chemical, Time Warner, and Sears Roebuck are turning over large portions of their logistics operations to outside suppliers. Third party logistics providers are finding it hard to persuade small companies to employ their services, although this may change as the use of 3PL becomes more prevalent and as 3PL providers make a larger effort to develop relationships with smaller companies [13].

6.3.2   Advantages and Disadvantages of 3PL

Most of the general advantages and disadvantages of strategic alliances described in Section 6.2 apply here.

Focus on Core Strengths

The most frequently cited benefit of using 3PL providers is that it allows a company to focus on its core competencies. With corporate resources becoming increasingly limited, it is often difficult to be an expert in every facet of the business. Logistics outsourcers provide a company with the opportunity to focus on that company's particular area of expertise, leaving the logistics expertise to the logistics companies. (Of course, if logistics is one of the company's areas of expertise, then outsourcing may not make sense.)

Example 6.3.1	The partnership between Ryder Dedicated Logistics and General Motors' Saturn division is a good example of these benefits. Saturn focuses on automobile manufacturing and Ryder manages most of Saturn's other logistics considerations. Ryder deals with vendors, delivers parts to the Saturn factory in Spring Hill, Tennessee, and delivers finished vehicles to the dealers. Saturn orders parts using electronic data interchange (EDI), and sends the same information to Ryder. Ryder makes all the necessary pickups from 300 different suppliers in the United States, Canada, and Mexico, using special *decision-support software* to effectively plan routes to minimize transportation costs [27].

Example 6.3.2	British Petroleum (BP) and Chevron Corp. also wished to stick to their core competencies. To do this, they formed Atlas Supply, a partnership of about 80 suppliers, to deliver items such as spark plugs, tires, window-washing fluid, belts, and antifreeze to their 6,500 service stations. Rather than use the distribution networks of either BP or Chevron or create a new one, Atlas outsourced all logistics to GATX, which is responsible for running five distribution centers and maintaining inventory of 6,500 SKUs at each service station. Each service station orders supplies through its oil company, which forwards the order to Atlas and then to GATX. Each station has a preassigned ordering day to avoid system bottlenecks. GATX systems determine appropriate routes and configurations and transmit orders to the DC. The next day, the DC selects and packs the orders, and trucks are loaded in the appropriate order based on the delivery schedule. As deliveries are made, returns and deliveries from Atlas suppliers are picked up. GATX electronically informs Atlas, Chevron, and BP of the status of all deliveries. The companies save enough on transportation costs alone to justify this partnership, and the two oil companies have managed to reduce the number of DCs from 5 to 13 and significantly improve service levels [1].

Provides Technological Flexibility

The ever-increasing need for technological flexibility is another important advantage of the use of 3PL providers. As requirements change and technology advances, the better 3PL providers constantly update their information technology and equipment. Often individual companies do not have the time, resources, or expertise to constantly update their technology. Different retailers may have different, and changing, delivery and information technology requirements, and meeting these requirements may be essential to a company's survival. Third party logistics providers can often meet these requirements in a quicker, more cost-effective way [45]. Also, third-party providers may already have the capability to meet the needs of a firm's potential customers, allowing the firm access to certain retailers that might not otherwise be possible or cost effective.

Provides Other Flexibilities

Third parties may also provide greater flexibility to a company. One example is flexibility in geographic locations. Increasingly suppliers are requiring rapid replenishment, which in turn may require regional warehousing. By utilizing third-party providers for this warehousing, a company can meet customer requirements without committing capital and limiting flexibility by constructing a new facility or committing to a long-term lease. Also, flexibility in service offerings may be achieved through the use of third parties, which may be equipped to offer retail customers a much larger variety of services than the hiring firm. In some cases, the volume of customers demanding these services may be low to the firm, but higher to the 3PL provider, who may be working for several different firms across different industries [109]. In addition, flexibility in resource and workforce size can be achieved through outsourcing. Managers can change what would be fixed costs into variable costs, in order to react more quickly to changing business conditions.

| Example 6.3.3 | Working with the Simmons Company, a mattress manufacturer, Ryder Dedicated Logistics provided new technology that allowed Simmons to completely change the way it does business. Before its involvement with Ryder, Simmons warehoused between 20,000 and 50,000 mattresses at each of its manufacturing facilities to meet customer demand in a timely fashion. Now, Ryder maintains an on-site logistics manager at Simmons' manufacturing plant. When orders arrive, the logistics manager uses special software to design an optimal sequence and route to deliver the mattresses to customers. This logistics plan is then transmitted to the factory floor where the mattresses are manufactured in the exact quantity, style, and sequence required—all in time for the shipment. This logistics partnership has virtually eliminated the need for Simmons to hold inventory at all [27]. |

| Example 6.3.4 | SonicAir, a division of UPS, provides an even more sophisticated third-party service. This company serves specialized customers who supply equipment for which every hour of downtime is very expensive; SonicAir rapidly delivers service parts where they are needed. SonicAir maintains 67 warehouses and uses specialized software to determine the appropriate inventory level for each part at each warehouse. When an order is placed, the system determines the best way to deliver the |

part and sends it out, usually on the next flight, where it is delivered by one of the company's ground couriers. This service enables customers to store fewer parts at each field service bureau than would otherwise be necesssary—and still provide the same level of service. With some parts valued at hundreds of thousands of dollars, this is clearly a cost savings to the customer. At the same time, this business is very profitable for SonicAir because customers are willing to pay well for this level of service [27].

Important Disadvantages of 3PL

The most obvious disadvantage of the use of 3PL providers is the *loss of control* inherent in outsourcing a particular function. This is especially true for outbound logistics where 3PL company employees themselves might interact with a firm's customers. Many third party logistics firms work very hard to address these concerns. Efforts include painting company logos on the sides of trucks, dressing 3PL employees in the uniforms of the hiring company, and providing extensive reporting on each customer interaction.

Also, if logistics is one of the core competencies of a firm, it makes no sense to outsource these activities to a supplier who may not be as capable as the firm's in-house expertise. For example, Wal-Mart built and manages its own distribution centers and Caterpillar runs its parts supply operations. These are competitive advantages and core competencies of these firms, so outsourcing is unnecessary. In particular, if certain logistics activities are within the core competencies of the firm and others are not, it might be wise to employ 3PL providers for only those areas that outside providers can handle better than the hiring firm. For example, if VMI replenishments strategies and materials handling are core competencies of a company but transportation is not, a 3PL firm could be contacted to handle shipments from the dock to the customer exclusively. Similarly, pharmaceutical companies build and own DCs for controlled drugs, but often use public warehouses located closer to the customer for items that are less expensive and easier to control [5].

6.3.3   *3PL Issues and Requirements*

A third party logistics contract is typically a major and complex business decision. Other than the pros and cons listed above, there are many considerations that are critical in deciding whether an agreement should be entered into with a particular 3PL provider.

1. Know your own cost. Among the most basic issues to consider in selecting a 3PL provider is to know your own costs so they can be compared with the cost of using an outsourcing firm. Often it is necessary to use activity based costing techniques, which involve tracing overhead and direct costs back to specific products and services [45].

2. Customer orientation of the 3PL. Of course, it is not enough to select a provider based on costs alone. Many of the advantages listed above involve intangibles such as flexibility. Therefore the strategic logistics plan of the company and how a 3PL provider would fit into this plan must be considered carefully. A 1995 survey of 3PL providers [59] identified the following characteristics as most critical to the success of a 3PL agreement. The most important was the customer orientation of the provider; that is, the value of a 3PL relationship is directly related to the ability of the provider to understand the needs of the hiring firm and to adapt its services to the special requirements of that firm. The second most important factor was reliability. The flexibility of the provider, or its ability to react to the changing needs of the hiring firm and the needs of that firm's customers, was third. Significantly further down the list was cost savings.

3. Specialization of the 3PL. When choosing a potential 3PL provider, some experts suggest that companies should consider firms whose roots lie in the particular area of logistics that is most relevant to the logistics requirements in question. For example, Roadway Logistics, Menlo Logistics, and Yellow Logistics evolved from major LTL carriers; Exel Logistics, GATX, and USCO started as warehouse managers; and UPS and Federal Express have expertise in the timely handling of small packages. Some firms have even more specialized requirements, and these should be considered carefully when choosing a 3PL partner [5]. Sometimes, a firm can use one of its trusted core carriers as its third party logistics provider. For example, Schneider National, a firm that already worked closely with Baxter Healthcare Corp., recently agreed to take over Baxter's dedicated fleet routes [70].

4. Asset-owning versus non–asset-owning 3PL. There are also advantages and disadvantages to utilizing an asset-owning versus a non–asset-owning 3PL company. Asset-owning companies have significant size, access to human resources, a large customer base, economies of scope and scale, and systems in place, but they may tend to favor their own divisions in awarding work, to be bureaucratic, and to have a long decision-making cycle. Non–asset-owning companies may be more flexible and able to tailor services, and have the freedom to mix and match providers. They may also have low overhead costs and specialized industry expertise at the same time, but limited resources and lower bargaining power [5].

6.3.4 3PL Implementation Issues

Once a potential partner has been selected, the process has only begun. Agreements need to be reached and appropriate efforts must be made by both companies to initiate the relationship effectively. Experts point to one lesson in particular that has come from failed 3PL agreements: Devote enough time to start-up considerations; that is, starting the relationship started effectively during the first six months to a year is both the most difficult, and the most critical, part of any 3PL alliance. The company purchasing the services must identify exactly what it needs for the relationship to be successful, and be able to provide specific performance measures and requirements to the 3PL firm. The logistics provider must, in turn, consider and discuss these requirements honestly and completely, including their realism and relevance [13]. Both parties must be committed to devoting the time and effort needed to making a success of the relationship. It is critical that both parties remember that this is a mutually beneficial third party alliance, with shared risk and reward. The parties are partners—neither party can take a "transaction pricing" mentality [4].

In general, *effective communication* is essential for any outsourcing project to succeed. First, within the hiring company, managers must communicate to each other and to their employees exactly why they are outsourcing and what they expect from the outsourcing process, so that all relevant departments are on the "same page" and can become appropriately involved. Obviously, communication between the firm and the 3PL provider is also critical. It is easy to speak in generalities, but specific communication is essential if both companies are to benefit from the outsourcing arrangement [13]. On a technological level, it is usually necessary to enable communications between the 3PL supplier's systems and those of the hiring customer. Along the same line, a firm should avoid 3PL providers who utilize proprietary information systems, because these are much more difficult to integrate with other systems.

Other important issues to discuss with potential 3PL providers include the following:

- The third party and its service providers must respect the confidentiality of the data that you provide them.
- Specific performance measures must be agreed upon.
- Discuss specific criteria regarding subcontractors.
- Consider arbitration issues before entering into a contract.
- Negotiate escape clauses into the contract.
- Ensure that performance goals are being met through periodic reporting by the logistics provider [4].

6.4 Retailer-Supplier Partnerships

The formation of strategic alliances between retailers and their suppliers is becoming ubiquitous in many industries. We saw in Chapter 4 that variations in demand to suppliers from retailers in traditional retailer-supplier relationships is far greater than the variation in demand seen by retailers. In addition, suppliers have far better knowledge of their lead times and production capacities than retailers do. Thus, as margins get tighter and customer satisfaction becomes even more important, it makes sense to create cooperative efforts between suppliers and retailers in order to leverage the knowledge of both parties.

6.4.1   Types of RSP

The types of retailer-supplier partnerships can be viewed on a continuum. At one end is information sharing, which helps the vendor plan more efficiently, and at the other is a consignment scheme, where the vendor completely manages and owns the inventory until the retailer sells it.

In a basic *quick response* strategy, suppliers receive POS data from retailers and use this information to synchronize their production and inventory activities with actual sales at the retailer. In this strategy, the retailer still prepares individual orders, but the POS data is used by the supplier to improve forecasting and scheduling.

Example 6.4.1	Among the first companies to utilize this scheme was Milliken and Company, a textile and chemicals company. Milliken worked with several clothing suppliers and major department stores, all of which agreed to use POS data from the department stores to "synchronize" their ordering and manufacturing plans. The lead time from order receipt at Milliken's textile plants to final clothing receipt at the department stores was reduced from 18 weeks to 3 weeks [103].

In a *continuous replenishment* strategy, sometimes called *rapid replenishment*, vendors receive POS data and use these data to prepare shipments at previously agreed upon intervals to maintain specific levels of inventory. In an advanced form of continuous replenishment, suppliers may gradually decrease inventory levels at the retail store or distribution center as long as service levels are met. Thus, in a structured way, inventory levels are continuously improved. In addition, the inventory levels need not be simple levels, but could be based on sophisticated models which change the appropriate level based on seasonal demand, promotions, and changing consumer demand [108].

In a *vendor managed inventory (VMI)* system, sometimes called a *Vendor Managed Replenishment (VMR)* system, the supplier decides on the appropriate inventory levels of each of the products (within previously agreed upon bounds), and the appropriate inventory policies to maintain these levels. In the initial stages, vendor suggestions must be approved by the retailer, but eventually the goal of many VMI programs is to eliminate retailer oversight on specific orders. This type of relationship is perhaps most famously exemplified by Wal-Mart and Procter & Gamble, whose partnership, begun in 1985, has dramatically improved P&G's on-time deliveries to Wal-Mart while increasing inventory turns [15]. Other discount stores followed suit, including Kmart, which by 1992 had developed over 200 VMI partners [103]. These VMI projects have in general been successful: projects at Dillard Department Stores, JCPenney, and Wal-Mart have shown sales increases of 20 to 25 percent, and 30 percent inventory turnover improvements [15].

Example 6.4.2	First Brands, Inc., the maker of such products as Glad sandwich bags, has successfully partnered with Kmart. In 1991, the company entered Kmart's Partners in Merchandise Flow program, in which vendors are responsible for ensuring appropriate inventory levels to Kmart at all times, at Kmart's insistence. Initially Kmart provided a three-year sales history, followed later by daily POS data to First Brands, which uses special software to convert these data into a production and delivery plan to each of Kmart's 13 distribution centers [26].

6.4.2   Requirements for RSP

The most important requirement for an effective retailer supplier partnership, especially one toward the VMI end of the partnership spectrum, is *advanced information systems*, on both the supplier and retailer sides of the supply chain. Electronic data interchange, or EDI—to relay POS information to the supplier and delivery information to the retailer—is essential to cut down on data transfer time and entry mistakes. Bar coding and scanning are essential to maintain data accuracy. And inventory, production control, and planning systems must be online, accurate, and integrated to take advantage of the additional information available.

As in all initiatives that can radically change the way a company operates, top management commitment is required for the project to be a success. This is especially true because information, which has been kept confidential up to this point, will now have to be shared with suppliers and customers, and cost allocation issues will have to be considered at a very high level (this is covered in more detail below). It is also true because such a partnership may shift power within the organization from one group to another. For instance, when implementing a VMI partnership, the day-to-day contacts with retailers shift from sales and marketing personnel to logistics personnel. This change in power may require significant involvment of top management.

Finally, RSP requires the partners to develop a certain level of trust without which the alliance is going to fail. In VMI, for example, suppliers need to demonstrate that they can manage the entire supply chain; that is, they can manage not only their own inventory but also that of the retailer. Similarly, in quick response, confidential information is provided to the supplier, which typically serves many competing retailers. In addition, strategic partnering in many cases results in significant reduction in inventory at the retailer outlet. The supplier needs to make sure that the additional available space is not used to benefit the supplier's competitors. Furthermore, the top management at the supplier must understand that the immediate effect of decreased inventory at the retailer will be a *one-time loss in sales revenue.*

6.4.3   *Inventory Ownership in RSP*

Several important issues must be considered when entering into a retailer-supplier partnership. One major issue is the decision concerning who makes the replenishment decisions. This places the partnership on the continuum of strategic partnership possibilities described above. This can be done in stages, first with information and, later, decision making, which is shared between the partners.

Inventory ownership issues are critical to the success of this kind of strategic alliance effort, especially one involving vendor-managed inventory. Originally, ownership of goods transferred to the retailer when goods were received. Now, some VMI partnerships are moving to a consignment relationship in which the supplier owns the goods until they are sold. The benefit of this kind of relationship to the retailer is obvious—lower inventory costs. Furthermore, since the supplier owns the inventory, it will be more concerned with managing it as effectively as possible. One possible criticism of the original VMI scheme is that the vendor has an incentive to move to the retailer as much inventory as the contract allows. If this is a fast-moving item and the partners had agreed upon two weeks of inventory, this may be exactly what the retailer wants to see in stock. If, however, this is a more complex problem of inventory management, the vendor needs to have an incentive to keep inventories as low as possible, subject to some agreed upon service level. For example, Wal-Mart no longer owns the stock for many of the items it carries, including most of its grocery purchases. It only owns them briefly as they are being passed through the checkout scanner [24].

It is less clear, however, why this consignment arrangement is beneficial to the supplier since the supplier owns inventory for a longer period of time. Many times, as in the case of Wal-Mart, the supplier has no choice because the market dictates this kind of arrangement. Even if this is not the case, such an arrangement is beneficial to the supplier because it allows the supplier to coordinate distribution and production, thus reducing total cost. To better understand this issue, recall from Chapter 4 the discussion of the difference between *global optimization* and *local optimization*. In the traditional supply chain, each facility does what is best for that facility; that is, the retailer manages its own inventory without regard to the impact on the supplier. The supplier in turn identifies a policy that will optimize its own cost subject to satisfaction of the retailer demand. In VMI, one tries to optimize the entire system by coordinating production and distribution. In addition, the supplier can further decrease total cost by coordinating production and distribution for several retailers. This is precisely why global optimization allows for significant reductions in total system costs.

Sometimes, depending on the relative power of the supplier and the retailer, the supply contract must be negotiated so that the supplier and the retailer share *overall system savings*. Retailers must also take this into account when comparing the cost of competing vendors: Different logistics schemes have different costs.

Example 6.4.3 | Ace Hardware, a retail hardware dealer co-op, has successfully implemented a consignment VMI scheme for lumber and building materials. In this program, Ace maintains financial ownership of these goods at the retailer, but the retailer has custodial ownership that makes it responsible if the product is damaged or destroyed [2]. The program is considered extremely successful, with service levels increasing from 92 to 96 percent on VMI items. Ace would eventually like to expand it to other product lines [3].

In addition to inventory and ownership issues, advanced strategic alliances can cover many different areas. Issues such as joint forecasting, meshed planning cycles, and even joint product development are sometimes considered [95].

6.4.4 Issues in RSP Implementation

For any agreement to be a success, performance measurement criteria must also be agreed to. These criteria should include nonfinancial measures as well as the traditional financial measures. For example, nonfinancial measures could include point-of-sale (POS) accuracy, inventory accuracy, shipment and delivery accuracy, lead times, and customer fill rates.

When information is being shared between retailers and suppliers, *confidentiality* becomes an issue. Specifically, a retailer who deals with several suppliers within the same product category may find that category information is important to the supplier in making accurate forecasts and stocking decisions. Similarly, there may be a relationship between stocking decisions made by several suppliers. How can these potential conflicts be managed, with the retailer maintaining the confidentiality of each partner?

When entering any kind of strategic alliance, it is important for both parties to realize that there will initially be problems that can only be worked out through *communication* and *cooperation*. For example, when First Brands started partnering with Kmart, Kmart often claimed that its supplier was not living up to its agreement to keep two weeks of inventory on hand at all times. It turned out that the problem arose from different forecasting methods employed by the two companies. This problem was eventually solved by direct communication between Kmart's forecasting experts and those from First Brands—this type of communication would have occurred through salespeople before the VMI partnership began [26].

In many cases, the supplier in a partnership commits to fast response to emergencies and situational changes at the retailer. If the manufacturing technology or capacity do not currently exist at the supplier, they may need to be added. For example, VF Mills, the maker of Wrangler jeans and a pioneer of quick response methods in the clothing industry, had to completely reengineer its production processes, including retraining and additional capital investment [15].

6.4.5   Steps in RSP Implementation

The important points listed above can be summarized in the following steps in VMI implementation [50]:

1. Initially, the contractual terms of the agreement must be negotiated. These include decisions concerning ownership and when it is to be transferred, credit terms, ordering responsibilities, and performance measures such as service or inventory levels, when appropriate.

2. Next, the following three tasks must be executed:

   • If they do not exist, integrated information systems must be developed for both supplier and retailer. These information systems must provide easy access to both parties.

   • Effective forecasting techniques to be used by the vendor and the retailer must be developed.

   • A tactical decision support tool to assist in *coordinating* inventory management and transportation policies must be developed. The systems developed will of course depend on the particular nature of the partnership.

6.4.6   Advantages and Disadvantages of RSP

One advantage of VMI relationships is nicely illustrated by the following example.

Example 6.4.4	Whitehall Robbins (WR), which makes over-the-counter drugs such as Advil, has an RSP relationship with Kmart. Like First Brands, WR initially disagreed with Kmart about forecasts. In this case, it turned out that WR forecasts were more accurate because the company has an much more extensive knowledge of its products than Kmart does. For example, Kmart's Chap Stick forecasts did not take the seasonality of the product into account. In addition, WR planners can take production issues, such as planned downtime, into account when planning shipments.

Also, WR benefits in another way. In the past Kmart would order large quantities of seasonal items at the beginning of the season, often linked to a promotion. This practice often lead to returns because it was difficult for Kmart to accurately forecast the amount it would sell. Now WR supplies weekly demand at an "everyday low cost," so large orders and preseason promotions have been eliminated, which in turn has greatly reduced returns. Inventory turns for seasonal items have gone from 3 to more than 10, and for nonseasonal items from 12–15 to 17–20 [26] .

Thus, in general, a huge advantage of RSPs is the knowledge the supplier has about order quantities, implying an ability to control the bullwhip effect (see Chapter 4). This of course varies from one type of partnership to another. In quick response, for instance, this knowledge is achieved through transfer of customer demand information that allows the supplier to reduce lead time, while in VMI the retailer provides demand information and the supplier makes ordering decisions, thus completely controlling the variability in order quantities. Of course, this knowledge can be leveraged to reduce overall system costs and improve overall system service levels. The benefits to the supplier in terms of better service levels, decreased managerial expenses, and decreased inventory costs are obvious. The vendor should be able to reduce forecast uncertainties and thus better coordinate

TABLE 6.1 **Main Characteristics of RSP**

Criteria → Types ↓	Decision Maker	Inventory Ownership	New Skills Employed by Vendors
Quick response	Retailer	Retailer	Forecasting skills
Continuous replenishment	Contractually agreed to levels	Either party	Forecasting & inventory control
Advanced continuous replenishment	Contractually agreed to & continuously improved levels	Either party	Forecasting & inventory control
VMI	Vendor	Either party	Retail management

production and distribution. To be more specific, reduced forecast uncertainties lead to reduced safety stocks, reduced storage and delivery costs, and increased service levels [50] as we noted in our discussion of the bullwhip effect in Chapter 4, Section 4.2.

In addition to the important benefits listed above, implementing a strategic partnership provides side benefits that cannot be understated. It provides a good opportunity for the reengineering of the retailer-supplier relationship. For example, redundant order entries can be eliminated, manual tasks can be automated, tasks such as ticketing merchandise and designing displays can be reassigned for systemwide efficiency, and unnecessary control steps can be eliminated from the process [15]. Many of these advantages stem from the same changes and technology needed to implement partnerships in the first place.

Many of the problems with retailer-supplier partnerships have been discussed above and are summarized here.

- It is necessary to employ advanced technology, which is often expensive.
- It is essential to develop trust in what once may have been an adversarial supplier-retailer relationship.
- In a strategic partnership, the supplier often has much more responsibility than formerly. This may force the supplier to add personnel to meet this responsibility.
- Finally, and perhaps most critically, expenses at the supplier often increase as managerial responsibilities increase. Also, inventory may initially be shifted back to the supplier; if a consignment arrangement is used, inventory costs in general may increase for the supplier. Thus, it may be necessary to work out a contractual relationship in which the retailer shares decreased system inventory costs with the supplier.
- Float is another issue with any EDI implementation, and it needs to be carefully considered when committing to a VMI partnership. Retailers who have become accustomed to waiting 30 to 90 days to pay for goods may now have to pay upon delivery. Even if they pay only when their goods are sold, this could be much sooner than their usual period of float [40].

6.4.7 Successes and Failures

We have cited several examples of RSP in the sections above. We include several other examples of successes—and one example of a failure—next.

Example 6.4.5 | Western Publishing is using VMI for its Golden Books line of children's books at several retailers, including more than 2,000 Wal-Mart locations. In this program, POS data automatically trigger reorders when inventory falls below a reorder point.

This inventory is delivered either to a distribution center or, in many cases, directly to a store. In this case, ownership of the books shifts to the retailer once deliveries have been made. In the case of Toys "R" Us, Western Publishing has even managed the entire book section for the retailer, including inventory from suppliers other than Western Publishing. The company has generated significant extra sales in both cases, although the program has increased costs significantly: These are costs related to the additional inventory management duties, as well as the extra freight costs incurred by shipping directly to stores. Nonetheless, management believes that VMI has provided a net benefit for the company [2].

Example 6.4.6	After Wal-Mart included supplier Mead-Johnson in its VMI program, the results were dramatic. Mead-Johnson has complete POS information to which it reacts instead of orders. Since this program was implemented, inventory turns at Wal-Mart have gone from under 10 to more than 100, and at Mead-Johnson from 12 to 52. Similarly, Scott Paper Company has been managing inventory in 25 of its customer distribution centers. In this effort, inventory turns at the customers have increased from about 19 to somewhere between 35 and 55, inventory has been eliminated, and service levels have improved. One caveat can be drawn from the experiences of Schering-Plough Healthcare Products (SPHP) with Kmart's Partners in the Merchandise Flow Program. In the first year of implementation, SPHP did see decreased stockouts at Kmart, but not substantially improved sales or profits. By patiently continuing with the program, however, SPHP eventually did realize substantial benefits in these areas [110].
Example 6.4.7	VF Corporation's Market Response System provides another success story of VMI. The company, which has many well-known brand names (e.g., Wrangler, Lee, and Girbaud), began its program in 1989. Currently, about 40 percent of its production is handled through some type of automatic replenishment scheme. This is particularly notable because the program encompasses 350 different retailers, 40,000 store locations, and more than 15 million levels of replenishment. Each division uses automatic software to manage the huge influx of data, and special techniques developed at VF to cluster the data so that it is more manageable. VF's program is considered one of the most successful in the apparel industry [101].
Example 6.4.8	Spartan Stores, a grocery chain, shut down its VMI effort about one year after its inception. In examining the reasons for the failure of the program, some important ingredients for a successful VMI program became clear. One problem was that buyers were not spending any less time on reorders than they had before because they didn't trust the suppliers enough to stop their careful monitoring of the inventories and deliveries of the VMI items. Buyers intervened at the slightest hint of trouble. Further, the suppliers didn't do much to allay these fears. The problems were not with the suppliers' forecasts; instead they were due to the suppliers' inability to deal with product promotions, which are a key part of the grocery business. Because suppliers were unable to account for promotions appropriately,

delivery levels were often unacceptably low during these periods of peak demand. In addition, Spartan executives felt that the inventory levels achieved by the VMI program were no lower than the levels the company could have achieved with a well-managed traditional supplier program. It should be noted that Spartan considered the VMI program successful with some suppliers. These were the suppliers with better forecasting skills. In addition, Spartan intends to maintain the continuous replenishment programs, in which inventory levels automatically trigger fixed delivery quantities with some of its suppliers [76].

6.5 Distributor Integration

For years business experts have advised manufacturers, particularly industrial manufacturers, to treat their distributors like partners [84]. Typically, this meant appreciating the value of the distributors and their relationship with the end users, and providing them with the necessary support to be successful. Distributors have a wealth of information about customer needs and wants, and successful manufacturers use this information when developing new products and product lines. Similarly, distributors typically rely on manufacturers to supply the necessary parts and expertise.

Example 6.5.1	The chairman and CEO of Caterpillar Corporation, Donald Fites, credits Caterpillar dealers with much of his company's recent success. Fites points out that dealers are much closer to customers than to the corporation, and can respond more rapidly to customer needs. They arrange financing when the product is purchased and carefully monitor, repair, and service the product. Fites says that, "the dealer creates the image of a company that doesn't just stand behind its products but with its products anywhere in the world." Caterpillar believes that its dealer network gives the company a tremendous advantage over its competition, especially the big Japanese construction and mining equipment manufacturers such as Komatsu and Hitachi [37].

This view of distributors is changing, however, as customer service needs present new challenges, and information technology rises to meet these challenges. Even a strong and effective distributor network can't always meet the needs of customers. A rush order might be impossible to meet from inventory or the customer might require some specialized technical expertise that the distributor does not have.

In the past these issues were addressed by adding inventory and personnel, either to each distributor or to the manufacturer. Modern information systems technology leads to a third solution, in which distributors are integrated so that the expertise and inventory located at one distributor is available to the others.

6.5.1   Types of Distributor Integration

Distributor integration (DI) can be used to address both inventory and service related issues. In terms of inventory, DI can be used to create a large pool of inventory across the entire distributor network, lowering total inventory costs while raising service levels. Similarly, DI can be used to meet a customer's specialized technical service requests by steering these requests to the distributors best suited to address them.

As we have pointed out in previous chapters, increased inventory is traditionally used to meet unusual rush orders and to provide spare parts quickly to facilitate repairs. In more sophisticated companies, risk-pooling concepts might be used to keep inventory earlier in the supply chain, where it can be distributed as needed. In a DI arrangement, each distributor can check the inventories of other distributors to locate a needed product or part. Dealers are contractually bound to exchange the part under certain conditions and for agreed-upon remuneration. This type of arrangement improves service levels at each of the distributors and lowers the total system inventory required. Of course, this type of arrangement is possible only because sophisticated information systems allow distributors to review each others' inventory, and integrated logistics systems allow parts to be delivered cheaply and efficiently.

Example 6.5.2   Machine tool builder Okuma America Corporation has implemented a DI system. Okuma carries many expensive machine tools and repair parts, but the high cost of carrying the full line makes it impossible for Okuma's 46 distributors in North and South America to do so. Instead Okuma requires each of its dealers to carry a minimum number of machine tools and parts. The company manages the entire system so that each tool and part is in stock somewhere in the system, either in one of the company's two warehouses or at one of the distributors. A system called Okumalink allows each of the distributors to check the warehouse inventories and to communicate with other distributors in finding a required part. Once a part is found, the company ensures that it is delivered quickly to the requesting dealer. There are plans to upgrade the system so that each distributor has full knowledge of the inventory held by all distributors. Since the system's implementation, inventory costs throughout the system have been reduced, the chance that a distributor will lose a sale because of inventory shortages has decreased, and customer satisfaction has increased [85].

Similarly, DI can be used to improve each distributor's perceived technical ability and ability to respond to unusual customer requests. In this kind of alliance, different distributors build expertise in different areas. A customer's specific request is routed to the distributor with the most expertise. For example, Otra, a large Dutch holding company with about 70 electrical wholesale subsidiaries, has designated some of them as *centers of excellence* in particular areas, such as warehouse layouts or point-of-sale materials. The other subsidiaries, as well as customers, are directed to these centers of excellence to meet particular requests [85].

6.5.2 Issues in Distributor Integration

There are two major issues involved in implementing a DI alliance. First, distributors may be skeptical of the rewards of participating in such a system. There is the chance that they will feel they are providing some of their expertise in inventory control to less skilled partners, especially when some of the distributors are larger and have bigger inventories than others. In addition, participating distributors will be forced to rely upon other distributors, some of whom they may not know, to help them provide good customer service.

This new kind of relationship also tends to take certain responsibilities and areas of expertise away from certain distributors, and concentrate them on a few distributors. It is not surprising that distributors might be nervous about losing these skills and abilities.

This explains why establishing a DI relationship requires a large commitment of resources and effort on the part of the manufacturing company. Distributors must feel sure that this is a long-term alliance. Organizers must work hard to build trust among the participants. Finally, the manufacturer may have to provide pledges and guarantees to ensure distributor commitment.

Example 6.5.3 | **Dunlop-Enerka** is a Dutch company that supplies conveyer belts to mining and manufacturing companies worldwide. Traditionally, the company met maintenance and repair requirements by storing vast quantities of inventory at distributors throughout Europe. To reduce inventories, the company installed a computer-based information system, Dunlocomm, to monitor inventory at the warehouses of each of its distributors. When a part is needed, a distributor uses the system to order the part and arrange for its delivery. To ensure distributor participation, Dunlop-Enerka guaranteed 24-hour delivery of each part to each distributor—if a part wasn't in stock, Dunlop-Enerka custom-manufactured and shipped it within the available time window. This guarantee reassured distributors enough so they committed to the system and, over time, inventory throughout the system dropped by 20 percent [85].

SUMMARY

In this chapter, we examined various types of partnerships that can be used to manage the supply chain more effectively. We started off by discussing the different paths a firm can take to ensure that particular supply chain related issues are addressed, including performing them internally or outsourcing them completely. Obviously, many different strategic and tactical issues play a part in the selection of the most appropriate strategy. We discussed a framework that can help in selecting the most appropriate way to address a particular logistics issue.

More and more frequently, third party logistics providers are taking over some of a firm's logistics responsibilities. There are both advantages and disadvantages to outsourcing the logistics function, as well as many important issues to consider once the decision has been made and a 3PL agreement is being implemented.

Retailer-supplier partnerships, in which the supplier manages a portion of the retailer's business—typically retail inventories—are also becoming common. There is a spectrum of possible types of retailer-supplier partnerships, ranging from agreements that cover only information sharing, to agreements in which the supplier has complete control over the retailer's inventory policy. We considered various issues and concerns relating to the implementation of these types of arrangement.

Finally, we discussed a class of alliances, called distributor integration, in which manufacturers coordinate the efforts of their (potentially competing) distributors to create risk-pooling opportunities across the various distributors and to enable different distributors to develop different areas of expertise.

CHAPTER

7

International Issues in Supply Chain Management

CASE: WAL-MART CHANGES TACTICS TO MEET INTERNATIONAL TASTES

São Bernardo, Brazil. Wal-Mart Stores Inc. is finding out that what plays in Peoria isn't necessarily a hit in suburban São Paulo.

Tanks of live trout are out; sushi is in. American footballs have been replaced by soccer balls. The fixings for *feijoada*, a medley of beef and pork in black bean stew, are now displayed on the deli counter. American-style jeans priced at $19.99 have been dropped in favor of $9.99 knock-offs.

But adapting to local tastes may have been the easy part. Three years after embarking on a blitz to bring "everyday low prices" to the emerging markets of Brazil and Argentina, Wal-Mart is finding the going tougher than expected.

Brutal competition, markets that don't play to Wal-Mart's ability to achieve efficiency through economies of scale, and some of its own mistakes have produced red ink. Moreover, the company's insistence on doing things "the Wal-Mart way" has apparently alienated some local suppliers and employees.

Deep Pockets

No one is counting Wal-Mart out, of course. With sales of nearly $105 billion last year and profits of $3.1 billion, the Bentonville, Arkansas, behemoth has deep pockets. And it has revised its merchandising in Brazil and Argentina and made other changes. Its four newest stores are smaller than the initial outlets in São Paulo and Buenos Aires and are in mid-size cities where competition isn't so fierce.

Bob L. Martin, Wal-Mart's head of international operations, is confident that the company will eventually become the dominant retailer in South America. "There is low-hanging fruit all over the place," he says. "The market is ripe and wide open for us." He adds that Wal-Mart plans to add eight stores in both Argentina and Brazil next year, doubling the number now in each country.

Source: Jonathan Friedland and Louise Lee, *The Wall Street Journal* (interactive edition), October 8, 1997. Copied with permission.

A lot is riding on Wal-Mart's global expansion drive, which is targeting not only South America but also China and Indonesia, two other markets full of promise and pitfalls. With opportunities for growth dwindling at home, the company is opening fewer than 100 domestic stores a year, down from as many as 150 in the early 1990s. The current rate of openings can't generate the profit gains that Wal-Mart wants, and its main hopes lie overseas.

"If we're good enough in international, we can duplicate Wal-Mart," chief executive David D. Glass said in an interview in June. "We have very high expectations."

A Small Operation So Far

So far, though, the six-year-old international operation is relatively tiny; it accounted for only 4.8 percent of Wal-Mart's 1996 sales. Most of the company's international revenue comes from Canada, where Wal-Mart purchased 120 stores from Woolworth Corp. in 1994, and from Mexico, where earlier this year it bought a controlling stake in Cifra, SA, its partner, and now has about 390 stores. Last year, the international unit had an operating profit of $24 million, its first, compared with a $16 million loss in 1995. Mr. Martin says he expects further improvement this year.

Mr. Glass said he expects international growth to account for a third of Wal-Mart's annual increase in sales and profits within three to five years.

The performance of Wal-Mart's 16 South American stores may well indicate the future outlook. In Canada and Mexico, many customers were familiar with the company from cross-border shopping trips, and by acquiring local retailers, Wal-Mart quickly reached the size necessary to hold down costs. In South America and Asia, by contrast, Wal-Mart is building from scratch in markets already dominated by savvy local and foreign competitors such as Grupo Pão de Acucar SA of Brazil and Carrefour SA of France.

Losses Forecast

Wal-Mart doesn't break out financial data on its South American Operations. However, retail analysts, citing the accounts of Wal-Mart's Brazilian partner, Lojas Americanas SA, expect Wal-Mart to lose $20 million to $30 million in Brazil this year, on top of an estimated $48 million in losses since starting up in South America in 1995. In Argentina, where the company doesn't have a partner, Wal-Mart executives concede that it is losing money but say its performance meets expectations. The company expects operations in both countries to be profitable by early 1999.

"What counts is that we are finding great customer acceptance," Mr. Martin says. Wal-Mart says its supercenter in Osasco, Brazil, was the top-grossing store in the entire company last year. And at a recent supercenter opening in the mid-size Brazilian city of Ribeirão Prêto, shoppers practically beat down the doors to scoop up bargain-priced microwave ovens and television sets.

But such enthusiasm is hard to sustain. At an older supercenter in Avellaneda, a suburb of Buenos Aires, a few shoppers are in the store during peak hours one Sunday. Hugo and Mariana Faojo help explain why. Browsing in the shoe section, the young couple say they see little difference between the goods at Wal-Mart and those at nearby Carrefour. For groceries, they prefer Supermercados Jumbo SA, a Chilean-owned chain, where they say they find high-quality products and fresh meats. Clothes and household goods, Wal-Mart's mainstays, are similar in quality and price to those at Carrefour, says Mr. Faojo, a government surveyor.

Not only did Carrefour arrive first—it now has a total of about 60 stores in Argentina and Brazil—but it is maneuvering with prices and promotions to keep Wal-Mart off balance. When Thomas Gallegos, who manages Wal-Mart's new store here, prints up fliers advertising bargains, the nearby Carrefour responds in just a few hours by offering the same product for a few cents less—and its fliers are handed out at the entrance to the Wal-Mart parking lot. "Geez, the competition is aggressive," says Mr. Gallegos, who previously ran a Wal-Mart in Harlingen, Texas.

Carrefour, which, like Wal-Mart in the United States, drives hard bargains with its suppliers, can afford to play low-ball because it has the critical mass that Wal-Mart lacks here. And it holds down its overhead by stocking a far-narrower selection of merchandise; for example, the Carrefour in La Plata, Argentina, stocks 22,000 items, while the Wal-Mart next door carries 58,000.

Mr. Martin contends that Carrefour's advantage is ephemeral and that customers value Wal-Mart's broader choice. "It's costing them something to fight us," he adds. Carrefour didn't respond to requests for an interview.

Distribution Problems

Right now, however, Wal-Mart's effort to stock such a wide variety of merchandise is hurting it. Squeezing out costs in the supply chain is crucial to its "everyday low pricing" formula. In the United States, the company runs like a well-oiled machine, maintaining a highly sophisticated inventory-management system and its own network of distribution centers.

But timely delivery of merchandise is a relative concept in the bumper-to-bumper traffic of São Paulo, where Wal-Mart depends on suppliers or contract truckers to deliver most of its goods directly to stores. Because it doesn't own its distribution system, it can't control deliveries nearly as well as it does in the United States, vendors say. Stores here sometimes process 300 deliveries daily, compared with seven a day at U.S. locations, and some shipments have mysteriously disappeared somewhere between the port and the store.

"The biggest issue Wal-Mart has is shipping product on time and getting on the shelf," says Jim Russel, a national account manager for Colgate-Palmolive Co. in Bentonville. Wal-Mart recently built a warehouse in Argentina and one in Brazil that it says will eventually reduce its distribution problems.

But logistics aren't the only issue. Some local suppliers have difficulty meeting Wal-Mart's specifications for easy-to-handle packaging and quality control, forcing the retailer to rely so heavily on imported goods that it could have problems if Brazil's economic stabilization policies falter. Eleven South American suppliers have taken umbrage at Wal-Mart's aggressive pricing policies and for a time refused to sell goods to the chain.

Wal-Mart also has sought to drive hard bargains with divisions of its major suppliers back in the United States. The pitch hasn't been altogether successful. Wal-Mart doesn't get special deals just because it's a big U.S. customer, some large domestic suppliers say.

Various Mistakes

Wal-Mart's troubles in South America stem partly from its own mistakes. Analysts say it failed to do its homework before plunging in. In addition to the live trout and American footballs, the company initially imported items such as cordless tools, which few South Americans use, and leaf blowers, which are useless in a concrete jungle such as São Paulo.

And merchandise flubs weren't the only mistakes. In Brazil, Wal-Mart brought in stock-handling equipment that didn't work with standardized local pallets. It also installed a computerized bookkeeping system that failed to take into account Brazil's wildly complicated tax system. Vincente Trius, who heads Wal-Mart's Brazilian operations, says, however, that the company hasn't lost money as a result of tax miscalculations.

Wal-Mart has also been slow to adapt to Brazil's fast-changing credit culture. Not until last February did the company start accepting postdated checks, which have become the most common form of credit since Brazil stabilized its currency in 1995. Pão de Acucar, whose Extra hypermarkets compete with Wal-Mart, has been taking postdated checks since they first became popular and has installed a sophisticated credit-checking system at its registers. Wal-Mart is hurrying to do so, too.

The six South American Sam's Club locations, the members-only warehouse stores that sell merchandise in bulk, got off to a slow start largely because shoppers weren't used to paying a membership fee and don't have enough room at home to store bulk purchases. In Argentina the clubs have faced another barrier: Small-business customers are reluctant to sign up for fear Wal-Mart could provide tax information to the authorities on their purchases.

Wal-Mart won't disclose Sam's Club membership data in South America. But it now offers shoppers free one-day memberships tied to specific purchases. Mr. Martin says that Wal-Mart is "disappointed" in the club's performance in Argentina but that it is improving in Brazil. The company says it plans more Sam's outlets in South America but hasn't disclosed details.

Problems Called Temporary

Wal-Mart's Mr. Glass characterized the missteps as temporary problems and inevitable in entering a new market. "It's a lengthy process to go to South America, recruit good managers, bring them to Wal-Mart and train them and indoctrinate them and teach them what you want to teach them," he said in June. "It's slow going early on, and you spend a lot of money. You pay a lot of tuition to learn what you need to learn."

Wal-Mart says that it is developing a strong group of young executives and hasn't suffered high turnover. But Francisco de Narvaez, the owner of Argentine supermarket chain Casa Tia SA, says some managers have left because Wal-Mart "didn't listen to their senior-level local employees." In the past six months, Wal-Mart has hired two managers who had worked at its Mexican operations to take over two São Paulo locations.

Mr. Trius, a Spanish-born executive who earlier turned around Dairy Farm Ltd.'s Spanish supermarket chain, says he believes the criticisms of Wal-Mart's South

American operations go too far. "If Joe Blow was to open in Brazil with the same concept and within two years had everything in place, people would say 'What an incredible job,' " he says. "People expected us to snap our fingers and be Wal-Mart in the United States overnight. To me, the criticisms are more related to expectations than to reality."

By the end of this chapter, you should be able to answer the following questions:

- Other than a need to expand, what other reasons would Wal-Mart have for opening stores globally?
- Why would it be beneficial for Wal-Mart to have suppliers in different countries?
- Why would Wal-Mart want strong centralized control of its stores? Why would Wal-Mart want strong local control of stores?
- What pitfalls and opportunities other than those mentioned in *The Wall Street Journal* article would Wal-Mart face over the next few years?

7.1 Introduction

It is readily apparent that global operations and supply chains are becoming increasingly significant. Dornier et al. [29] collected the following statistics which help to indicate the magnitude of this trend:

- About one-fifth of the output of U.S. firms is produced overseas.
- One-quarter of U.S. imports are between foreign affiliates and U.S. parent companies.
- Since the late 1980s, over half of U.S. companies increased the number of countries in which they operate.

In many ways, international supply chain management is the same as domestic supply chain management spread over a larger geographic area. However, as we will discuss in the remainder of this chapter, international supply chain networks can provide a wealth of additional opportunities if they are managed effectively. At the same time, there are many additional potential problems and pitfalls to be aware of.

International supply chains can run the gamut from a primarily domestic business with some international suppliers to a truly integrated global supply chain. Some of the advantages and disadvantages that we will discuss apply equally to all of the systems in the following list, while others apply only to the most complex integrated systems.

International distribution systems. In this type of system, manufacturing still occurs domestically, but distribution and typically some marketing take place overseas.

International suppliers. In this system, raw materials and components are furnished by foreign suppliers, but final assembly is performed domestically. In some cases, the final product is then shipped to foreign markets.

Offshore manufacturing. In this type of system, the product is typically sourced and manufactured in a single foreign location, and then shipped back to domestic warehouses for sale and distribution.

Fully integrated global supply chain. Here products are supplied, manufactured, and distributed from various facilities located throughout the world. In a truly global supply chain, it may appear that the supply chain was designed without regard to national boundaries. Of course this is far from the truth! As we shall see, the true value of a global supply chain is realized by taking advantage of these national boundaries.

Clearly, a supply chain can fit more than one of these categories. Throughout the following discussion, consider how each of the issues discussed applies differently to firms, depending on their position in this global supply chain spectrum.

In any event, many firms cannot help but become involved in global supply chain issues. Dornier et al. [29] identified the following forces that collectively drive the trend toward globalization:

- Global market forces
- Technological forces
- Global cost forces
- Political and economic forces

7.1.1   Global Market Forces

Global market forces involve the pressures created by foreign competitors, as well as the opportunities created by foreign customers. Even if companies don't do business overseas, the presence of foreign competitors in home markets can affect their business significantly. To defend domestic markets successfully, companies may find it necessary to move into foreign markets. Sometimes the threat of a presence is sufficient, as in the dry breakfast cereal business, dominated by Kellogg Co. in the United States and Nestle in Europe. Apparently, failed attempts in the past to penetrate each other's home markets, combined with the threat of retaliation, are enough to maintain the status quo.

In addition, much of the demand growth available to companies is in foreign and emerging markets. Recently, companies have made great sacrifices (particularly in terms of proprietary technology) and taken on considerable business risk to become involved in ventures in mainland China. Indeed, the United States is accounting for less and less of the total consumption of goods in the world.

One cause of this increasing demand for products throughout the world is the global proliferation of information. Television introduces products to Europeans. Japanese vacation abroad. Businesses send overnight mail between continents. Most recently, the Internet provides instant international exposure, as well as the ability to purchase goods in one country that will be delivered in another without leaving home or office.

Example 7.1.1	In Brazil thousands of people move from preindustrial villages to rapidly growing cities. Once there, their first goal is to install television sets, even as they continue to "make sacrificial offerings of fruit and fresh-killed chickens to Macumban spirits by the candlelight" [65].

As Kenichi Ohmae, head of management consulting firm McKinsey's Japanese office, points out, people have "all become global citizens, and so must the companies that want to sell us things" [87]. Products are universally desired, and many companies are willing to sell them globally. This is clearly a self-amplifying trend for an industry, because, as companies become global, their competitors must also become global in order to compete. Thus, many companies are becoming global citizens with universal products and the opportunity to hire talented employees worldwide.

Along similar lines, particular markets often serve to drive technological advances in some areas. By participating in these competitive markets, companies are forced to develop and enhance leading-edge technologies and products. These products can then be used to increase or maintain market position in other areas or regions where the markets are not as competitive. To be a leader in software, for example, you have to compete in the U.S. market. Similarly, the German machine tools market and the Japanese consumer electronics market are hotly contested.

7.1.2   *Technological Forces*

Technological forces are related to the products themselves. Various subcomponents and technologies are available in different regions and locations around the world, and many successful firms need to have the ability to use these resources quickly and effectively. To achieve this, it may be necessary for firms to locate research, design, and production facilities close to these regions. This is often particularly useful if suppliers are involved in the design process, as discussed in Chapter 8. The same logic applies to collaborations and interfirm development projects. To gain access to markets or technology, companies in different regions frequently collaborate, resulting in the location of joint facilities close to one of the partners.

Along similar lines, global location of research and development facilities is becoming more common, primarily for two reasons. First, as product cycles become shorter and time more important, companies have discovered how useful it is to locate research facilities close to manufacturing facilities. This helps transfer technology from research facilities to manufacturing facilities, and speeds up the resolution of problems that inevitably arise during this transfer. In addition, specific technical expertise may be available in certain areas or regions. For example, Microsoft recently opened a research lab in Cambridge, England, to take advantage of the expertise available in Europe.

7.1.3   Global Cost Forces

Cost forces often dictate global location decisions. In the past the low cost of unskilled labor was a decisive factor in determining factory location. Recently, studies have found that in many cases, the costs of cheaper unskilled labor were more than offset by the increase in other costs associated with operating facilities in remote locations. In some cases, of course, cheaper labor is sufficient justification for overseas manufacturing. More recently, however, other global cost forces have become more significant.

For example, cheaper *skilled labor* is drawing an increasing number of companies overseas. Many of the analyses and programs that U.S. consulting firms are undertaking to address the Year 2000 problem (in which computer programs might fail when the year changes from 1999 to 2000) are being done in India, where programming skills are much cheaper.

We have discussed how a supplier and the customer supply chain must often be tightly integrated to deliver certain products effectively. Often this can be accomplished most cost effectively if the various participants are located close together. This may necessitate establishing integrated supply chains in different markets.

Finally, the capital costs of building a new facility often dominate labor costs. Many governments are willing to provide tax breaks or cost-sharing arrangements to lower the cost of the new facility. In addition, supplier price breaks and cost-sharing joint ventures may dictate these types of decisions.

7.1.4   Political and Economic Forces

Political and economic forces may greatly affect the drive toward globalization. In Section 7.2.1, we will discuss exchange rate fluctuation and the operational approaches to dealing with this issue. There are also several other political and economic factors. For example, regional trade agreements may drive companies to expand into one of the countries in the regional group. It may be to a company's advantage to obtain raw materials from or to manufacture within European, Pacific Rim, or North American trading blocks. In some cases, production processes may even be redesigned to avoid tariffs; for example, almost-finished goods may be shipped into a trading block to avoid tariffs on "finished goods."

Similarly, various trade protection mechanisms can affect international supply chain decisions. Tariffs and quotas affect what can be imported, and may lead a company to decide to manufacture within the market country or region. More subtle regulations, including local content requirements, affect supply chains. To address local content requirements, for example, TI and Intel, both U.S. firms, make microprocessors in Europe, and various Japanese automakers produce cars in Europe. Even voluntary export restrictions can affect the supply chain—Japanese manufacturers began to manufacture more expensive cars after agreeing voluntarily to limit exports to the United States. Recall that this is why brands such as Infiniti and Lexus came into existence. Government procurement policies can affect the ability of international companies to be successful in various markets. In the United States, for example, the Department of Defense gives as much as a 50 percent advantage to U.S. companies in the bidding on contracts.

7.2   Risks and Advantages of International Supply Chains

We have looked at the various forces that drive companies to develop international supply chains. In this section, we take a slightly different perspective by examining the various advantages and risks inherent in different types of international supply chains. Certain advantages of sourcing, manufacturing, and selling globally are immediately obvious.

Clearly, the world is converging in many instances toward standardized products. This means that more and more, vast markets have opened up for products—far greater than anything managers in the past could have imagined. By taking advantage of this trend, companies can realize vast economies of scale in terms of production, management, distribution, marketing, and so forth [65].

Indeed, as we discussed in the previous section, costs can be lowered with greater potential raw material, labor, and outsourcing sources and a greater number of potential manufacturing sites. At the same time, the increase in potential markets allows for an increase in sales and profits. These advantages are due to the increase in the size and scope of the supply chain—they are independent of the specific characteristics of the global supply chain.

To utilize these advantages, it is essential that management understand the different *demand characteristics* and *cost advantages* of different regions. We will discuss this issue in more depth in the next section. This discussion is greatly influenced by Kogut [56].

Most important, the global supply chain can provide a firm the *flexibility* to address the uncertainty in international markets. In particular, this flexibility can be used to counteract the inherent risks from various factors that are particularly relevant to global companies.

7.2.1 Risks

So what are these risks? First, fluctuating exchange rates change the relative value of production and the relative profit of selling a product in a particular country. Relative costs change so that manufacturing, storing, distributing, or selling in a particular region at a particular price can change from being extremely profitable to a total loss.

The same is true domestically. In many cases, certain regions within the same country may be less expensive for storage or manufacturing than others. However, the cost differences between domestic regions are not typically as dramatic as those across countries and, more importantly, they don't change as frequently.

It should be stressed that although managers typically think of exchange rates as affecting the dollar value of assets and liabilities denominated in foreign currencies, it is the *operating exposure* described in the previous paragraphs that can have the most dramatic effect on annual operating profit. This operating exposure reflects the fact that in the short run, changes in currency exchange rates do not necessarily reflect changes in relative inflation rates between countries. Thus, over the short term, regional operations can become relatively more or less expensive in terms of dollars. Note that this operating exposure is not only a function of a firm's global supply chain, but also its competition's global supply chain. If a competitor's relative costs decrease more, a firm can be underpriced in the market [64].

Indeed, Dornier et al. [29] identified several factors that affect the impact of operating exposure on a firm. *Customer reactions* influence how a firm adjusts prices in various markets in response to changes in operating expenses. As discussed above, *competitor reactions* also influence how a firm can react to changes in the relative cost of doing business. Competitors can react to price increases by raising their own prices to increase profitability or gain market share. As we discuss in the next section, *supplier reaction*—the ability of suppliers to respond with flexibility to varying demands—is a strong factor in the effectiveness of certain strategies that help firms address the risk of operating exposure. Finally, *government reactions* play a large role on the global stage. Governments can intervene to stabilize currencies or even directly support endangered firms by providing subsidies or tariffs. In addition, other political instabilities can also affect multinational companies. Tax situations can change rapidly because politics dictates different treatment of corporations, particularly foreign corporations, in various regions.

Likewise, foreign companies can enter domestic markets. These companies may even use domestic profits to subsidize low-priced goods in foreign markets. This could even affect companies that have decided not to compete on the global stage.

7.2.2   Addressing Global Risks

Bruce Kogut [56] identified three ways a global supply chain can be employed to address global risks: speculative, hedge, and flexible strategies.

Speculative Strategies
Using *speculative strategies*, a company bets on a single scenario, with often spectacular results if the scenario is realized, and dismal ones if it is not. For example, in the late 1970s and early 1980s, Japanese automakers bet that if they did all of their manufacturing in Japan, rising labor costs would be more than offset by exchange rate benefits, rising productivity, and increased levels of investment and productivity. For a while these bets paid off, but then rising labor costs and unfavorable exchange rates began to hurt manufacturers, and it became necessary to build plants overseas. Of course, if it had remained favorable to do all the manufacturing in Japan, the Japanese manufacturers would have "won the bet" because building new facilities is time-consuming and expensive.

Hedge Strategies
Using *hedge strategies*, a company designs the supply chain in such a way that any losses in part of the supply chain will be offset by gains in another part. For example, Volkswagen operates plants in the United States, Brazil, Mexico, and Germany, all of which are important markets for Volkswagen products. Depending on macroeconomic conditions, certain plants may be more profitable at various times than others. Hedge strategies, *by design*, are simultaneously successful in some locations and unsuccessful in others.

Flexible Strategies
When properly employed, *flexible strategies* enable a company to take advantage of different scenarios. Typically, flexible supply chains are designed with multiple suppliers and excess manufacturing capacity in different countries. In addition, factories are designed to be flexible, so that products can be moved at minimal cost from region to region as economic conditions demand.

When considering the implementation of a flexible strategy, managers have to answer several questions:

1. Is there enough variability in the system to justify the use of flexible strategies? Clearly, the more variability in international conditions, the more a company can benefit from utilizing flexible strategies.
2. Do the benefits of spreading production over various facilities justify the costs, which may include loss of economies of scale in terms of manufacturing and supply?
3. Does the company have the appropriate coordination and management mechanisms in place to take rapid advantage of flexible strategies?

If the supply chain is appropriately designed, several approaches can be utilized to implement flexible strategies effectively:

Production shifting. Flexible factories and excess capacity and suppliers can be used to shift production from region to region to take advantage of current circumstances. As exchange rates, labor cost, and so on change, manufacturing can be relocated.

Information sharing. Having an increased presence in many regions and markets will often increase the availability of information, which can be used to anticipate market changes and find new opportunities.

Global coordination. Having multiple facilities worldwide provides a firm with a certain amount of market leverage that it might otherwise lack. If a foreign competitor attacks one of your main markets, you can attack back. Of course, various international laws and political pressures place limits on this type of retaliation.

Example 7.2.1	When Michelin began to target North American markets aggressively, Goodyear was able to drop its tire prices in Europe. This forced Michelin to slow its overseas investment program.

Political leverage. The opportunity to move operations rapidly gives firms a measure of political leverage in overseas operations. For example, if governments are lax in enforcing contracts or international law, or present expensive tax alternatives, firms can move their operations. In many cases, the implicit threat of movement is sufficient to prevent local politicians from taking unfavorable actions.

7.2.3   Requirements for Global Strategy Implementation

Any company, even a huge global company, is not immediately ready for integrated global supply chain management on this scale. Michael Mc-Grath and Richard Hoole [77] discuss important developments that are necessary to set the stage for this kind of massive global integration. These developments are outlined below for each of the **five basic functions of firms:** product development, purchasing, production, demand management, and order fulfillment.

1. Product development. It is important to design products that can be modified easily for major markets, and which can be manufactured in various facilities. As we discuss in the next section, this is not always possible, but it is certainly helpful in those cases where it is achievable. While it is dangerous to design a product to be the "average" of what several markets require, it may be possible to design a base product or products that can be more easily adapted to several different markets. An international design team may be helpful in this regard.

2. Purchasing. A company will find it useful to have management teams responsible for the purchase of important materials from many vendors around the world. In this way, it is much easier to ensure that the quality and delivery options from various suppliers are compatible, and that a qualified team is present to compare the pricing of various suppliers. Also, these teams can work to guarantee that sufficient suppliers in different regions are at hand to ensure the flexibility necessary to take full advantage of the global supply chain.

3. Production. As we discussed above, excess capacity and plants in several regions are essential if firms are to take full advantage of the global supply chain by shifting production as conditions warrant. To utilize this kind of strategy, however, effective communications systems must be in place so that this global supply chain can be managed effectively. Centralized management is thus essential to this system, which implies that centralized information must be available. Indeed, knowledge of the current status of factories, supplies, and inventory is essential when making the types of decisions described above. In addition, since factories are typically supplying each other in a complex supply chain, it is important that interfactory communication is solid and that centralized management makes each factory aware of the system status.

4. Demand management. Often demand management, which involves setting marketing and sales plans based on projected demand and available product, is carried out on a regional basis. For the supply chain to be managed in an integrated way, demand management clearly has to have at least some centralized component. On the other hand, much of this sensitive, market-based information is best supplied by analysts located in each region. Thus, once again communication is a critical component of the success of global supply chain management.

5. Order fulfillment. To successfully implement a truly flexible supply chain management system, a centralized system must be in place so that regional customers can receive deliveries from the global supply chain with the same efficiency as they do from local or regionally based supply chains. All the flexibility in the world is of little use if it makes the system so cumbersome and unpleasant that customers turn elsewhere. We discuss the kinds of advanced information systems that this centralized order fulfillment requires in Chapter 10.

Only when a company is sufficiently prepared to implement flexible strategies can it take advantage of all that the global supply chain has to offer.

7.3   Issues in International Supply Chain Management

In this section, we will discuss other important issues of international supply chains that were not appropriate for the previous sections.

7.3.1   *International versus Regional Products*

The preceding discussion suggests that the ideal company builds "universal products" that can be sold in many markets. In many cases, however, this is not that simple. Ohmae [87] pointed out that there are several categories of products, each of which has different "international requirements."

> **Region-specific products.** Some products have to be designed and manufactured specifically for certain regions. For example, automobile designs are often region specific. The 1998 Honda Accord has two basic body styles—a smaller body style tailored to European and Japanese tastes, and a larger body style catering to American tastes. Of course, even if regional designs are different, effective supply chain management can take advantage of common components or subassemblies within the different designs. We discuss this issue in detail in Chapter 8.

Example 7.3.1 | Nissan designates "lead-country" status to each of its car models. For example, the Maxima and Pathfinder are designed for American tastes, often by American design studios. Similar designs are developed primarily for Japanese and European markets. Once regional product managers ensure that vehicles meet lead-country requirements, other regional product managers suggest slight changes that might promote local sales. But the focus is on developing cars for regions. Otherwise, Nissan fears "the trap of pleasing no one well by pleasing everyone half way." There is no effective way to average size, color, and other aesthetic and substantive differences in cars across regions without ending up with a model that no customers in that region particularly like. Of course, if models can be modified slightly to increase sales in other regions, it helps, but that isn't the primary focus [87].

True global products. These products are truly global, in the sense that no modification is necessary for global sales. For example, Coca-Cola is essentially the same throughout the world, as are Levi's jeans and McDonald's burgers. Similarly, luxury brands like Coach and Gucci are essentially the same worldwide. It should be noted, however, that some of these brands and products, such as Coke and McDonald's, depend on very specific regional manufacturing and bottling facilities and distribution networks, while others are essentially distributed and sold in the same way throughout the world [65].

The difference between region-specific products and global products does not imply that one is inherently better than the other. However, it is important to consider carefully which of the two product types is more appropriate for a particular situation because employing strategies for regional products that are designed for global products, or vise versa, can lead to disastrous results.

7.3.2 Local Autonomy versus Central Control

Centralized control can be important in taking advantage of some of the strategies we have discussed, but in many cases it makes sense to allow local autonomy in the supply chain. Sometimes, after independent regional operations have proven to be successful, headquarters can't resist the temptation to tamper with the system, and performance suffers.

In addition, it is important to temper expectations for regional business depending on the characteristics of the region involved. For example, companies typically experience, in the short term, relatively low returns in Japan, medium returns in Germany, and higher returns in the United States. Indeed, those companies that are successful in Japan had often settled initially for low returns [87].

On the other hand, managers may be tempted to follow local conventional wisdom, and thus miss some of the opportunities derived from the knowledge acquired in the operation of a global supply chain.

| Example 7.3.2 | When it first introduced the decongestant Contac 600 to Japanese markets, SmithKline Corporation was advised to use the traditional approach, involving more than 1,000 distributors with which the firm would have little contact. Rather than accept this advice, SmithKline used 35 wholesalers, with whom it remained in close contact. SmithKline had used this approach successfully elsewhere. Despite the naysayers, the introduction was highly successful [65]. |

7.3.3   Miscellaneous Dangers

To be sure, there are many potential dangers that firms must face as they expand their supply chains globally. Exchange rate fluctuations, discussed earlier as an opportunity, can just as easily be a risk if not properly managed. It may be harder to administer offshore facilities, especially in less developed countries. Similarly, the promise of cheap labor may mask the threat of reduced productivity [74]. Expensive training may be required, but even then productivity may not reach domestic levels.

Often local collaboration occurs in the global supply chain. In this case, collaborators can ultimately become competitors.

| Example 7.3.3 | **COLLABORATORS WHO BECAME COMPETITORS**

 • Hitachi, which used to manufacture under license from Motorola, now makes its own microprocessors.
 • Toshiba, which manufactured copiers for 3M, is now a major supplier of copiers under the Toshiba brand name.
 • Sunrise Plywood and Furniture, of Taiwan, was for many years a partner of Mission Furniture in California. Now it is one of Mission's major competitors [74]. |

Similar dangers exist with foreign governments. To deal with China and gain access to that country's huge markets, many companies are handing over critical manufacturing and engineering expertise to the Chinese government or to Chinese partners. It is only a matter of time until these Chinese companies, or other companies selected by the government, begin to compete under favorable terms with their original partners. The only question is whether the overseas firms that gave away their technology will still be able to compete successfully in the Chinese market, or if they will lose this opportunity even as Chinese companies begin to compete on the world stage.

Indeed, this serves to highlight only one of the dangers that foreign governments pose to the international supply chain. Although world markets are becoming more open all the time, the world is far from becoming a giant free trade zone. At any time the threat of *protectionism* might appear, and if the global supply chain is not set up with some kind of counter to this threat, companies will not be able to do much about it. Sometimes the threat comes not from the foreign government, but from the domestic government, dealing with the concerns of smaller local firms.

Example 7.3.4	In 1986 Taiwan had a $15.7 billion trade surplus with the United States, heightening domestic pressure on the U.S. government to impose trade restrictions on Taiwanese products. This occurred despite the fact that the vast majority of Taiwanese imports were parts to supply American companies, such as GE, IBM, Hewlett-Packard, and Mattel, which had moved manufacturing offshore to take advantage of lower costs. In response, Taiwan was forced to increase the value of its currency relative to the U.S. dollar, thus effectively removing much of the cost advantage of manufacturing to Taiwan [74].

7.4 Regional Differences in Logistics

In the previous sections, we discussed the general advantages, disadvantages, and strategies for utilizing global supply chains effectively. Of course, it is important to be aware of the cultural, infrastructure, and economic differences between regions when decisions are made about particular foreign links in the global supply chain. Wood et al. [112] identified several categories of differences that managers must consider when designing international supply chains. In particular, major differences can be highlighted between the so called *triad*, or First World, nations: Japan, the United States, and the nations of western Europe; *emerging nations* such as Thailand, Taiwan, China, Brazil, Argentina, and the countries of eastern Europe; and the *Third World* nations. These differences are summarized in Table 7.1 and analyzed below.

7.4.1 Cultural Differences

Cultural differences can critically affect the way international subsidiaries interpret the goals and pronouncements of management. Wood et al. [112] highlighted beliefs and values, customs, and language, all of which play a big role in global business and can strongly affect negotiation and communication.

TABLE 7.1   **Major Differences between Different Regions**

	First World	*Emerging*	*Third World*
Infrastructure	Highly developed	Under development	Insufficient to support advanced logistics
Supplier operating standards	High	Variable	Typically not considered
Information system availability	Generally available	Support system not available	Not available
Human resources	Available	Available with some searching	Often difficult to find

Language consists not only of words but also of expressions, gestures, and context. Many times, the words appear to be translated correctly, but the meaning is not. We've all heard stories of American businesspeople using the wrong gestures in Asia, leading to disastrous consequences. It is important to utilize appropriate resources to make sure that communication is effective.

Beliefs, or specific values about something, can differ widely from culture to culture. The belief that effective communication is important, for instance, can vary from culture to culture. Similarly, values, or more general conceptions, can vary. For example, American manufacturers value "efficiency" in ways that some other cultures do not [112]. Also, some cultures may value time more than others, so that late delivery may be viewed in some places as a serious problem, while in others it is not particularly important.

Customs, of course, vary greatly from country to country. In many cases, it is important for the businessperson to adhere to local customs to avoid offending anyone. For example, the practice of gift giving varies greatly from country to country.

7.4.2   *Infrastructure*

In First World countries, the manufacturing and logistics infrastructure is highly developed. Highway systems, ports, communication and information systems, and advanced manufacturing techniques allow the development of advanced supply chains. Regional differences do exist, primarily for geographical, political, or historical reasons. For example, road widths, bridge heights, and communications protocols may differ from region to region but, in general, techniques have been developed to overcome these differences.

Regardless of the infrastructure, geography also affects supply chain decisions, even within First World countries. In the United States, for example, where large distances often exist between major cities, more inventory might be held than in countries such as Belgium, where the distance between cities is small.

Similarly, relative economic conditions have affected the mix of logistics and supply chain components in many First World countries. For example, countries with relatively cheap land and cheap labor, such as France, have built many large, "low-tech" warehouses, while the Scandinavian countries have developed warehouse automation because labor in those countries is so expensive [33].

In the emerging nations, the supply chain infrastructure is usually not fully in place. Most domestic companies in emerging nations see logistics as a necessary expense and not a strategic advantage, so they limit investments in logistics infrastructure. In many cases, gross national income in an emerging nation may not yet be sufficient to fully implement an advanced logistics infrastructure. In addition, the focus of infrastructure development may have been on exports instead of building a system appropriate for imports and exports. This is true in China [112]. Nonetheless, these nations are "emerging" because they have begun to address these issues. For example, many countries have national transportation policies in place, and are beginning or continuing to implement them.

In the Third World, the infrastructure is generally insufficient to support advanced logistics operations. Roads are often in poor shape. Warehousing facilities are frequently unavailable. Distribution systems may be nonexistent. In general, specific supply chain decisions have to be considered carefully, because many of the things taken for granted in the triad or emerging nations may not exist here.

7.4.3   *Performance Expectation and Evaluation*

Although regional differences remain among First World nations, operating standards are generally uniform and high. For example, overnight carriers are expected to make deliveries overnight. Contracts are legally binding documents. Environmental regulations and constraints are typically present, and companies are expected to obey them.

However, the approaches to developing and enforcing relationships do differ from region to region. For example, European and American companies use formal partnership contracts more frequently than Japanese firms, which tend to favor informal partnership agreements built over time [16].

In emerging nations, operating standards typically vary greatly. Some firms may have—and meet—high expectations, and place great value on contracts and agreements. Others, however, might not be so scrupulous. Research and negotiation are essential to successful deal making in the emerging nations. In addition, the government typically plays a large role in business, so foreign partners and corporations often must be ready to respond to the government's changing whims.

In the Third World, traditional performance measures have no meaning. Shortages are common and customer service measures that are used in the West (e.g., stock availability, speed of service, and service consistency) are irrelevant; given this situation, a firm has little control of the timing and availability of inventory [112].

7.4.4   Information System Availability

Within the triad nations, computer technology has increased at more or less the same rate across different nations. In most cases, POS data, automation tools, personal computers, and other information system tools are just as available in Spain as in California.

Of course, there may be incompatibilities in various systems. For example, European EDI standards may vary from country to country and industry to industry. In addition, legal standards relating to data protection and document authentication vary from country to country. Nevertheless, efforts are underway to overcome these hurdles, and technology exists to overcome the technical incompatibilities [81].

Support systems in the emerging nations may not be in place to implement efficient information systems. Communications networks may be incomplete and not reliable enough to support the traffic. Technical support expertise may not be available to utilize and maintain the equipment. However, governments in these nations typically have plans or programs in place to address these issues.

Advanced information technology is simply not available in Third World countries. Systems such as EDI and bar coding cannot be supported in this type of environment. Even the value of a personal computer is limited because of inefficient communications systems. In addition, data on the economy and population typically are unavailable.

7.4.5   Human Resources

Within most First World countries, technically and managerially competent workers are available. As Wood et al. [112] pointed out, "Cultural differences aside, a logistics manager from Japan would be functionally at home in a counterpart's position in America." Unskilled labor, however, is relatively expensive in these regions.

While it may be true that skilled managerial and technical personnel are frequently not available in emerging nations, sometimes this is not the case. It might take some searching, but employees with the appropriate skills can often be found. In particular, the eastern European countries have generally well-educated populations [43]. In addition, the wages of skilled workers in emerging nations are generally competitive on the world market. On the other hand, many Chinese managers have been selected for political reasons, rather than technical or managerial expertise, so experience in this case may not be an appropriate indicator of ability [43].

Although it may be possible to find employees that are appropriate to the available technology level, it is often difficult to find trained logistics professionals and managers familiar with modern management techniques in Third World countries. Thus, training becomes especially important in this type of environment.

SUMMARY

In this chapter, we examined issues specific to *global* supply chain management. First, we discussed various types of international supply chains, covering the spectrum from primarily domestic supply chains with some international product distribution all the way to fully integrated global supply chains. We then examined the various forces compelling companies to develop international supply chains. Both advantages and risks are inherent in global supply chains. Besides the obvious cost advantages, we discussed the advantages of having a truly flexible global supply chain to address the inherent risks in operating a global company. However, even with a flexible supply chain, the strategies and approaches used to address these risks will work only if the appropriate infrastructure is in place.

We next surveyed some of the many issues in global supply chain management, including the concepts of international and regional products, and the issue of centralized versus decentralized control in an international context. We concluded with a discussion of regional logistics differences which influence the design of effective supply chains in different parts of the world.

CHAPTER 8

Coordinated Product and Supply Chain Design

CASE: HEWLETT-PACKARD: DESKJET PRINTER SUPPLY CHAIN

Brent Cartier, manager for special projects in the Materials Department of Hewlett-Packard (HP) Company's Vancouver Division, clicked off another mile. It had been a long week and it looked like it would be a long weekend as well, based on the preparation that needed to be done for Monday's meeting with group management on worldwide inventory levels for the DeskJet Printer product line. Even when he was busy, he always took time for the 25-mile bike ride to work—it helped reduce stress in times like this.

The DeskJet printer was introduced in 1988 and had become one of HP's most successful products. Sales had grown steadily, reaching a level of over 600,000 units in 1990 ($400 million). Unfortunately, inventory growth had tracked sales growth closely. Already, HP's distribution centers had been filled with pallets of the DeskJet printer. Worse yet, the organization in Europe was claiming that inventory levels there needed to be raised even further to maintain satisfactory product availability.

Each quarter, representatives from the production, materials, and distribution organizations in Europe, Asia-Pacific, and North America met to discuss "the I-word"—as they referred to it—but their conflicting goals prevented them from reaching consensus on the issues. Each organization had a different approach to the problem. Production had not wanted to get involved, claiming it was "just a materials issue," but had taken the time to rant about the continued proliferation of models and options. The distribution organization's pet peeve was forecast accuracy. They didn't feel that the distribution organization should have to track and store warehouses of inventory, just because the Vancouver Division couldn't build the right products in the right quantities. The European distribution organization had even gone so far as to suggest that they charge the

Source: Copyright 1993 by the Board of Trustees of the Leland Stanford Junior University. All rights reserved. This case was written by Laura Kopczak and Professor Hau Lee of the Department of Industrial Engineering and Engineering Management at Stanford University.

167

cost of the extra warehouse space that they were renting back to Vancouver Division directly, instead of allocating it among all the products that they shipped. Finally, Brent's boss, David Arkadia, the materials manager at the Vancouver Division, had summarized the perspective of group management at the last meeting when he said, "The word is coming down from corporate: We can't run our business with this level of unproductive assets. We're just going to have to meet customer needs with less inventory."

As Brent saw it, there were two main issues. The first issue was to find the best way to satisfy customer needs in terms of product availability while minimizing inventory. The second and stickier issue involved how to get agreement among the various parties that they had the right level of inventory. They needed to develop a consistent method for setting and implementing inventory goals and get everyone to sign off on it and use it. It was not going to be easy. The situation was especially urgent in Europe. His mind was still filled with the faxed picture that he had received the previous day, showing the dip in product availability levels for some versions of the product at the European Distribution Center (DC), yet he was sure that loads and loads of DeskJets had been shipped to Europe in the past months. His voice mail had been filled with angry messages from the sales offices, and yet the European DC was telling Vancouver that it had run out of space to store Vancouver's products.

Brent parked his bike and headed for the company showers. His morning shower was another ritual—this was the time he had to review his plans for the day and play out different scenarios. Perhaps a solution would come to him...

Background

Hewlett-Packard Company was founded in 1939 by William Hewlett and David Packard, with headquarters in Palo Alto, California. It grew steadily over the next 50 years, diversifying from its base in electronic test and measurement equipment into computers and peripherals products, which now dominated its sales. In 1990 HP had over 50 operations worldwide, with revenues of $13.2 billion and net income of $739 million.

HP was organized partially by product group and partially by function. The Peripherals Group was the second largest of HP's six product groups, with 1990 revenues of $4.1 billion. Each of the group's divisions acted as a strategic business unit for a specific set of products. Products included printers, plotters, magnetic disk and tape drives, terminals, and network products.

The Peripherals Group had set technological standards with many of its products, with innovations such as the disposable print head used in its ink-jet printers and moving-paper plotters. While these innovations contributed to its success, the Peripherals Group was also recognized for its ability to identify and profitably exploit market opportunities, as in the case of its most successful product, the LaserJet printer.

The Retail Printer Market

Worldwide sales of small workgroup/personal printers in 1990 were about 17 million units, amounting to $10 billion. The market tracked personal computer sales closely; the market was mature in the United States and western Europe but was still developing in eastern Europe and in the Asia-Pacific region. Small workgroup/personal printers were sold almost exclusively through resellers. The reseller channels were changing rapidly, particularly in the United States. Traditionally, printers had been sold through computer dealers, but as personal computers became commodity products, more and more sales were flowing through superstores and consumer mass merchandisers such as Kmart and Price Club.

The retail printer market was composed of three technology segments: impact/dot matrix (40 percent), ink-jet (20 percent) and laser (40 percent). Dot matrix was the oldest technology, and was viewed as noisy and of lower print quality compared to the other two types. The dot-matrix printer market share was expected to fall to 10 percent during the next few years as the technology was replaced by either ink-jet or laser printers in all applications except multipart forms and wide-carriage printing. Prior to 1989 most customers were not aware of ink-jet technology. However, customers were discovering that ink-jet print quality was almost as good as laser print quality—and at a much more affordable price. Sales had increased dramatically. In the monochrome market, it remained to be seen which technology would eventually dominate at the low end. Much would depend on the pace at which technology developed in both areas, and on the relative costs.

HP and Canon pioneered ink-jet technology separately at their respective corporate laboratories during the early 1980s. The key technological breakthroughs had been ink formulation and the disposable printhead. HP had introduced its first disposable head model, the ThinkJet printer, in the late 1980s, while Canon had just introduced one in 1990.

HP led the ink-jet market in the United States, while Canon led the market in Japan. European competitors included Epson, Mannesmann-Tally, Siemens, and Olivetti, though only Olivetti had introduced a printer with a disposable printhead by 1991. Some dot-matrix printer companies were also starting to offer ink-jet printer products.

Ink-jet printers were rapidly becoming commodity products. The end customer, choosing between two ink-jet printers of equal speed and print quality, increasingly used general business criteria such as cost, reliability, quality, and availability to decide. Product loyalty continued to decrease.

The Vancouver Division and its Quest for Zero Inventory

In 1990 Vancouver Division's mission statement read: "Our Mission Is to Become the Recognized World Leader in Low Cost Premium Quality Printers for Printed Communications by Business Personal Computer Users in Offices and Homes."

The Vancouver Division, located in Vancouver, Washington, was established in 1979. HP saw an opportunity to provide personal printers for the relatively new, fast-growing personal computer market. HP consolidated personal printer activities from four divisions (Fort Collins, Colorado; Boise, Idaho; Sunnyvale, California; and Corvallis, Oregon) to the Vancouver site. The new division became part of HP's Peripherals Group and was chartered with the design and manufacturing of ink-jet printers.

As Bob Foucoult, the production manager and one of Vancouver's first employees, recalled, "Management was pulled from all over HP and plopped down in

Vancouver. There was no cohesive staff and no cohesive set of business practices—perhaps that's why we were so open to new ideas."

The manufacturing organization realized early on that a fast, high-volume manufacturing process would be required for success in the printer market. With the current (1979) 8 to 12 week manufacturing cycle time and 3.5 months of inventory, the Vancouver Division would be doomed to fail. They looked within HP for knowledge of high-volume processes, but found none. HP, being an instrument company, only had experience building low-volume, highly customized products using batch processes.

One day in mid-1981 two Vancouver managers happened to take seats on a plane next to two professors—Richard Schoenberger (Nebraska University) and Robert Hall (Indiana University). Schoenberger had just written a rough draft for a paper called "Driving the Productivity Machine" about a manufacturing process being used in Japan: *kanban*. Vancouver's management recognized the promise of this "new" manufacturing concept and Robert Hall recognized an opportunity to have his ideas tested in the United States. They decided to work together.

Within a year Vancouver had converted the factory to stockless production just-in-time (JIT) and had reduced inventory from 3.5 months to 0.9 months, with a drastic reduction in cycle time. Vancouver became a showcase factory for the *kanban* process; between 1982 and 1985 more than 2,000 executives from within and outside HP toured the process. Vancouver impressed visitors by having them sign a raw printed circuit board as they arrived, then presenting them with a finished printer, made with that PC board using the standard process, an hour and a half later.

There was one key element missing, however. As Bob Foucoult puts it, "We were all dressed up but had no one to take us to the dance." Vancouver had not yet introduced a successful, high-volume product that would take full advantage of the advanced production line. Vancouver had introduced products based on HP's latest ink-jet technology but, as with any new technology, they had to gain experience to work the bugs out. The early models had poor resolution and required special paper for printing, resulting in limited success in the marketplace. In 1988 things started to change. Vancouver introduced the DeskJet printer, a new model with near letter-quality resolution which used standard paper. The introduction was a wild success. Since the manufacturing process had been in place and had been thoroughly exercised, all that was needed was to "flip the switch." HP's knowledge and implementation of the ink-jet technology, combined with its streamlined manufacturing process, gave it the edge needed to become the market leader in the ink-jet printer market.

The DeskJet Supply Chain

The network of suppliers, manufacturing sites, distribution centers (DCs), dealers, and customers for the DeskJet product comprised the DeskJet supply chain (Figure 8.1). Manufacturing was done by HP in Vancouver. There were two key stages in the manufacturing process: (1) printed circuit board assembly and test (PCAT) and (2) final assembly and test (FAT). PCAT involved the assembly and testing of electronic components like ASICs (application-specific integrated circuits), ROM (read-only memory), and raw printed circuit boards to make logic boards and printhead driver boards for the printers. FAT involved the assembly of other subassemblies like motors, cables, keypads, plastic chassis and "skins," gears, and

FIGURE 8.1

The Vancouver supply chain

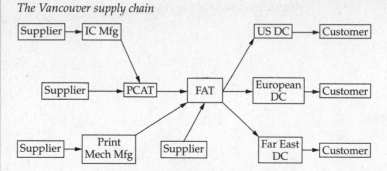

Key: IC Mfg = Integrated circuit manufacturing
PCAT = Printed circuit assembly and test
FAT = Final assembly and test
Print Mech Mfg = Print mechanism manufacturing

the printed circuit assemblies from PCAT to produce a working printer, as well as the final testing of the printer. The components needed for PCAT and FAT were sourced from other HP divisions as well as from external suppliers worldwide.

Selling the DeskJet in Europe required customizing the printer to meet the language and power supply requirements of the local countries, a process known as "localization." Specifically, the localization of the DeskJet for different countries involved assembling the appropriate power supply module, which reflected the correct voltage requirements (110 or 220) and power cord terminator (plug), and packaging it with the working printer and a manual written in the appropriate language. The design of the product was such that the assembly of the power supply module had to be done as part of the final assembly and test process, and therefore the localization of the printer was performed at the factory. Hence, the finished products of the factory consisted of printers destined for all of the different countries. These products were then sorted into three groups destined for the three distribution centers: North America, Europe, and Asia-Pacific. Figure 8.2 details the bill of materials and the various options available.

Outgoing products were shipped to the three distribution centers by ocean. In Vancouver, inventories of the components and raw materials were maintained to meet production requirements, but otherwise, no significant buffer inventories between the PCAT and FAT stages were kept. Management had continued to prefer to maintain no finished goods inventory at the factory, a tradition that was started in 1985 as described in the previous section.

The total factory cycle time through the PCAT and FAT stages was about a week. The transportation time from Vancouver to the U.S. DC, located in San Jose, California, was about a day, whereas it took four to five weeks to ship the printers to Europe and Asia. The long shipment time to the DCs in Europe and Asia was due to ocean transit and the time to clear customs and duties at ports of entry.

The printer industry was highly competitive. Customers of HP's computer products (resellers) wanted to carry as little inventory as possible, yet maintaining

FIGURE 8.2

Bill of material in the Vancouver supply chain

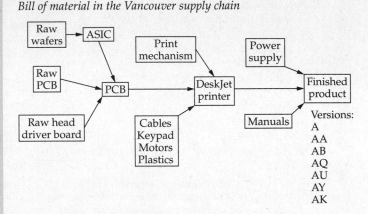

a high level of availability to end users (consumers) was critical to them. Consequently there had been increasing pressure for HP as a manufacturer to provide high levels of availability at the DCs for the resellers. In response, management had decided to operate the DCs in a make-to-stock mode in order to provide very high levels of availability to the dealers. Target inventory levels, equal to the forecasted sales plus some safety stock level, were set at the three DCs.

As mentioned earlier, Vancouver prided itself as an almost "stockless" factory. Hence, in contrast to distribution, manufacturing of the Deskjet printer operated in a pull mode. Production plans were set weekly to replenish the DCs "just in time" to maintain the target inventory levels. To ensure material availability, safety stocks were also set up for incoming materials at the factory.

There were three major sources of uncertainty that could affect the supply chain: (1) delivery of incoming materials (late shipments, wrong parts, etc.), (2) internal process (process yields and machine downtimes), and (3) demand. The first two sources of uncertainties resulted in delays in the manufacturing lead time to replenish the stocks at the DCs. Demand uncertainties could lead to inventory buildup or back orders at the DCs. Since finished printers were shipped from Vancouver by ocean, the consequence of the long lead time for the European and Asian DCs was that the DC's ability to respond to fluctuations in the demand for the different versions of the product was limited. In order to assure high availability to customers, the European and Asian DCs had to maintain high levels of safety stocks. For the North American DC the situation was simpler; since an overwhelming majority of demand was for the U.S. version of the DeskJet printer, there was little localization-mix fluctuation.

The Distribution Process

At HP, while a typical DC shipped hundreds of different peripheral and computer products, a small number of products accounted for a large share of the unit volume. The DeskJet printer was one of these high-volume products.

The Operations Manager of each regional DC reported to a Worldwide Distribution Manager, who reported directly to HP's Vice President of Marketing, and by dotted line to the Peripherals Group Manager (peripherals made up the bulk of shipments through distribution centers). Each Operations Manager had a staff of six functional managers, representing Finance, NGS, Quality, Marketing, Physical Distribution, and Distribution Services. The first three functions were similar to their respective functions in a manufacturing organization. Marketing was responsible for interactions with customers. Physical Distribution was responsible for the "physical process," that is, from receiving through shipping. Distribution Services was responsible for planning and procurement.

The major performance measures for a typical DC included Line Item Fill Rate (LIFR) and Order Fill Rate (OFR). LIFR was calculated as the total number of customer order line items filled on time divided by the total number of customer line items attempted. (Each time HP tried to pull material for a line item, it was counted as an attempt.) OFR was a similar measure, but was based on orders completed, where an order contains multiple line items. Secondary performance measures included inventory levels and distribution cost per gross shipment dollar. The two major costs were outbound freight and salaries. Freight was charged back to the product lines based on the actual number of pounds of product shipped. In addition, the DC estimated the "percentage of effort" required to support a particular product line and charged that percentage of nonfreight costs back to that product line. The system was somewhat informal, and major negotiations took place between the DCs and the major product lines during the budget-setting process to determine the percentage allocation that was appropriate for each product line.

The DCs had traditionally envisioned their process as a simple, straight-line, standardized process. There were four process steps:

1. Receive (complete) products from various suppliers and stock them.
2. Pick the various products needed to fill a customer order.
3. Shrink-wrap the complete order and label it.
4. Ship the order by the appropriate carrier.

The DeskJet printer fit well into the standard process. In contrast, other products, such as personal computers and monitors, required special processing, called "integration," which included addition of the appropriate keyboard and manual for the destination country. Although this extra processing didn't require much additional labor, it was difficult to accommodate in the standard process and disrupted the material flow. Furthermore, the DCs' materials management systems supported distribution (pass-through processing of "end-items" in the form of individual models and options) and did not support manufacturing (assembly of components into a final product). There were no MRP (material resource planning) nor BOM (bill of materials) explosion systems, and the DCs did not have adequate people trained in component procurement.

There was considerable frustration within the distribution organization regarding the support of assembly processes. In general, top management stressed the DC's role as a warehouse, and the need to continue to "do what they were best at—distribution." Tom Beal, the U.S. DC materials manager, expressed the general concern when he said, "We have to decide what our core competency is and what value we add. We need to decide whether we are in the business of warehousing or integration, then adopt strategies to support our business. If we want to take on manufacturing processes (here), we have to put processes in place to support them."

The Inventory and Service Crisis

To limit the amount of inventory throughout the DeskJet supply chain and at the same time provide the high level of service needed had been quite a challenge to Vancouver's management. The manufacturing group in Vancouver had worked hard on supplier management to reduce the uncertainties caused by delivery variabilities of incoming materials, on improving process yields, and on reducing downtimes at the plant. The progress made had been admirable. However, improvement of forecast accuracy remained a formidable task.

The magnitude of forecast errors were especially alarming in Europe. It was becoming quite common to have product shortages for model demands from some countries, while inventory of some other models kept piling up. In the past, the target inventory levels at the DCs were based on safety stocks that were a result of some judgmental rule of thumb. It seemed like the increasing difficulty of getting accurate forecasts meant that the safety stock rules would have to be revisited.

David Arkadia had solicited the help of a young inventory expert from corporate HP, Dr. Billy Corrington, to help him put in place a scientifically based safety stock system which would be responsive to forecast errors and replenishment lead times. Billy had formed a team consisting of Laura Rock, an industrial engineer, Jim Bailey, the planning supervisor, and José Fernandez, the purchasing supervisor from Vancouver, to overhaul the safety stock management system. They were to recommend a method for calculating appropriate safety stock levels for the various models and options at the three DCs. Gathering appropriate data turned out to be a task that the team spent a lot of time at. They now felt that they had a good sample of demand data (see Table 8.1) and were developing the safety stock methodology. Brent was hoping that this new methodology would solve the inventory and service problem. It would be nice if he could tell his management that all this inventory and service mess was due to their lack of a sound safety stock methodology, and Billy's expertise would then be their savior.

One issue that continually came up was the choice of inventory carrying cost to be used in safety stock analyses. Estimates within the company ranged from 12

TABLE 8.1   **Some Sample DeskJet Demand Data: Europe**

Option	Nov.	Dec.	Jan.	Feb.	Mar.	Apr.	May	June	July	Aug.	Sept.	Oct.
A	80	0	60	90	21	48	0	9	20	54	84	42
AA	400	255	408	645	210	87	432	816	430	630	456	273
AB	20,572	20,895	19,252	11,052	19,864	20,316	13,336	10,578	6,096	14,496	23,712	9,792
AQ	4,008	2,196	4,761	1,953	1,008	2,358	1,676	540	2,310	2,046	1,797	2,961
AU	4,564	3,207	7,485	4,908	5,295	90	0	5,004	4,385	5,103	4,302	6,153
AY	248	450	378	306	219	204	248	484	164	384	384	234
Total	29,872	27,003	32,344	18,954	26,617	23,103	15,692	17,431	13,405	22,692	30,735	19,455

percent (HP's cost of debt plus some warehousing expenses) to 60 percent (based on the return on investment [ROI] expected of new product development projects). Another issue was the choice of target line item fill rate to be used. The company target was 98 percent, a number which had been "developed" by marketing.

As faxes and phone calls about the worsening situation at the European DC kept pouring in, Brent also began receiving other suggestions from his colleagues that were more aggressive in nature. Talks about Vancouver's setting up a sister plant in Europe had surfaced. Would the volume in Europe be large enough to justify such a site? Where should it be located? Brent knew that the European sales and marketing folks would like such an idea. He also liked the idea of having a European plant to take care of the inventory and service problem in Europe. Maybe that would put a halt to his recent loss of sleep.

There was certainly a group that advocated more and more inventory. It was simple logic, according to them. "When it comes down to real dollars, inventory costs do not enter into the P&L statements, but lost sales hurt our revenues. Don't talk to us about inventory-service trade-offs. Period."

Kay Johnson, the Traffic Department supervisor, had long suggested the use of air shipment to transport the printers to Europe. "Shortening the lead time means faster reaction time to unexpected changes in product mix. That should mean lower inventory and higher product availability. I tell you, air freight is expensive, but it is worth it."

Brent recalled his conversation at lunch with a summer intern from Stanford University. The enthusiastic student was lecturing Brent that he should always try to tackle the "root of the problem." Going to the root of the problem, according to the intern, is what the professors taught at school, and was also what a number of quality gurus preached. "The root of the problem is that you have a horrible forecasting system. There is no easy way out. You've got to invest in getting the system fixed. Now, I know this marketing professor at Stanford who could help you. Have you ever heard of the Box-Jenkins method?" Brent also remembered how he lost his appetite at that lunch, as he was listening to the student who was so eager to volunteer his advice.

What Next?

Brent reviewed his schedule for the day. At 11:00 he planned to meet with Billy, Laura, Jim, and José to review the recommended inventory levels they had calculated using the safety stock model. He was somewhat concerned about what level of change the model would recommend. If it suggested small changes, management might not feel the model was useful, but if it suggested large changes they might not accept it either.

After lunch he would meet briefly with the materials and manufacturing managers to review the results and sketch out their recommendations. At 2:00 he would talk with the U.S. DC materials manager by phone. That night he could reach Singapore and Saturday morning he could reach Germany. Hopefully he could get buyoff from everyone.

He wondered, too, if there wasn't some other approach that he should be considering. He knew that whatever numbers he came up with would be too high.

By the end of this chapter, you should be able to answer the following questions:

- How can design for logistics concepts be used to control logistics costs and make the supply chain more efficient?
- What is delayed differentiation and how can Hewlett-Packard use delayed differentiation to address the problems described in the case above? How can the advantages of delayed differentiation be quantified?
- When should suppliers be involved in the new product development process?
- What is mass customization? Does supply chain management play a role in the development of an effective mass customization strategy?

For many years manufacturing engineering was the last stop in the product engineering process. The researchers and design engineers worked on developing a product that worked, and perhaps one that used materials as inexpensively as possible. Then manufacturing engineers were charged with determining how to make this design efficiently. In the 1980s this paradigm began to change. Management began to realize that product and process design were key product cost drivers, and that taking the manufacturing process into account early in the design process was the only way to make the manufacturing process efficient. Thus, the concept of design for manufacturing (DFM) was born.

Recently, a similar transformation has begun in the area of supply chain management. We have discussed appropriate strategies for supply chain design and operation, assuming that *product design decisions were already made* by the time the supply chain is designed. Designing the supply chain, we have assumed, involves determining the best way to supply existing products using existing manufacturing processes. In the last few years, however, managers have started to realize that by taking logistics and supply chain management concerns into account in the product and process design phase, it becomes possible to operate a much more efficient supply chain. Obviously, this is analogous to the Design For Manufacturing (DFM) practice of taking manufacturing into account during the product design phase. In the following sections, we discuss various approaches that leverage product design in order to manage the supply chain more effectively.

In the next section, we discuss a series of concepts introduced by Professor Hau Lee [63] and known collectively as design for logistics (DFL). These concepts suggest product and process design approaches that help to control logistics costs and increase customer service levels.

Following that, we discuss the advantages of including suppliers in the product design process. This discussion is based on an extensive report issued by The Global Procurement and Supply Chain Benchmarking Initiative at Michigan State University, which is titled *Executive Summary: Supplier Integration into New Product Development: A Strategy for Competitive Advantage.*

Finally, we discuss the concept of mass customization, developed by Joseph Pine II with several coauthors. In particular, we focus on the ways in which advanced logistics and supply chain practices help to enable this exciting new business model.

8.1 Introduction

8.1.1 Design for Logistics: Overview

Transportation and inventory costs, as we have seen, are often critical supply chain cost drivers, particularly when inventory levels must be kept fairly high to ensure high service levels. These are exactly the issues that DFL addresses, using the following three key components [63]:

- Economic packaging and transportation
- Concurrent and parallel processing
- Postponement/delayed differentiation

Each of these components addresses the issue of inventory or transportation costs and service levels in complementary ways. They are discussed in detail in the following subsections.

8.1.2 Economic Packaging and Transportation

Of the various DFL concepts, perhaps the most obvious involves designing products so that they can be efficiently packed and stored. Products that can be packed more compactly are cheaper to transport, particularly if delivery trucks "cube out" before they "weigh out." In other words, if the space taken up by a product and not its weight constrains how much can fit in a delivery vehicle, products that can be stored more compactly can be transported less expensively.

Example 8.1.1 | Swedish furniture retailer Ikea, with $5.8 billion in sales, is the world's largest furniture retailer. Started in Sweden by Ingvar Kamprad, Ikea currently has 131 stores in 27 countries [54]. It has grown so dramatically by "reinventing the furniture business" [71]. Traditionally, furniture sales were split between department stores and small, locally owned shops. Typically, customers would place an order, and delivery could take place up to two months after the order was placed.

Ikea changed that formula by displaying all of its 10,000 products in large warehouse-like spaces in out-of-town stores, and keeping all of these items in the warehouse. This was accomplished by designing products so that they can be packed compactly and efficiently in kits, which customers take from the stores and assemble at home. These kits are easy and cheap to transport, so products can be manufactured efficiently in a small number of factories, and then shipped relatively cheaply to stores all over the world. Since Ikea has so many stores, each of which is very large, the company is able to take advantage of vast economies of scale. This has enabled the firm to sell good-quality furniture at prices lower than that of its competitors [71].

Ikea continues to work toward improved design and packaging to continue its dramatic growth—"recently the company figured out how to shave one-third off the width of bookcase packing boxes by making the back panels a separate assembly piece" [90].

There are other reasons to design products to pack compactly. For example, many major retailers favor products that take up less storage space and stack easily. Efficient storage reduces certain components of inventory cost because handling costs typically decrease, space per product (and thus rent per product) decreases, and revenue per square foot can increase. For example, many of the large plastic items available in discount stores, such as garbage pails, are designed to stack, so that they take up less shelf (or floor) space in the store. Thus, while it might not be enough to design packaging efficiently after the product design is completed, it may be valuable to redesign the product itself in order to take these issues into account.

Example 8.1.2 | Recently Rubbermaid won several design awards from *Business Week* magazine. When describing why the Clear Classics food storage containers won an award, the writers mention that "Wal-Mart loves products designed to fit 14-by-14-inch shelves," which is one of the reasons these products were so successful. In addition, when describing the children's Icy Rider sled designed by Rubbermaid (which also won the award) the writers state, "Of course, not all products sold in Wal-Mart can fit into 14-by-14 shelving. But if designers create them to stack and save space, they have a shot of selling to Wal-Mart... After researching Wal-Mart's needs, Rubbermaid made the Icy Rider thin and stackable" [86].

Similarly, it is often possible to ship goods in bulk and only complete final packaging at the warehouse or even at the retailer. This may save on transportation costs because bulk goods tend to be shipped more efficiently.

Example 8.1.3	The Hawaiian sugar industry switched over to bulk transportation after World War II, when costs began to increase. They estimate that the cost of transporting a bulk ton of sugar is about $0.77 today, whereas the cost of transporting the same quantity of sugar in bags would be about $20.00 [25].

In some cases, final packaging can even be delayed until the goods are actually sold. For example, many grocery stores now sell flour, cereal, and many other goods in bulk, allowing consumers to package as much as they want.

Recall that cross-docking (see Chapter 3) involves moving goods from one truck (e.g., from the supplier) to another set of trucks (e.g., perhaps going to individual retail stores). In some cases, boxes or pallets are taken off an incoming truck and moved directly to an outgoing one. However, it is often necessary to repackage some of the products. In many cases, bulk pallets of single items come in from suppliers, but mixed pallets with many different items have to go out to individual retailers. In this case, goods must be repacked at the cross-dock point, so more identification or labeling also might be needed if packages are broken up [104]. In general, packaging and products that are designed to facilitate this type of cross-docking operation by making repacking easier will clearly help to lower logistics costs.

8.1.3   Concurrent and Parallel Processing

In the previous section, we focused on simple ways that redesign of the product and packaging could help control logistics costs. In this subsection, we will focus on modifying the manufacturing *process*—which may also require modification of the product design.

We have seen that many difficulties in operating supply chains are due to long manufacturing lead times. Most manufacturing processes consist of manufacturing steps performed in sequence. The requirements of short start-up times and ever-shorter product life cycles often dictate that certain manufacturing steps be performed in different locations to take advantage of existing equipment or expertise. *Concurrent and parallel processing* involves modifying the manufacturing process so that steps that were previously performed in a sequence can be completed at the same time. This obviously helps reduce manufacturing lead time, lower inventory costs through improved forecasting, and reduce safety stock requirements, among other benefits.

A key to keeping the manufacturing process parallel is the concept of modularity or decoupling. If many of the components of the product can be decoupled, or physically separated, during manufacturing, it is possible that these components can be manufactured in parallel. If manufacturing each of the individual components takes the same amount of time in the newly decoupled design, but the manufacturing steps are performed in parallel, lead time will decrease. Even if some of these modular components take slightly more time to manufacture, the overall lead time may still decrease since various components are being manufactured in parallel. An added advantage of this manufacturing strategy of decoupling is that it may be possible to design different inventory strategies for the various decoupled components. If the supply of raw materials or manufacturing yield is uncertain for a particular component, a higher inventory level can be held of that single component, rather than for the entire end product.

Example 8.1.4

A European manufacturer produces network printers for the European market in alliance with a manufacturer in the Far East. The main printer PC board is designed and assembled in Europe. It is then shipped to Asia, where it is integrated with the main printer housing in a process that involves building the printer, including the motor, printhead, housing, and so forth, around the board. The finished product is then shipped to Europe. The manufacturer is concerned with the long production and transportation lead times, which make it essential to maintain a large safety stock in Europe. However, much of the long manufacturing lead time is due to the sequential manufacturing process.

Redesigning the printer manufacturing process and product so that the board can be integrated with the rest of the printer at the end of the manufacturing process will decrease lead times by allowing parallel manufacturing in Europe and the Far East. In addition, moving final assembly to Europe can serve to further increase responsiveness and decrease lead times. The two manufacturing processes are diagrammed in Figure 8.3 [63].

FIGURE 8.3

Concurrent processing

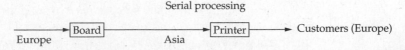

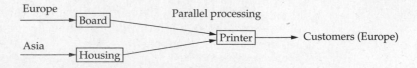

8.1.4 Postponement

As we have discussed above, it is possible in some cases to shorten lead times (e.g., by taking advantage of parallel processing) in order to reduce inventory levels and increase the accuracy of forecasts. Sometimes, however, it is impossible to reduce the lead time beyond a certain point. In these cases, it may be possible to get some of the benefits of reduced lead time using a postponement, or delayed differentiation, strategy.

Recall the second rule of inventory management described in Chapter 3: aggregate demand information is always more accurate than disaggregate data. Thus, we can better forecast demand for a continent than a country or for a product family (e.g., ski jackets) than a specific product or style. Unfortunately, in a traditional manufacturing environment, aggregate forecasts are not of much use—the manufacturing manager has to know exactly what needs to be made before starting the process.

However, by utilizing postponement techniques, it is possible to make effective use of the information in aggregate forecasts. Specifically, these techniques involve designing the product and manufacturing process so that decisions about which specific product is being manufactured—differentiation—can be delayed until after manufacturing is under way. The manufacturing process starts by making a generic or family product which is later differentiated into a specific end product. For this reason, this approach is also known as *delayed product differentiation* [63]. To use this approach, it is usually necessary to redesign products specifically. Delayed differentiation can be used to address many of the different forms of forecast aggregation we discussed in Chapter 3. Thus, design for delayed product differentiation can be effectively used to address the uncertainty in final demand even if forecasts cannot be improved.

Implementing Delayed Differentiation

Hau Lee identified several concepts important to implementing delayed differentiation [63]. One or more may be appropriate, depending on the specific issues being addressed. These include resequencing, commonality, modularity, and standardization. Each concept is described in more detail below.

1. Resequencing. *Resequencing* refers to modifying the order of product manufacturing steps so that those operations that result in the differentiation of specific items or products are postponed as much as possible. The most famous and dramatic example of a firm utilizing resequencing to improve its supply chain operation is Benetton Corporation.

Example 8.1.5 | Benetton is a major supplier of knitwear, at one point (in 1982) the largest consumer of wool in the world, supplying hundreds of shops. The nature of the fashion industry is that consumer preferences change rapidly. However, because of the long manufacturing lead time store owners frequently had to place orders for wool sweaters up to seven months in advance before the sweaters would appear in their stores. The wool sweater manufacturing process typically consists of acquiring yarn, dyeing it, finishing it, manufacturing the garment parts, and then joining those parts into a completed sweater. Unfortunately, this left little flexibility to respond to the changing tastes of consumers.

To address this issue, Benetton revised the manufacturing process, postponing the dyeing of the garments until *after* the sweater was completely assembled. Thus, color choices could be delayed until after more forecasting and sales information was received. Thus, because of the postponement of the dyeing process, yarn purchasing and manufacturing plans could be based on aggregate forecasts for product families, rather than forecasts for specific sweater/color combinations. This revised process made sweater manufacturing about 10 percent more expensive and required the purchasing of new equipment and the retraining of employees. However, Benetton was more than adequately compensated by improved forecasts, lower surplus inventories, and, in many cases, higher sales [9].

A U.S. disk drive manufacturer provides another notable example. Notice in this example that although lower levels of inventory need to be held to achieve specific service levels, the per unit inventory cost tends to be more expensive.

Example 8.1.6	A major U.S. manufacturer of mass storage devices makes different unique hard-drive products for each of a variety of customers. Orders are placed to be delivered by a certain time and, since lead times are very long, the manufacturer has to keep a variety of products in process in order to meet promised delivery dates. Since variability of demand is high and each product is unique, the manufacturer has to maintain high levels of in-process inventory to meet demand reliably.

The manufacturing process involves a brief generic segment, through which products intended for all customers must go, and then an extensive customization portion. Clearly, the ideal point to hold inventory is before customization begins. Unfortunately, however, the majority of manufacturing time, due particularly to time-consuming testing, occurs after differentiation has started. This testing has to take place after differentiation starts because a particular circuit board has to be added to the assembly for the testing to take place, and this circuit board is different for each customer.

In order to delay differentiation, it is possible to insert a generic circuit board into the assembly, complete much of the testing, remove the generic circuit board, and add the customer-specific boards later. In this way, disk drive differentiation can be delayed until more order information is available. Clearly, this will decrease the level of required in-process inventory needed to meet demand reliably. However, this will add some additional manufacturing steps. In particular, the generic board has to be added and removed. Thus, it is necessary to compare the manufacturing inefficiencies caused by adding and removing this circuit board with the gains in inventory savings. The manufacturing processes are illustrated in Figure 8.4 [63].

FIGURE 8.4

Delaying differentiation

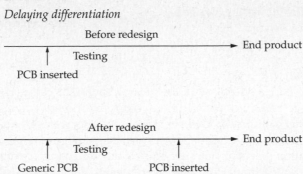

2. **Commonality.** Example 8.1.6 also indicates why *commonality* is an important concept in the implementation of delayed differentiation. If the disk drive products did not have common components (with differentiation achieved by insertion of the PC board), the approach described above would be impossible. Sometimes, it is necessary to redesign product lines or families to achieve commonality, which can then be used to implement postponement strategies.

| Example 8.1.7 | A major printer manufacturer was preparing to introduce a new color printer into the market. Demand for the new printer and an existing printer was expected to be highly variable and negatively correlated. The manufacturing processes for the two products were similar, except that different circuit boards and printhead assemblies were used. Differences in head assemblies and circuit boards led to very different manufacturing processes. To implement delayed differentiation, it will be necessary to ensure that the manufacturing processes are similar until the final step. To do this, the printers have been redesigned so that both products share a common circuit board and printhead. This ensures that differentiation can be delayed as late as possible. Thus, commonality can enable delayed differentiation in this case [63]. |

In some cases, the concepts of resequencing and commonality allow some of the final manufacturing steps to be completed at distribution centers (DCs) or warehouses instead of at the factory. One of the advantages of this approach is that if DCs are much closer to the demand than the factories, products can be differentiated closer to the demand, thus increasing the firm's ability to respond to rapidly changing markets. This is one of the approaches we will discuss in more detail in the next section, when we analyze the case from the beginning of this chapter.

3. Modularity. Sometimes commonality can be so advanced that the differentiating steps don't have to be performed in a manufacturing facility or distribution center at all, but can take place in the retailer after the sale is made. Often this is accomplished by focusing on modularity during the design phase, placing functionality in *modules* which can be easily added to a product. For example, some printers are sold in generic Macintosh/PC versions. Along with the printer, each retail store stocks separately packaged modules which differentiate the product for the Mac or PC. Obviously, this can greatly lower required inventory since only modules have to be stocked in Mac and PC versions, instead of entire printers. Similarly, many color ink-jet printers are black-and-white printers with added "color kits."

4. Standardization. Finally, it is sometimes possible to replace a family of products by a *standard product*. One way to accomplish *standardization* is to build in several of the possible options that particular customers might need. For example, as we have seen previously, many products are similar, except that power supplies have to be different for different markets. Instead of manufacturing two versions of a product, however, manufactures can utilize a standardized product, with a switchable power supply. Hewlett-Packard successfully implemented such a standardization strategy for its LaserJet printers. Initially, the printer had an internal power supply of either 110 or 220 volts, and a specific choice had to be made *before* initiating manufacturing. By switching to a universal power supply, HP was able to decrease the total cost of delivering the final product to the customer by 5 percent annually [32].

Many of these DFL approaches have additional benefits. In the example above, the customer can use the product in different countries. In one of the earlier examples, the customer can buy a black-and-white printer, and later convert it to a color printer by him or herself.

8.1.5   Important Considerations

In the previous sections, we discussed many of the advantages of implementing a design for logistics strategy and the many considerations involved. Frequently, it may not be possible or cost effective to implement these strategies in the context of a particular product or supply chain. In addition, even if implementing such a strategy would theoretically be cost effective, there are many issues and concerns that have to be considered during the design and implementation of this approach.

For example, there are many processes for which resequencing or modularization is not possible. Some products simply don't lend themselves to this kind of manufacturing. Even if it is technically possible, in many cases the expenses resulting from product and packaging redesign may not compensate for the savings under the new system. In addition, capital expenditures are likely to be required to retool assembly lines. Sometimes, as we discussed above, it may even be necessary to add manufacturing capability at distribution centers. Typically, the value of these types of changes is higher at the start of the product life cycle, when expenditures can be amortized over the entire life of the product. It is possible that DFL initiatives that make a great deal of sense at the start of the product life cycle don't pay for themselves when implemented later [63].

It also may be more expensive to manufacture a product using a newly designed process or a modular design. In many of the examples mentioned above, the products and manufacturing processes became more expensive. It is therefore necessary to estimate the savings produced by a more effectively designed product or process, and compare these savings to the increased cost of manufacturing. Many of the benefits of implementing such a system are very difficult to quantify; increased flexibility, more efficient customer service, and decreased market response times may be hard to place a value on, which only serves to make the analysis more difficult. To add to the difficulty, engineers are often forced to take a broader perspective than they have been trained to take when they are making these kinds of decisions.

To add to these complications, resequencing will cause the level of inventory in many cases to go down, but the value of inventory being held will be higher per item. For example, in the sweater example, it may be possible to hold less wool in inventory because it doesn't have to be dyed before it is assembled. However, much of this wool will be held in the form of sweaters, which have a higher value than dyed wool.

On the other hand, if manufacturing or customized steps are postponed, the generic products may have a lower value than customized products, so value is added later in the supply chain than it would be otherwise.

Finally, in some cases tariffs and duties are lower for semifinished or nonconfigured goods than for final products [63]. Thus, implementing a strategy of completing the manufacturing process in a local distribution center may help to lower costs associated with tariffs and duties.

All of these issues have to be taken into consideration when making design for logistics implementation decisions. Nevertheless, it is clear that in many cases DFL can help to improve customer service and greatly reduce the costs of operating the supply chain.

8.1.6 The Push-Pull Boundary

Recall our discussion of push versus pull systems in Chapter 5. In push-based systems, production decisions are based on long-term forecasts, while in pull-based supply chains, production is demand driven. We listed many advantages of pull-based systems, and concluded that compared to push-based systems, pull-based systems typically lead to a reduction in supply chain lead times, inventory levels and system costs, while simultaneously making it easier to manage system resources.

Unfortunately, it is not always practical to implement a pull-based system throughout the entire supply chain. Lead times may be too long, or it may be necessary to take advantage of economies of scale in production or transportation. The delayed differentiation strategies we have been discussing in this section can be viewed as a method to combine push and pull systems within a single supply chain. Indeed, that portion of the supply chain prior to product differentiation is typically a push-based supply chain. That is, the undifferentiated product is built and transported based on long-term forecasts. In contrast, differentiation occurs as a response to market demand. Thus, the portion of the supply chain starting from the time of differentiation is a pull-based supply chain.

For instance, in the Benetton example, Example 8.1.5, uncolored sweaters are made to forecast, but dyeing takes place as a reaction to customer demand. The point of differentiation is thus known as the **push-pull boundary**, since this is the point where the system changes from a push-based system to a pull-based system.

One way to view the push-pull boundary concept is through the second rule of inventory management discussed in Chapter 3. Since aggregate demand information is more accurate than disaggregate data, the push portion of the supply chain includes only activities and decisions made prior to product differentiation. These activities and decisions are based on aggregate demand data.

Clearly, then, an additional advantage of postponement is that it allows firms to realize many of the advantages of pull-based systems, while at the same time allowing for the economies of scale inherent in push-based systems. Often, when implementing a postponement strategy, if there is more than one possible differentiation point, it may be useful to think in terms of locating the push-pull boundary in order to achieve a balance between the advantages of the push and the pull-based systems.

8.1.7   *Case Analysis*

Consider the Hewlett-Packard case which you read at the beginning of this chapter. Although several problems and issues are outlined in the case, we will focus on analyzing the inventory problems in the European distribution center. In particular, HP faces long delivery lead times of about four to five weeks from its production facility in Vancouver, Washington, to Europe. The Vancouver plant is a high-speed, high-volume facility where manufacturing takes about a week.

In particular, HP is concerned about high inventory levels and inventory imbalance in Europe. One of the characteristics of the DeskJet product line is that it is customized for local markets, a process called *localization*. This involves adding labeling and documentation in the correct language, and customizing the power supply for the correct voltage level and plug. Customization is done in Vancouver many weeks before the products arrive in Europe. Furthermore, once the printers arrive in Europe inventory imbalance might occur in the following sense: The European DC often finds itself with too much inventory of printers customized for certain markets, and not enough inventory of printers customized for others.

What are the causes of these problems? Based on the case and material we have discussed in previous chapters, the following issues are clear:

- There is significant uncertainty about how to set the correct inventory level.
- The many different localization options make inventory difficult to manage.
- Long lead times lead to difficulty in forecasting and high safety stocks.
- Uncertainty in the many local markets makes forecasting difficult.
- Maintaining cooperation between the various HP divisions is challenging.

In the short term, the first issue can be addressed by rationalizing safety stock utilizing the methods we discussed in Chapter 3. To address these problems in the longer term, the following solutions have been proposed:

- Switch to air shipments of printers from Vancouver.
- Build a European factory.
- Hold more inventory at the European DC.
- Improve forecasting practices.

Unfortunately, there are significant problems with each of these suggestions. Air shipments are prohibitively expensive in this competitive, low-margin business. European volumes are not sufficient to justify building a new factory. Inventory is already a problem; more would simply magnify the problem. Finally, it is unclear how to improve forecasts.

Thus, HP management is motivated to consider another option, *postponement*. Specifically, this option involves shipping "unlocalized" printers to the European DC, and localizing them after observing local demand. The question is, what are the inventory savings of such a strategy? To address this issue, we utilize the inventory management policies detailed in Chapter 3. Specifically, using the data in Table 8.1 on page 174, we calculate the average monthly and weekly demand, and the standard deviation of monthly and weekly demand, for each of the European customization options using the approach discussed in Chapter 3.

Recall that we can calculate required safety stock for each of the customized products by noting that safety stock must equal $z \times STD \times \sqrt{L}$, where z is selected to maintain the required service level (see Table 3.2). In the analysis below, we assume that lead time is five weeks, and we require a 98 percent service level. By dividing this quantity by average demand, we determine the number of weeks of safety stock required. Thus, the first six rows of Table 8.2 contain the results of these calculations for each of the customization options specified in Table 8.1. The second to last row totals all of the required safety stock. We see that by utilizing effective inventory management strategies and the current distribution system, HP needs over three-and-a-half weeks of safety stock on hand to meet the 98 percent service level requirement.

The table also shows the effect of postponing localization until after demand is observed. In this case, the DC keeps safety stock of only the generic printer, customizing the printers as demand is realized. This allows the DC to focus on aggregate demand levels and therefore, as we saw in the section on risk pooling in Chapter 3, aggregate demand has a much smaller standard deviation than individual demand. The standard deviation of the aggregate demand is calculated in the last row of the table. This new standard deviation is used to determine safety stock for the generic model. Observe that this new system, in which localization is postponed, requires less safety stock than the currently existing system.

The dollar savings in inventory carrying cost obviously depends on the rate of carrying cost used. For example, if carrying cost is taken to be 30 percent and a product value of $400 is assumed, annual savings is about $800,000. In addition, there are other benefits to implementing a postponement strategy. These include:

- The value of inventory in transit, and thus insurance costs, goes down.
- It may be possible to reduce freight handling costs.
- Some of the localization materials can be locally sourced, reducing costs and meeting "local content" requirements.

On the other hand, there are costs associated with implementing such a strategy. First, the product and packaging have to be redesigned so that

TABLE 8.2 Inventory Analysis

Parameter	Average Monthly Demand	Standard Deviation Monthly Demand	Average Weekly Demand	Standard Deviation Weekly Demand	Safety Stock	Week of Safety Stock
A	42.3	32.4	9.8	15.6	71.5	7.4
AA	420.2	203.9	97.7	98.3	450.6	4.6
AB	15,830.1	5,624.6	3,681.4	2,712.4	12,433.5	3.4
AQ	2,301.2	1,168.5	535.1	563.5	2,583.0	4.8
AU	4,208.0	2,204.6	978.6	1,063.2	4,873.6	5.0
AY	306.8	103.1	71.3	49.7	227.8	3.2
Total	23,108.6		5,373.9		20,640.0	3.8
Generic	23,108.6	6,244	5,373.9	3,011.1	13,802.6	2.6

localization can be delayed. This entails expense and requires research and development work on a product that is already working well. Also, the European distribution center has to be modified to facilitate localization there. Recall that in addition to capital investments, the mind-set of the distribution operation—"Distribution, not manufacturing, is our core competency"—has to be changed.

Hewlett-Packard did indeed implement such a strategy, with great success. Inventory declined while service levels rose, leading to significant cost savings and increased profitability. To achieve these results, the printer was redesigned for localization and the distribution center took on more work and responsibilities.

8.2 Supplier Integration into New Product Development

Another key supply chain issue involves the selection of appropriate suppliers for components of the new product. Traditionally, this has been done after design and manufacturing engineers have determined the final design for a product. Recently, a study in *The Global Procurement and Supply Chain Benchmarking Initiative*, Michigan State University, [82] found that firms often realize tremendous benefits from involving suppliers in the design process. Benefits include a decline in purchased material costs, an increase in purchased material quality, a decline in development time and cost and in manufacturing cost, and an increase in final product technology levels.

In addition to the competitive forces that drive managers to seek out all types of supply chain efficiencies, several competitive forces are specifically encouraging managers to find opportunities to work with suppliers during the product design process. These forces include the continuing focus on strategies that encourage companies to focus on their core competencies and outsource other business capabilities, and to continually reduce the length of product life cycles. Both of these forces encourage companies to develop processes that make the design process more efficient. Taking advantage of supplier competencies is certainly one way to do this.

8.2.1 The Spectrum of Supplier Integration

The supplier integration study [82] notes that there is no single "appropriate level" of supplier integration. Instead, they develop the notion of a *spectrum of supplier integration*. In particular, they identify a series of steps from least to most supplier responsibility as follows:

None. The supplier is not involved in design. Materials and subassemblies are supplied according to customer specifications and design.

White Box. This level of integration is informal. The buyer "consults" with the supplier informally when designing products and specifications, although there is no formal collaboration.

Grey Box. This represents formal supplier integration. Collaborative teams are formed between the buyer's and supplier's engineers, and joint development occurs.

Black Box. The buyer gives the supplier a set of interface requirements and the supplier independently designs and develops the required component.

Of course, just because the Black Box approach is at one end of the continuum doesn't mean that it is the best approach in all cases. Instead, firms must develop a strategy that helps them determine the appropriate level of supplier integration for different situations.

The Global Procurement and Supply Chain Benchmarking Initiative has developed a strategic planning process to help firms make this determination [82]. The first several steps of the process are summarized below:

- Determine internal core competencies.
- Determine current and future new product developments.
- Identify external development and manufacturing needs.

These three steps help management determine what is going to be procured from suppliers, and what level of supplier expertise is appropriate. If future products have components which require expertise that the firm does not possess, and development of these components can be separated from other phases of product development, then taking a Black Box approach makes sense. If this separation is not possible, then it makes more sense to use the Grey Box development. If the buyer has some design expertise but wants to ensure that the supplier can adequately manufacture the component, perhaps a White Box approach is appropriate.

8.2.2 Keys to Effective Supplier Integration

Simply selecting an appropriate level of supplier integration is not sufficient. Much work goes into ensuring that the relationship is a success. The next steps of the strategic planning process [82] help to ensure this success:

- Select suppliers and build relationships with them.
- Align objectives with selected suppliers.

Selecting suppliers in general involves various considerations, such as manufacturing capacity and response time. Since supplier integration partners typically supply components (in addition to cooperating in their design), all of the traditional considerations still apply. In addition, the special nature of supplier integration presents an additional set of supplier requirements.

The same study identifies many of these, including:

- The capability to participate in the design process.
- The willingness to participate in the design process, including the ability to reach agreements on intellectual property and confidentiality issues.
- The ability to commit sufficient personnel and time to the process. This may include colocating personnel if appropriate.
- Sufficient resources to commit to the supplier integration process.

Of course, the relative importance of these requirements depends on the particular project and type of integration. Once suppliers are identified, it is critical to work on building relationships with them. For example, firms have found it useful to involve suppliers early in the design process. Companies that do so report greater gains than those that involve suppliers only after design concepts have been generated.

Sharing future plans and technologies with suppliers helps to build this relationship, as does a joint continuous improvement goal. Separate organizational groups dedicated to managing the relationship are also useful. In all of these cases, the goals of the purchasing firm revolve around building long-term, effective relationships with trusted suppliers. These will naturally lead to the alignment of buyer and supplier objectives, which will result in more effective integration.

8.2.3   A "Bookshelf" of Technologies and Suppliers

The Michigan State group also develops the idea of a "bookshelf" of technologies and suppliers within the context of supplier integration. This involves monitoring the development of relevant new technologies, and following the suppliers that have demonstrated expertise in these technologies. Then, when appropriate, a buyer firm can quickly introduce these technologies into new products by integrating the supplier design team with its own. This enables a firm to balance the advantages and disadvantages of being on the cutting edge of new technology. On one hand, there is no need to use the technology immediately in order to gain experience with it—suppliers are developing this knowledge with other customers. On the other hand, the danger of being slow to introduce cutting-edge technology and concepts is lessened. The bookshelf concept is a dramatic example of the power of supplier integration.

8.3   Mass Customization

8.3.1   What Is Mass Customization?

In his book *Mass Customization* [93], Joseph Pine II introduced a concept that is becoming important to more and more businesses: *mass customization*.

In this section, we will first review the idea of mass customization, and then discuss how logistics and supply chain networks play an important role in the implementation of related concepts.

Mass customization has evolved from the two prevailing manufacturing paradigms of the 20th century, craft production and mass production. Mass production involves the efficient production of a large quantity of a small variety of goods. Spurred by the Industrial Revolution, so-called *mechanistic firms* developed in which management put a high priority on automating and measuring tasks. A very bureaucratic management structure, with rigid, functionally defined groups and tasks, and tightly supervised employees, is common. This kind of organization enables tight control and predictability, which tends to lead to high degrees of efficiency. The quality of a small number of items can be quite high and prices can be kept relatively low. This is particularly critical for commodity products, where firms have typically competed on price and, more recently, on quality.

Craft production, on the other hand, involves highly skilled and flexible workers, often craftsmen in the manufacturing setting, who are governed by personal or professional standards, and motivated by the desire to create unique and interesting products or services. These workers, found in so-called *organic organizations*, are typically trained through apprenticeships and experience; the organization is flexible and continually changing. This type of organization is able to produce highly differentiated and specialized goods, but it is very difficult to regulate and control. As a consequence, the quality and production rates of these goods are hard to measure and reproduce, and they are typically much more expensive to manufacture [94].

In the past managers often had to make a decision between these two types of organizations with their inherent trade-offs. For some products, a low-cost, low-variety strategy was appropriate while for others, a higher-cost, higher-variety, more adaptable strategy was more effective. The development of mass customization demonstrates that it is not always necessary to make this trade-off.

Mass customization involves the delivery of a wide variety of customized goods or services quickly and efficiently at low cost. Thus, it captures many of the advantages of both the mass production and craft production systems described above. Although not appropriate for all products (e.g., commodity products may not benefit from differentiation), mass customization gives firms important competitive advantages and helps to drive new business models.

8.3.2 *Making Mass Customization Work*

Pine points out [94] that the key to making mass customization work is highly skilled and autonomous workers, processes, and modular units, so that managers can coordinate and reconfigure these modules to meet specific customer requests and demands. Each module continually strives to upgrade its capabilities; a module's success depends on how effectively, quickly, and efficiently it completes its task, and how good it is at expanding its capabilities. Managers are charged with determining how these capabilities "fit together" efficiently. Thus, management's success depends on how effectively it can develop, maintain, and creatively combine the links between modules in different ways to meet different customer requests, and on the creation of a work environment that encourages the development of a variety of different modules.

Since each unit has highly specialized skills, workers can develop expertise and efficiency in the manner of mass production. Since these units or modules can be assembled in many ways, the differentiation of craft production is achievable. Pine calls this type of organization a *dynamic network*.

There are several key attributes that a company, or more specifically, the *systems within a company that link different modules*, must possess to implement mass customization successfully [94]. They are:

Instantaneousness. Modules and processes must be linked together very quickly. This allows rapid response to various customer demands.

Costless. The linkages must add little if any cost to the processes. This attribute allows mass customization to be a low-cost alternative.

Seamless. The linkages and individual modules should be invisible to the customer, so customer service doesn't suffer.

Frictionless. Networks or collections modules must be formed with little overhead. Communication must work instantly, without taking time for the team building which is necessary in so many other types of environments.

With these attributes in place, it becomes possible to design and implement a dynamic, flexible firm that can respond to varying customer needs quickly and efficiently.

Example 8.3.1   National Bicycle is a subsidiary of Matsushita that sells bicycles under the Panasonic and National brand names in Japan. Several years ago management found that sales were not at acceptable levels, primarily because the company was unable to predict and satisfy varying customer demand. In the year before beginning the mass customization efforts, 20 percent of bicycles from the previous year remained in inventory. Rather than market to a particular niche or try to improve forecasts, National became a mass customizer.

The company developed a highly flexible bicycle frame manufacturing facility, noting that painting, and installation and tuning components, were separate functions which could be performed by other "modules" in its manufacturing facility. Next, they installed a sophisticated custom-order system called the Panasonic Order System at retailers. This system includes a unique machine that measures customer weight and size, and the appropriate dimensions of the frame, position of the seat, and extension of the bar stem. The customers can also select model type, color patterns, and various components. Information from the dealer is instantaneously transmitted to the factory, where a computer-aided design (CAD) system produces technical details in three minutes. The information is transmitted automatically to the appropriate modules, where manufacturing is completed. The bike is then delivered to consumers two weeks later.

Thus, by noting that the production process could be separated into independent production modules in a seamless and essentially costless manner, and by installing sophisticated information systems, National Bicycle was able to increase sales and customer satisfaction without significantly increasing manufacturing costs [34].

8.3.3   Mass Customization and Supply Chain Management

Clearly, many of the advanced supply chain management approaches and techniques which we have discussed in this and earlier chapters are essential if mass customization is to be successfully implemented. This is particularly true if the components in the network stretch across several companies.

The same information technology that is so critical for effective supply chain management is also critical for coordinating the different modules in the dynamic network, and ensuring that together they meet customer requirements. The required system attributes listed above make effective information systems mandatory.

Similarly, in many cases the modules in the dynamic network exist across different firms. This makes concepts like strategic partnerships and supplier integration essential for the success of mass customization. Finally, as many of the printer-related examples indicate, postponement can play a key role in implementing mass customization. For instance, postponing regional differentiation until products have reached regional distribution centers facilitates regional customization. As the following example illustrates, postponing differentiation until orders have been received allows customer-specific customization.

Example 8.3.2 | Dell Computer has become one of the dominant players in the PC industry—in 1998 it was the second largest manufacturer of PCs for business—by adopting a unique strategy based on mass customization. Dell never builds a PC for a customer until the customer's order has been placed. This allows the customer to specify unique requirements, and Dell builds the computer to these requirements. A growing majority of orders come in over the Internet. The order-taking system interfaces with Dell's own supply chain control system, which ensures that inventory is where it needs to be for the computer to be quickly manufactured. In addition, Dell stores very little inventory. Instead, Dell's suppliers have built warehouses close to Dell's facilities, and Dell orders parts on a just-in-time basis. By implementing these strategies, Dell has been able to provide customers with exactly what they want very quickly. In addition, inventory costs are low and Dell minimizes the danger of parts obsolescence in the rapidly changing computer industry. In this way, Dell has become one of the dominant players in the desktop PC market, and is well on its way to doing so in the laptop and server markets.

Dell has utilized many of the important concepts we have discussed to achieve its goals. The company is driven by advanced information systems which do everything from taking many of the orders (over the web) to managing inventory in the supply chain. Strategic partnerships have been established with many of Dell's suppliers. Dell is even establishing supplier integration partnerships with some of its key suppliers (e.g., 3Com, the network equipment supplier) to ensure that new computers and networking devices are compatible. Finally, Dell has utilized the concept of postponement, deferring final assembly of computers until orders have been received, to achieve mass customization [79].

SUMMARY

In this chapter, we focused on various ways that product design interacts with supply chain management. First, we considered various design for logistics concepts, in which product design is used to lower the costs of logistics. Products designed for efficient packaging and storage obviously cost less to transport and store. Designing products so that certain manufacturing steps can be completed in parallel can cut down on manufacturing lead time, leading to a reduction in safety stocks and increased responsiveness to market changes. Finally, postponing product differentiation enables risk pooling across products leading to lower inventories, and allows firms to use the information contained in aggregate forecasts more effectively.

Another critical design/supply chain interaction involves integrating suppliers into the product design and development process. We discussed different ways that suppliers can be integrated into the development process, and considered keys to managing this integration effectively.

Finally, advanced supply chain management helps to facilitate mass customization. Mass customization involves the delivery of a wide variety of customized goods or services quickly and efficiently at low cost. Obviously, this approach helps to provide firms important competitive advantages and, just as obviously, effective supply chain management is critical if mass customization is to be successful.

CHAPTER
9

Customer Value and Supply Chain Management

CASE: DELL'S DIRECT BUSINESS MODEL

Michael Dell started a computer business in his dormitory room in 1984 with this simple insight: He could bypass the dealer channel through which personal computers were being sold and instead sell directly to customers and build their personal computers (PCs) to order. This idea, now called the *direct business model*, eliminated the cost of inventory and the reselling expenses. The model had other benefits that were not apparent when Dell founded his company, Dell Computer Corporation. "You actually get to have a relationship with the customer," Michael Dell explains, "and this creates valuable information which, in turn, allows us to leverage our relationships with both suppliers and customers. Couple that information with technology, and you have the infrastructure to revolutionize the fundamental business models of major global companies."

Dell Computer's model involves building computers based on components that are available in the market. The decision not to manufacture the computer components has relieved Dell of the burden of owning assets, research and development risks, and managing a large number of employees. Spreading the development and manufacturing risk among several suppliers allowed Dell to grow much faster than if these functions were performed inside the company.

Dell's use of technology and information to blur the traditional boundaries in the supply chain between suppliers, manufacturers, and end users, has been named *virtual integration*. In a traditional computer company, such as Digital Computer, processes were *vertically integrated*, with all the research, development, manufacturing, and distribution capabilities in-house. This allowed for a high level of communication and ability to develop products based on the company's interaction with its clients. The disadvantage was the high risk and costs of development and the ownership of assets in a volatile industry. To achieve the advantages of an integrated company, Dell treats suppliers and service providers as if they were inside the company. Their systems are linked in real time to Dell's

Source: The case above is based on [69].

197

system and their employees participate in design teams and product launches. Technology enhances the economic incentives to collaborate because it makes it possible to share design databases and methodologies and speed the time to market.

Dell measures *inventory velocity*, the reciprocal of the average amount of time a product spends in inventory. For this purpose, each component is marked with a date stamp. Accumulating inventory in the fast-moving PC industry is a high-risk proposition since the components can become obsolete very quickly. In some cases, such as Sony monitors, Dell does not keep any inventory but has UPS or Airborne Express pick up the monitors from Sony's Mexican factory, the computer from Dell's Austin, Texas, facility, and then match and deliver them to the customers. Dell suppliers benefit from the real-time information about demand and a commitment from Dell for a certain level of purchases. The results are impressive. While Compaq, IBM, and Hewlett-Packard all announced plans in late 1998 to emulate portions of Dell's business model, with various build-to-order plans, all have had difficulty in making the transition. Most are moving to a target inventory level of four weeks, while Dell maintains just eight days of inventory, allowing it to turn over inventory 46 times a year.

On the customer side, Dell has segmented its customer base so that it can offer value-added services to different customers. Dell configures PCs and supports them for large customers. It will also load standard software and place asset stickers on the machines based on customer requests. For some clients, Dell has an on-site team that assists in PC purchasing and servicing. "The whole idea behind virtual integration is that it lets you meet customers' needs faster and more efficiently than any other model." Furthermore, it allows Dell to be efficient and responsive to change at the same time. By spending time with customers and following technological trends, Dell tries to be a few steps ahead of the change, and even create and shape it.

By the end of this chapter, you should be able to answer the following questions:

- What is customer value?
- How is customer value measured?
- How is information technology used to enhance customer value in the supply chain?
- How does supply chain management contribute to customer value?

9.1 Introduction

Not long ago this chapter would have been titled "Customer Service and Logistics." In today's customer-driven market, however, it is not the product or service itself that matters but the perceived value to the customer of the entire relationship with the company. The way companies measure the quality of their product and services has evolved from internal quality assurance to external customer satisfaction and from there to *customer value*. Internal quality measures, such as the number of defects, dominated company goals in the era of supply-driven manufacturing. Customer satisfaction concentrated on the company's current customers and their use of a company's product and impression of its service. This provided valuable information about current customers and generated ideas for areas of improvement and ways to compensate for performance in the company. The current emphasis on customer value goes a step further and tries to establish the reasons a customer chooses one company's product over another's, and looks at the entire range of product, services, and intangibles that constitute the company's product and image.

Thinking in terms of customer value promotes a broader look at a company's offerings and customers. It requires learning why customers purchase, continue to purchase, or defect from a company. What are their preferences and needs and how can they be satisfied? Which customers are profitable and have potential for revenue growth, and which customers may incur losses? Assumptions about customer value need to be examined carefully to make sure the trade-offs made are the correct ones. Some examples of these trade-offs include:

Does the customer value low prices more than superior customer support services?

Does the customer prefer next day delivery or lower prices?

Does the customer prefer to purchase the item in a store that specializes in this type of item or from a large megastore that allows one-stop shopping?

These are critical questions for any business, and should be the driving force behind business strategy.

Indeed, logistics, previously considered a back-office function, has evolved into the highly visible supply chain management partly because of this change of perspective. Supply chain management is naturally an important component in fulfilling customer needs and providing value. Equally important, supply chain management determines the availability of products, how fast they will arrive in the market, and at what cost. Our definition of *supply chain management* (see Chapter 1) implies that the ability to respond to customer requirements is the most basic function of this discipline. This function includes not only the physical attributes of product distribution, but also the related status information and access to this information.

Supply chain management can also impact the all-important customer value of price by significantly reducing costs. Dell's strategy to reduce its supply chain costs by postponing the final product assembly until after the purchase (i.e., by building to order) has allowed Dell to underprice its competitors in the personal computer industry (see Chapter 8). Wal-Mart has been able to lower costs by introducing the cross-docking strategy (see Chapter 5) and by engaging in strategic partnering with its suppliers (see Chapter 6). Finally, the policy of everyday low prices, applied by Wal-Mart and other retailers, is also motivated in large part by supply chain efficiencies, as we have seen in Chapter 4.

Customer value drives changes and improvements in the supply chain—some forced by demanding customers and competitor activities, and others undertaken to achieve competitive advantage. Furthermore, large manufacturers, distributors, or retailers place certain demands on their suppliers which force suppliers to adopt supply chains that will make these requests possible. Specifically, Wal-Mart demands many of its suppliers to practice vendor managed inventory (see Chapter 6). Large manufacturers such as Hewlett-Packard and Lucent Technologies demand that its parts manufacturers have 100 percent availability of stock for the parts they use. In return, they are willing to commit to one supplier that will provide the required products and services, or at least up to a certain volume of purchases.

Finally, customer value is also important in determining the type of supply chain required to serve the customer and what services are required to retain customers. A company's supply chain strategy is determined by the type of product or services it offers and the value of various elements of this offering to the customer. For example, if customers value one-stop shopping, that would entail carrying a large number of products and options, even if that is costly in terms of inventory management. If customers value innovative products, then companies who produce them need to apply their supply chain to supply these products efficiently while demand lasts. If a company offers personal customization of its products, then its supply chain needs to be flexible enough to provide the infrastructure for this offering. Thus, the supply chain needs to be considered in any product and sales strategy and could, in itself, provide competitive advantages leading to increased customer value.

9.2 The Dimensions of Customer Value

We have defined customer value as the way the customer perceives the entire company's offerings, including products, services, and other intangibles. The customer perception can be broken into several dimensions:

- Conformance to requirements
- Product selection
- Price and brand

- Value-added services
- Relationships and experiences

The list of dimensions starts with the essentials—that is, the first three items above—and goes on to more sophisticated types of features that may not always be critical. However, the less critical features can be mined for ideas to create a unique way to add value and differentiation to a company's offering. In this section, we suggest how each dimension is affected by supply chain management, and how supply chain management needs to take into account the customer values inherent in each dimension.

9.2.1   Conformance to Requirements

The ability to offer what the customer wants and needs is a basic requirement to which supply chain management contributes by creating availability and selection. Marshall Fisher calls it the *market mediation* function of the supply chain [36]. This function is distinct from the supply chain physical function of converting raw materials into goods and shipping them through the chain to the customer. The costs associated with the market mediation function occur when there are differences in supply and demand. If the supply exceeds demand, there are inventory costs throughout the supply chain; if demand exceeds supply, there are lost sales and possibly market share.

If product demand is predictable, as in *functional items* such as diapers, soup, or milk, market mediation is not a major issue, but when dealing with fashion items or other high variability items, the nature of demand can create large costs due to lost sales or excess inventory. Clearly, efficient supply chains for functional items can reduce costs by focusing on reducing inventory, transportation, and other costs. This is the strategy Campbell Soup and Procter & Gamble take for their supply chains.

On the other hand, high variability products require responsive supply chains, which stress short lead times, flexibility, and speed over cost efficiencies. When the supply chain strategy does not match the product characteristics, there are major implications in the ability to conform to the market, as illustrated in the following example.

Example 9.2.1 | Consider a Korean company that manufactures electronic relays. Since competition is intense in this industry, customers can pick and choose their supplier. Thus, if the manufacturer does not have the right products at the right time, it will lose customers to the competition. To make matters worse, forecasting customer demand is a challenge because variation in monthly demand is very high. To reduce cost, the manufacturer ships products from a number of manufacturing facilities in the Far East by sea. Unfortunately, by the time the product has arrived at the U.S. warehouse, the demand has changed and there is a shortage of one type of component and unsalable inventory of another. Therefore, the manufacturer is considering shipping the products by air, which would reduce lead times and hence inventory levels and costs, as well as improve customer sales and retention (see Chapter 3).

9.2.2 Product Selection

Many products come in a large variety of options, styles, colors, and shapes. For instance, a car may come in 5 styles, 10 different exterior colors, 10 interior colors, and, with automatic/manual transmission, a total of 1,000 configurations. The difficulty is that distributors and retailers need to stock most of the various configurations and combinations of products. As explained in Chapter 3, this proliferation of the product line makes it difficult to predict customer demand for a specific model, thus forcing retailers and distributors to build inventory.

The contribution of product proliferation to customer value is difficult to analyze and understand. Three successful business trends exist. They include:

- Specializing in offering one type of product. Examples include companies such as Starbucks or Subway.
- Megastores that allow one-stop shopping for a large variety of products. Examples include Wal-Mart and in particular Kmart, which has recently expanded its store capacity.
- Megastores that specialize in one product area. Examples here include Home Depot, Office Max, and Sportmart.

These trends have also emerged on the Internet where some World Wide Web sites have been successful in offering a large variety of different products while others specialize in a single offering. For instance, a new successful web site, at www.justballs.com, sells only balls for various sports.

The PC industry is an industry that has seen significant changes in the way products are sold. In the mid-1980s PCs were sold through specialized stores such as Egghead. At the beginning of the 1990s PCs were sold in department stores such as Sears. More recently, however, the direct business model has caught on. Finally, Gateway, one of the leaders in the direct business model, has just opened retail stores. This suggests that there may be a need for a company to sell its products through various outlets to reach the largest number of customers.

As observed earlier, the proliferation of products and the difficulty in predicting demand for a specific model forces retailers and distributors to stock a large inventory. We next discuss several ways to control the inventory problem of a large variety of configurations or products.

1. The approach pioneered by Dell is the build-to-order model, where the configuration is determined only when the order comes in. This is an effective way to implement the concept of postponement introduced and analyzed in Chapter 8. An interesting way to implement this strategy is described in the following example.

Example 9.2.2	Amazon.com sells a huge variety of books and music CDs. When a customer enters an order, Amazon.com requests the book from one of a dozen wholesalers and 20,000 publishers. The books arrive at Amazon.com's warehouse shipping dock. In most cases, they are packaged and out the door to a customer within hours. With the exception of a few hundred best-selling titles, the company keeps no inventory.

2. A different strategy suitable for products with long manufacturing lead times, such as vehicles, is to keep larger inventories at major distribution centers. These distribution centers allow the manufacturer to reduce inventory levels by taking advantage of risk pooling (see Chapter 3) and deliver the vehicles quickly to customers. General Motors has initiated this approach with its Cadillac unit in Florida. Dealers can send orders for cars that they do not have on their lot to a regional warehouse which can ship the car out in a day. Of course, two major issues need to be raised when considering this strategy:

a. Inventory costs of cars at the regional warehouse. Is the manufacturer (i.e., General Motors) going to pay for the inventory at the regional warehouse? If it is, then there is an incentive for the dealers to reduce inventory in their lots and reduce their cost while increasing that of the manufacturer.

b. Equalizing small and large dealers. If all dealers have access to the regional warehouse, then there is no difference between the different dealers. Thus, it is difficult to see why large dealers would be interested in participating in such an arrangement, especially if they are going to pay for inventory at the regional warehouse.

3. Another possibility is to offer a fixed set of options that covers most customer requirements. For instance, Honda offers a limited number of options on its cars. Dell offers few options for modems or software that can be installed on its machines, although the overall number of possible configurations remains quite high. Indeed, large product variety is not required in all cases. For example, M. L. Fisher noted how a dysfunctional level of variety exists in many grocery products—28 varieties of toothpaste, to give one example [36]. It is not clear whether this variety actually adds any customer value.

9.2.3   Price and Brand

Price of products and cost of services are an essential part of customer value. Although the price may not be the only factor a customer considers, there may be a narrow price range that is acceptable for certain products. When an item is a commodity—even sophisticated items like personal computers are commodities—there is very little flexibility in price. Therefore, companies achieve cost advantages through innovations in their supply chains. As we have seen in Dell's direct business model, allowing clients to configure their own systems and building a supporting supply chain not only can improve customer value but also reduce costs.

Wal-Mart has been a supply chain innovator, which has enabled it to provide low-cost merchandise and undercut its competition. We have also seen that the "everyday low pricing" policy applied by Procter & Gamble is an important tool in reducing the bullwhip effect (see Chapter 4). This policy appeals to customers who do not have to worry about buying at the wrong time, and to the retailer and manufacturer who do not need to plan for demand variations as a result of promotions.

Another factor in the price is the brand of the product. In today's market, there are fewer salespeople and more customers looking for supermarket-style shopping [98]. This is true of auto superstores as well as shopping on the Internet. This trend in customer behavior increases the importance of brand names, because a brand name is a guarantee of quality in the buyer's mind. Brand names like Mercedes cars, Rolex watches, and Coach purses can be promoted for high quality and prestige, and command much higher prices than products that lack this aura. Furthermore, the price itself may be a large part of the prestige and perceived quality. Since lost sales in this case are more expensive owing to higher margins, the supply chain needs to be more responsive; the increase in supply chain cost will be offset by the higher price margin.

Example 9.2.3 | One of the key elements in the rise of Federal Express as the most successful small package carrier is that it was the first carrier to narrow its focus to overnight delivery, thereby owning the word "overnight" in the market. Even though there are cheaper alternatives, customers are willing to pay a premium to ship by Federal Express because of the brand name and the perception of dependability it conveys [98].

Finally, in many industries "product" typically means both the "physical product" and associated "services." Typically, pricing the physical product is not as difficult as pricing services. At the same time, it is quite difficult to compare different services; as a result, variability in pricing increases. This suggests opportunities for companies that develop new offerings and services that are more difficult to turn into commodities. As we will see below, there is a challenge in turning these opportunities into offerings that customers are actually willing to pay for.

9.2.4   Value-Added Services

Many companies cannot compete on product price alone in an economy that has an overabundance of supply. Therefore, they need to look at other sources of income. This drives companies toward value-added offerings that differentiate them from competitors and provide them with more profitable pricing structures.

Value-added services, such as support and maintenance, can be a major factor in the purchase of some products, especially technical products. Indeed, many companies are now adding more services around their products [55]. This is due in part to:

1. The commoditization of products, where only the price matters and all other features are identical, reduce profitability and competitive advantage from the sale of products alone.
2. The need to get closer to the customer.
3. The increase in information technology capabilities that make this offering possible.

An example of a sophisticated service offering is illustrated in the following example.

Example 9.2.4 | Goodyear Tire & Rubber Co. provides truck manufacturer Navistar International Transportation Corp. with a full-blown automated supply chain service that includes delivering mounted tires sequenced for just-in-time use on automated assembly lines for automakers. Goodyear has a 13-person information technology group dedicated to the tire maker's materials management division. This division acts as systems integrator on supply chain projects it takes on with wheel manufacturer Accuride, Inc., in Henderson, Kentucky. Under a joint venture called AOT, Inc., Goodyear and Accuride furnish entire wheel assemblies, painted and ready for use, to Mitsubishi Motor Co. and Ford Motor Co. as well as Navistar. Those assemblies include Goodyear's or competitors' tires, depending on customer specifications [55].

For many years companies such as IBM did not charge for their services although the company's slogan was "IBM Means Service." Today service provides most of IBM's income! Companies that have not stressed customer support, such as Microsoft, are enhancing their capabilities in this area. In many cases, there is a charge associated with receiving support, such as a one-time call fee or a service agreement. As we saw in the Dell case, service and support not only can generate additional revenue, but, more importantly, bring the company closer to the customer and provide it with insight on how to improve its offering, tailor support, and find the next idea to add value to its products and services.

An important value-added service is information access. Allowing customers access to their own data—such as pending orders, payment history, and typical orders—enhances their experience with the company. For example, it is well known that customers value the ability to know the status of an order, sometimes even more than the actual turnaround time. This capability provides reliability and enables planning. FedEx pioneered the package tracking systems that are now standard in the package handling industry. As we will see below, this not only enhances service, but can result in large savings for the provider of the information by handing over to its customers some of the data entry and inquiry functions from its own employees.

The ability of customers to access information is becoming an essential requirement in supply chain management, as visibility of information is what an increasing number of customers expect. The Internet enables these capabilities and companies will need to invest in information systems that support it. In Chapter 10, we deal with these issues in more detail.

9.2.5   Relationships and Experiences

The final level of customer value is an increased connection between the firm and its customers through development of a relationship. This makes it more difficult for customers to switch to another provider since a relationship requires an investment of time from both the customer and the provider. For example, Dell configures PCs and supports them for large customers. When Dell manages the entire PC purchase for a large customer, including special custom features, it becomes more difficult for the customer to switch to another vendor.

Another type of relationship is the learning relationship, where companies build specific user profiles and utilize this information to enhance sales as well as retain customers [92]. Companies such as Individual Inc., which builds tailored information services, and USAA, which uses its databases to offer customers other services and products, are examples of this kind of organization.

| Example 9.2.5 | Peapod, Inc., is America's leading Internet grocer, providing consumers with broad product choices and local delivery services. The company currently provides such services in seven metropolitan markets in the United States and serves over 103,000 |

members. Shoppers use a personal computer that allows them to browse through Peapod's offerings. Peapod's computers are linked directly to the databases of the supermarkets from which it purchases the groceries. The shoppers can create their own virtual supermarket by accessing the information according to category and creating customized shopping lists that can be saved for repeated use. At the end of each shopping session, Peapod has the opportunity to learn about its service by asking, "How did we do on the last order?" and using the relatively high response rate of its customers (35 percent) to institute requested changes to its services [92].

The approach used by Peapod Inc. is an example of the *one-to-one enterprise* concept suggested in [89]. In this concept, companies learn about each customer through databases and interactive communications, and sell to one customer as many products and services as possible throughout the lifetime of the customer's patronage. Indeed, Peapod is using its databases to suggest new offerings to customers, tracking the customer's preferences and needs, and further tailoring the company's offering to the customer.

The learning process can take time, but this will make it difficult for competitors to emulate the strategy. In addition, it typically ensures that a customer who considers switching to another provider will have to take into account investing time and money in the process.

Indeed, some of the Internet sites, such as www.amazon.com, are applying new modes of learning, with suggestions to customers based on their own previous purchases or those of customers who make similar purchases. Dell has implemented this approach with programs tailored to large corporations, creating custom PCs loaded with specific software, tags, and other special requirements. Dell has also tailored its web site so that different types of users can access it according to their needs. In many ways, this approach is a more extensive application of mass customization, which we discussed in Chapter 8.

Beyond relationships, some companies are also designing, promoting, and selling unique experiences to their customers, which according to [91], is the trend in the new economy. The authors define experience as an offering distinct from customer service.

> An experience occurs when a company intentionally uses services as the stage, and goods as props, to engage individual customers in a way that creates a memorable events [91].

Some current examples include airline frequent flyer programs, theme parks, Saturn owner gatherings, and Lexus Sunday breakfast and car wash events. The Internet provides other opportunities for creating experiences which have not yet been fully explored. Some examples include offerings such as interactive communities, futures auctions, bidding sites, and others.

| **Example 9.2.6** | Silicon Graphics opened the Visionarium Reality Center in June 1996. The Visionarium is a virtual reality center intended for use as a sales and marketing tool. The idea is that designers who develop products using Silicon Graphics technology can simulate the experience achieved with new products. The virtual reality center is used in the design of automobiles, airplanes, and architecture. It allows the developers, or potential customers, to view, hear, touch, and even drive, walk, or fly various prototype product configurations. This enables customers to know what their products will look, feel, and sound like before manufacturing [91]. |

As with the initial introduction of services, companies do not yet charge for experiences. Before a company can charge for this offering, experiences must be seen by the customer as worth the price. This requires a large investment in making the experience valuable in itself. Disney's theme parks are the prime example of a successful experience which many are willing to pay for. The parks can be seen as a means to selling Disney's products—movies and various spin-off toys and accessories.

Evidently, the ability to provide sophisticated customer interactions (e.g., relationships and experiences) is very different from the ability to manufacture and distribute products. This suggests the emergence of firms that specialize in providing the former offerings. This may separate the market into "sizzle" and "steak" companies. Steak companies make products and move them to market; sizzle companies deal with the end customer. Dell is obviously a "sizzle" company, while its suppliers—such as Sony—are "steak" companies. Other examples of "sizzle" companies are Disney, Nike, and Sara Lee.

9.3   Customer Value Measures

Because customer value is based on customer perceptions, it requires measures that start with the customer. Typical measures include service level and customer satisfaction. Our objective in this section is to introduce various measures of customer value as well as supply chain performance measures. The latter are important since supply chain performance is an important contributor to customer value.

1. Service level. Service level is the typical measure used to quantify a company's market conformance. In practice, the definition of service level can vary from company to company, but *service level* usually is related to the ability to satisfy a customer's delivery date—for instance, the percent of all orders sent on or before the promised delivery date. Many companies consider this measure so critical to their ability to succeed in today's markets that they invest heavily in decision-support systems which allow them to quote delivery dates accurately by analyzing information from the entire supply chain.

There is a direct relationship between the ability to achieve a certain level of service and supply chain cost and performance. For instance, demand variability and manufacturing and information lead times determine the amount of inventory that needs to be kept in the supply chain (see Chapter 3). Clearly, when setting the level of service that should be used for a particular offering, it is important to understand customer value. For instance, customers may value low cost, information about the delivery date, and the ability to customize the product more than they value immediate delivery itself. This is definitely the case for PC buyers, where Dell's direct business model—with the extra time it takes to build and deliver the PC—seems to be winning over off-the-shelf store purchases.

2. Customer satisfaction. Customer satisfaction surveys are used to measure sales department and personnel performance as well as to provide feedback for necessary improvements in products and services. In addition, as in the Peapod example, there are other innovative ways to receive information about customer satisfaction. However, customer surveys may not be the best way to learn about customer value. As Reichheld [97] points out, relying on customer satisfaction surveys can often be misleading. These surveys are easy to manipulate and are typically measured at the selling point while nothing is said about retaining the customer.

Indeed, more important than what customers say about their satisfaction is *customer loyalty*, which is easier to measure than customer satisfaction. This can be accomplished by analyzing customer repurchase patterns based on internal databases.

Example 9.3.1 | Lexus is a consistent winner of auto satisfaction awards, but it refuses to consider surveys as the best measure of satisfaction. To Lexus the only meaningful measure of satisfaction is repurchase loyalty. Lexus considers the repurchase activities of cars and services as the only measure for its dealers' success. Each Lexus dealership has a satellite dish that keeps information flowing back and forth to headquarters, where these measures are constantly tracked [97].

An additional option is to learn from customer defections. Unfortunately, identifying those customers is not an easy task because dissatisfied customers seldom cancels an account completely. Instead they gradually shift their spending, making a partial defection. However, if this type of tracking is possible, it may provide the key to increasing customer value.

3. Supply chain performance measures. As we have seen, supply chain performance affects the ability to provide customer value, especially in the most basic dimension of availability of products. Therefore, there is a need to develop independent criteria to measure supply chain performance. The need for well-defined measures in the supply chain stems from the presence of many partners in the process and the requirement of a common language. This is precisely the motivation behind standardization initiatives such as the SCOR model (see Chapter 10).

The Supply Chain Operations Reference Model (SCOR) uses a *process reference model* that includes analyzing the current state of a company's processes and its goals, and quantifying operational performance and comparing it to benchmark data. For this purpose, SCOR has developed a set of metrics for supply chain performance and its members are in the process of forming industry groups to collect best-practice information that companies can use to evaluate their supply chain performance. Table 9.1 lists examples of metrics used to evaluate supply chain performance in SCOR based on [78].

Once a specific company's metrics are calculated, they are compared to those of industry benchmarks such as average and best-in-class. This enables identifying the company's advantages as well as opportunities for supply chain improvement.

TABLE 9.1   SCOR Level 1 Metrics

Perspectives	Metrics	Measure
Supply chain reliability	On time delivery	Percentage
	Order fulfillment lead time	Days
	Fill rate	Percentage
	Perfect order fulfillment	Percentage
Flexibility and responsiveness	Supply chain response time	Days
	Upside production flexibility	Days
Expenses	Supply chain management cost	Percentage
	Warranty cost as percentage of revenue	Percentage
	Value added per employee	Dollars
Assets/utilization	Total inventory days of supply	Days
	Cash-to-cash cycle time	Days
	Net asset turns	Turns

The SCOR model is a good example of supply chain metrics. It has the additional advantage of possibly becoming an industry standard. However, as we saw in the Dell case, every company needs to understand its own unique environment and determine its measures based on that insight. For instance, Dell measures inventory velocity and not inventory turns, which is the standard measure of inventory management performance (see Chapter 3).

9.4 Information Technology and Customer Value

Information technology has produced many valuable benefits for customers. We will briefly review three aspects below. The first is exchange of information between customers and businesses, the second is the use of information by companies to learn more about their customers so that they can better tailor their services, and the third is enhanced business-to-business capabilites. For more details on this subject see Chapter 10.

1. Customer benefits. Customer service has changed for many reasons. One of the most dramatic is the opening of corporate, government, and educational databases to the customer. This started with kiosks and voice mail and has accelerated significantly with the uniform data access tools of the Internet. These innovations have had the effect of increasing customer value while reducing costs for the supplier of the information. Banks were the first to realize that by installing automated teller machines (ATMs) they could reduce their workforce. Voice mail was at first derided as dehumanizing, preventing interactions with a live person, but it actually allowed unmediated access to a user's accounts at any time of the day from almost anywhere. The Internet has expanded these capabilities and allows users to access their accounts and perform transactions from any location at any time. This opening of the information boundaries between customer and company is part of the new customer value equation, where the information is part of the product.

The Internet has also had some less obvious effects [11].

- *Increased importance of intangibles.* Customers have become accustomed to ordering even high-priced products from unseen sales people over the phone or Internet. This increases the importance of brand names and other intangibles, such as service capabilities or community experience in purchasing decisions.
- *Increased ability to connect and disconnect.* The Internet makes it not only easier to identify business partners and connect to them but also to disconnect and find new partners. Increasing availability of information, including performance measures and data, reduces the need to develop long-term trust relationships. Companies can rely

on accessible, published track records to make decisions on quality of service. This ability is mainly important when there is no considerable investment in setting up the partnership. If there is, then frequent changes of partners may have a major impact on cost and available resources.

• *Increased customer expectations.* The ability to compare and the ease of performing various transactions over the phone and the Internet has raised expectations of similar services from every type of business as well as for business-to-business interactions.

2. Business benefits. One way to enhance customer value is to use the information captured in the supply chain to create new offerings for customers. The information now available allows companies to "sense and respond" to customers' desires rather than simply make and sell products and services. Indeed, as we have seen, learning about customers takes time, requires some of the customers' time, and eventually makes switching vendors more difficult. The learning process takes many forms from sophisticated data mining methods used to correlate purchasing patterns, to learning about each individual customer by keeping detailed data of preferences and purchases. The method applied depends on the industry and business model. Retailers would use the first method while service companies, as in the example below, would be more likely to track individual customer preferences and requirements.

Example 9.4.1 | In the 1930s it was difficult for military personnel to obtain reasonably priced insurance, so a group of officers formed United Services Automobile Association (USAA) to provide insurance for military officers. USAA still offers services only to active and former military officers and their families, and handles all transactions by mail and phone. USAA has used its extensive databases to expand into financial and shopping services for its members. When a customer calls USAA, the information about him or her can be accessed and updated and the customer can be offered a variety of services to match his or her needs. For instance, if a customer owns a boat purchased or financed through USAA, he or she could receive an offer to acquire insurance [92].

---

3. Business-to-business benefits. The Dell Computer case introduced at the beginning of the chapter illustrates how information technology allows companies to improve the performance of their suppliers and service providers. This makes it possible to outsource important parts of a company's business, but still keep close control over what it produces or services. For instance, strategic partnering relies heavily on information sharing while allowing the partners to achieve supply chain efficiencies (see Chapter 6).

Other examples of information sharing between businesses can be found in [85]. The authors describe various arrangements between manufacturers and distributors for sharing information on inventory that results in cost reduction. These arrangements, motivated by the risk-pooling concept introduced in Chapter 3, allow manufacturers and distributors to reduce overall inventory by sharing information about inventory in all locations and allowing any member of the channel to share the inventory.

SUMMARY

Creating customer value is the driving force behind a company's goals, and supply chain management is one of the means of achieving customer value. As we have seen, the Dell Computer case illustrates many of the current and future trends in creating customer value, in general, and using supply chain management, in particular. Below we summarize the major issues covered in the chapter and how they are illustrated in the Dell case.

Supply chain management strategy affects customer value. Such considerations affect every aspect of customer value and must be part of any strategy or plan, not an afterthought. It is important to choose the appropriate supply chain strategy to match customer value with the company's market. Excellence in supply chain management translates into customer value in many dimensions, from availability and selection to influencing the price at which a product can be sold. The supply chain strategy in the Dell case was the business model, and it created the customer value of low prices.

Customer access to information about the availability of products and the status of orders and deliveries is becoming an essential capability. This also creates opportunities to learn about customers and their preferences, and to create new modes of interaction. Dell uses this information to enhance its services.

Adding services, relationships, and experiences is a way for companies to differentiate their offerings in the market and learn about their customers. It also makes it difficult for the customers to switch to another service provider. Dell has added excellent customer support to its capabilities. Larger companies find that it provides more extensive options, from custom preloaded PCs to in-house service and support.

Measuring customer value is at the heart of company goals and objectives, but identifying the appropriate measure is not an easy task. Some companies are moving away from the classical concept of customer satisfaction to customer loyalty. Dell, for example, measures inventory velocity, not the classical inventory turnovers.

Specialization, the ability to provide sophisticated customer interactions—for example, relationships and experiences—is very different from the ability to manufacture and distribute products. Because a distinctive expertise is required for each function, companies will gain by specializing. This concept has been applied successfully by Dell, a "sizzle" company through virtual integration. Dell has relationships with many "steak" companies—its suppliers—which create the components of its product.

A virtually integrated company can lose some of its ability to innovate and collaborate if it does not pay close attention to its relationships with suppliers. This is also true for other third-party providers performing tasks for the company. Communication systems, ways of sharing information and resources, and proper incentives need to be in place to make these relationships work. Dell, a company built on outsourcing, has been working on this type of collaboration for many years. It has practices in place to make sure that the quality of work performed by its partners meets its own standards.

There is no real customer value without a close relationship with customers. Today this is possible not only through direct interaction, but also through information and communications technology. By allowing customers to state their preferences and learning from them—a true two-way interaction—a firm will develop the means to achieve greater customer value and therefore loyalty. Dell has inadvertently been able to achieve this because of its direct supply chain model. The company has taken full advantage of close relationships with its customers.

CHAPTER

10

Information Technology for Supply Chain Management

CASE: BACKUP IN THE ESPRESSO LANE

You have to admire the enthusiasm of Starbucks Corp. employees. Store managers have been known to stuff sacks of coffee beans into their cars and race over to help out other stores running low on java. Exceptional customer service, but certainly no way to run a business—especially one that's growing as quickly as Starbucks.

"With 2,000 stores, you can't have 2,000 people with coffee in their trunks," says Tim Duffy, director of supply chain systems and support for Starbucks in Seattle. The specialty coffee supplier plans to have 2,000 retail locations up and running by the turn of the century, up from 1,400 today. To make sure none of those locations is beholden to a distribution system backed by a fleet of employee cars, Starbucks is in the midst of overhauling its supply chain management system.

Unfortunately, what was supposed to be a three-year project is now slated to be finished in five, primarily because Starbucks chose a best-of-breed approach over an integrated ERP (enterprise resource planning) solution. With supply chain software vendors such as Manugistics Inc. bragging about full implementations of their applications being completed in less than a year, it's fair to ask what's taking Starbucks so long.

The answer to that question provides lessons for any IT executive looking to revamp his or her company's supply chain operations with a best-of-breed system. This approach, where companies hand-pick the best software product for each piece of the supply chain process, comes with its share of headaches. Among them: an extended vendor evaluation period, complex software integration hurdles, and version control problems. These issues are all the more pertinent since supply chains are top-of-mind these days. Purchases of supply chain management software will shoot up 45 percent, from $419 million today to $2.7 billion in 2001, according to a new report by Advanced Manufacturing Research Inc., of Boston.

Source: Lawrence Aragon, *PC Week*, November 10, 1997. Copied with permission.

"For a fast-growing company, even putting a single ERP system in place in three years would have been a pretty average time," says John Bermudez, group director of supply chain research for AMR. "I don't know that Starbucks really planned this thing out."

Recipe for Growth

To get a clear picture of Starbucks' situation, you have to fully appreciate its challenges. Although it's a 26-year-old company, the coffee powerhouse has been on its caffeine-jolted growth curve for only the past five years. Since it went public in 1992, the company has opened 1,235 retail locations. Sales from those stores account for 86 percent of the company's annual revenue.

But Starbucks' expansive retail operation is just a piece of its supply chain. As part of its effort to establish itself as a major brand, Starbucks launched joint ventures with Dreyer's Grand Ice Cream Inc., Pepsi-Cola Co., and Redhook Ale Brewery to create products based on its coffee. It also hammered out a deal with Capital Records to produce jazz compact disks, began selling its products through grocery stores, and struck a deal for its coffee to be carried by Aramark Food & Services Inc. Then there are the partnerships to sell its brew through other venues, including bookstore chain Barnes & Noble Inc. and United Airlines.

Amazingly, Starbucks was able to handle the growth—from $103 million in annual sales when it went public to about $700 million in 1996—with its original supply chain management systems. Duffy says the fact that Starbucks continued to thrive, even though it didn't have formal supply chain processes in place, is a tribute to the company's "ambitious and impassioned" employees.

That isn't hyperbole. Consider that the only real technology Starbucks used was a merchandise management system called JDA software, running on an AS/400. The rest of the supply chain processes were done manually. "For a long time, we didn't do production planning at the SKU level," Duffy says. Instead, planning was based around the company's 30-odd flavors of coffee. Today, Starbucks manages about 3,000 SKUs with software from Manugistics.

Forecasting was another area limited by the manual approach. Prior to the overhaul, it was essentially done through messages swapped between business unit managers and production managers on voice mail and e-mail, Duffy says. Now, business units use Retek Information Systems Inc.'s SkuPlan forecasting software to create a rolling monthly forecast for sales and a rolling 24-month forecast for SKUs in general. That data feeds into Manugistics' software, which draws up an enterprise supply chain plan.

Starbucks even had problems with the fundamental BOM (bill of materials). "There were as many BOMs in the company as the people who needed them," Duffy says. And that meant higher costs because of redundancies and multiple and divergent forecasts. Today, BOMs are part of a comprehensive process run by several applications, including Numetrix Laboratories Ltd.'s Schedule X software, which tells Starbucks the most efficient way to schedule its manufacturing resources.

Although it was getting by with its old system, Starbucks management knew it was spending more than it should to support its supply chain. "We had grown so much and had so much volume, what the employees had built up to that point wasn't good enough anymore," Duffy explains.

So, in early 1995, Starbucks resolved to revamp the technology behind the supply chain. The stated goal: to create a state-of-the art, integrated supply chain system that would reduce costs by an undisclosed amount, improve customer service, and maintain consistent quality.

Initially, Starbucks figured that an ERP package would be the best solution. With that in mind, the company's supply chain operations and IT groups defined the company's needs, in part by using Expert Buying Systems Inc.'s Choose Smart software to query more than 50 people inside and outside the company. The next step was to send out requests for information to top ERP vendors and consult with industry experts, such as Gartner Group Inc., AMR, and the American Production Inventory Control Society. Demos and customer visits followed for five ERP vendors–Baan Co., Datalogix International Inc. (now part of Oracle Corp.), Oracle, QAD Inc., and System Software Associates.

Some six months after the whole process began, however, Starbucks decided that none of these ERP packages could meet its needs. Instead, it opted for a best-of-breed approach, which meant pulling together nine separate components. (See Table 10.1.) "We're building this thing so that at any given point in time, if we need to upgrade any part of the supply chain, we can probably more readily pull and replace any one component than we could with an ERP system," Duffy says. "The overriding reason is functional flexibility—to be able to react to the dynamic needs of our business environment."

TABLE 10.1 Starbucks' Supply Chain Menu

Vendor	Product	Function
Retek Information Systems Inc. (subsidiary of HNC Software Inc.)	SkuPlan	Forecasting
Manugistics Inc.	Materials planning, deployment, constrained production planning Distribution planning, Manufacturing planning	Supply chain planning
Numetrix Laboratories Ltd.	Schedule X	Finite capacity scheduling
Oracle Corp.	GEMMS	Production activity control
Industri-Matematik International Corp.	System ESS	Order processing
TBD*	TBD*	Data warehouse for sales and operations
TBD*	TBD*	Purchasing
TBD*	TBD*	Warehousing/distribution
TBD*	TBD*	Transportation planning

* TBD = To be determined.

Although the project is taking longer than anticipated, Duffy hammers home the point that "we deliver something every six to nine months. We have an overall vision that has been sliced into phases."

So far, Starbucks has purchased five of the applications outlined in its nine-piece plan. Software from Manugistics and Numetrix has been in place for about a year. Retek's SkuPlan went live in September, and Oracle Corp.'s GEMMS (Global Enterprise Manufacturing Management System) was launched in October. IMI's order processing software is scheduled to be in place by the spring, while applications for transportation planning, purchasing, and warehousing/distribution are set to be purchased and installed between 1998 and 1999. The final piece will be a data warehouse for sales and operations planning—a project that Starbucks plans to do itself.

Best-of-Breed Challenges

Counter to what Starbucks is doing, most users today typically take a hybrid approach to automating their supply chains, says Ann Grackin, a partner in charge of the supply chain practice for Benchmarking Partners Inc., of Cambridge, Massachusetts. Most users purchase an ERP system as a "vine," then buy the "best fruit" in supply chain management software to hang onto it, she says.

Given that customers are demanding a bit of both worlds, ERP vendors have purchased, partnered, or made their products work with the top supply chain management software packages. For example, Oracle bought Datalogix last year for GEMMS, the company's client/server process manufacturing software. It also partnered in February with supply chain software vendors Manugistics and Industri-Matematik International Corp. to create Oracle CPG, an enterprisewide solution for the consumer packaged-goods industry.

While Starbucks' Duffy insists that an ERP package wasn't an option when Starbucks made its decision, he admits that the best-of-breed approach is the primary culprit for the extended supply chain overhaul. "We were able to deliver key functionality faster, but the overall length of the project is longer," he says.

In contrast, Green Mountain Coffee Roasters Inc., a $47-million specialty coffee roaster in Waterbury, Vermont, went with PeopleSoft Inc. to revamp its supply chain management system and expects the entire project to be finished in less than two years. (See related case, "ERP brews instant success.")

One of the reasons the best-of-breed method takes longer is that companies spend more time selecting and integrating packages. "Vendor management is a lot of work," says Duffy. "When you get into a partnership with each niche player, you have to establish a good, solid working relationship. That doesn't happen overnight."

As Starbucks works through its implementation—which it is doing by itself with a little help from consultants—the company faces a series of challenges typical of best-of-breed projects. One is retaining talent. If a project stretches into five years, "it can become a demotivating process," AMR's Bermudez says. "And when you have a hotshot company like Starbucks that's working with top-end applications like IMI, people become prime recruiting targets."

Duffy says he doesn't expect much poaching because Starbucks has a distinctive culture that is promoted by CEO Howard Schultz. "People are committed and driven to be a part of a fun time in our history," he says. "I think that alone is a key factor to keeping turnover low."

If headhunters weren't enough of a headache, companies pursuing best-of-breed projects face the migraine-inducing process of juggling new versions of each of their applications. It can be a political nightmare because certain departments may need a new version of an application, while those that don't could resent having to go through the upgrade process, says Benchmarking's Grackin.

The best-of-breed method also creates extra work. You have to constantly build "bridges" between applications, says Jim Prevo, CIO of Green Mountain. "Doing that once is one thing, but when you're faced with revisions as the best-of-breed applications evolve, you have to make sure your bridges hold together," he says. "For example, if you have an order management application from Vendor A and a warehouse management application from Vendor B, you have to make sure the interface to Vendor B holds up after a revision to Vendor A."

That could pose problems for Starbucks. "In pockets of the company, they will have superior performance, with, say, Manugistics," Grackin says. "But where they might fall down is keeping different business functions communicating with each other seamlessly."

Duffy concedes that "the challenge is managing integration and staying current on versions." But he says: "We have enough bright people, and we're confident that we'll find an effective solution."

The Upside

The best-of-breed approach does have some advantages, according to Grackin, who specifically cites flexibility. But Starbucks might do well to look into making Oracle its framework and plugging in select best-of-breed applications, since it is already using some of the components of Oracle CPG, she says. "It really depends on how far along they are. Either it's too late or they should run to the telephone," she says.

In fact, Starbucks is showing interest in CPG and is keeping a close eye on how Oracle develops it.

For now, Duffy says Starbucks is happy with its best-of-breed approach. The company has seen reductions in its overall inventory, inventory obsolescence, overtime hours and emergency orders, as well as in other areas, he says. Duffy declines to give specific numbers, but says that his department is still committed to a 40 percent return on investment. "I fully expect to be able to go back to our chief financial officer and say, 'These are what these dollars bought you,'" he says.

Evidence that the best-of-breed approach is working, Duffy says, is the fact that top management is watching the process closely and has not called him on the carpet even though the project is taking longer than expected. "If they weren't seeing improvement, we'd be seeing second-guessing today," he says. "But this company is twice the size it was two years ago and we're delivering. We've met or exceeded expectations to date."

CASE: ERP BREWS INSTANT SUCCESS

Green Mountain Coffee Roasters Inc. won't be catching up to Starbucks Corp. anytime soon. But that doesn't mean the small coffee roaster doesn't have the same double cappuccino-size supply chain problems as its larger competitor.

Source: Lawrence Aragon, *PC Week*, November 10, 1997. Copied with permission.

The main difference is that the $47-million Green Mountain went with an ERP (enterprise resource planning) system and is on track to finish the project in less than two years. Meanwhile, $700-million Starbucks opted for a best-of-breed approach that's taking it about two years longer than expected to implement.

Starbucks' approach is not necessarily wrong. But for smaller companies, an ERP solution may be just the ticket to solve supply chain woes without getting into the timely—and costly—process of cobbling together best-of-breed projects.

No More Homegrown

Green Mountain had been using a homegrown system that integrated its financial, manufacturing, and distribution systems. It worked well for about 10 years, but "as we started growing, we hit the wall on scalability," says Jim Prevo, CIO of Green Mountain, in Waterbury, Vermont. "For example, when we tried to bring on our four regional operation centers, we couldn't perform transactions outside the Waterbury area without locking up the database."

Green Mountain couldn't dally. In addition to about a dozen retail stores, 5,000 wholesale outlets depend on the roaster for their coffee, as well as a mail-order catalog and business partners such as the Delta Shuttle and Amtrak.

Prevo figured he and his skilled crew of programmers could write a new application, but they found tools lacking for building a three-tier client/server system. They pulled the plug on the project after four months.

The next decision was relatively simple: Find a suitable ERP system. Prevo didn't even entertain the thought of buying best-of-breed applications and integrating them because he had seen the high maintenance associated with his own homegrown application. "What happens is you have a lot of redundant maintenance of tables, or you have to build bridges to feed changes back and forth between systems," he says.

To choose an ERP vendor, Prevo and his team put together a software selection document outlining their functional requirements and a demonstration script. They followed that with invitations to top ERP vendors to make a one-day pitch and a two-day demo. The short list included SAP AG, Baan Co., and QAD Inc. It wasn't until Prevo went to an American Production Inventory Control Society conference in October 1996 that he gave serious consideration to PeopleSoft Inc.

After less than three months of evaluations, Green Mountain chose Enterprise Solutions from dark horse PeopleSoft. Prevo was impressed by PeopleSoft's track record for quality products, its flexibility, and its tool set.

Green Mountain purchased 17 modules of the Enterprise Solutions in late January, and by early June it went live with seven of them: general ledger, accounts payable, purchasing, production management, bill of materials and routing, cost management, and inventory management. Prevo expects the entire project to be completed within the two-year projection or possibly six months earlier.

Green Mountain has not yet seen a return on its $2 million investment, but Prevo expects the system to start paying for itself soon after it's fully installed.

One of the reasons the implementation has been speedy, according to Prevo, is because Green Mountain hired some PeopleSoft contractors and an integrator, Strategic Information Group, of San Jose, California. "Because we had a rapid deployment schedule, we knew that we'd need rapid knowledge transfer, and it takes way too long to send people to training classes and develop that purely internally," Prevo says.

Green Mountain is running Enterprise Solutions on an Oracle Corp. database sitting on a Windows NT server running atop a Compaq Computer Corp. ProLiant 5000 equipped with two 200MHz Pentium Pro processors, 640MB of RAM and 28GB of storage on a RAID 5 stack. "In general, the performance is adequate," Prevo says. He expects to see some improvements with the recent release of PeopleSoft 7 and the follow-on, PeopleSoft 7.5.

Prevo hopes to see further improvements as PeopleSoft continues to integrate planning software from Red Pepper Inc., a best-of-breed vendor PeopleSoft acquired last year. If all goes as planned, PeopleSoft will keep Green Mountain brewing for a while to come.

By the end of this chapter, you should be able to answer the following questions:

- What are the goals of software installations like the ones described at Starbucks and Green Mountain?
- Why have Starbucks and Green Mountain chosen such different approaches to the same problem?
- What is the relationship between ERP software and decision-support software used in the installations?
- How will current trends in the information technology area affect the companies' ERP implementations?

10.1 Introduction

Information technology (IT) is an important enabler of effective supply chain management. Much of the current interest in supply chain management is motivated by the possibilities that are introduced by the abundance of data and the savings inherent in sophisticated analysis of these data. The innovative opportunities coming to the fore with electronic commerce (e-commerce), especially through the Internet, have also increased the interest in IT.

Supply chain management spans the entire enterprise and beyond, encompassing suppliers on one end, and customers on the other. Therefore, our discussion of IT for supply chains will include both systems which are internal to an individual company as well as external systems, which facilitate information transfer *between* various companies and individuals.

In addition, supply chain management typically spans many functional areas within a company and is affected by the way the various groups communicate and interact. Thus, in this chapter we will also discuss topics that relate to company IT infrastructure, supply chain applications, and intercompany communications.

For many firms, IT provides a competitive advantage. Though this has been true for some time in service industries such as banks, it is also becoming more relevant for firms such as large retailers, airlines, and manufacturers. Prominent examples include Wal-Mart with its satellite-connected Information Technology, American Airlines with its innovative Sabre reservation system, and Federal Express with its superb tracking system.

Indeed, as we have observed in Chapters 3 and 4, when applying supply chain strategies that reduce cost and lead times and increase service level, the timeliness and availability of relevant information is critical. In addition, an increasing number of companies are providing value-added IT-based services to their customers as a way of differentiating themselves in the marketplace, and developing strong long-term relationships with their customers. Of course, once these kinds of services are offered by even one company within an industry, they can very quickly become a basic requirement for all others.

In many cases, current IT that supports the various components in the supply chain process is diverse and disconnected. It has typically evolved throughout the years based on various local and companywide requirements that were rarely integrated. This issue must be addressed if a company is to position itself to manage its supply chain effectively.

Various strategies are utilized by companies to overcome these problems and create systems that can use the multitude of data in the system effectively. In this chapter, we will explain how these systems are typically implemented in the supply chain management process, how different systems relate to each other, and how the systems and relationships are evolving.

As we will discuss in more detail in the next chapter, information flow between suppliers, manufacturers, and customers is critical for effective supply chain management. This entails information flow between different companies, a relatively new concept that is already widely practiced to varying degrees (e.g., e-mail, EDI, extranets). We will also discuss how developing standards for communications and user interfaces, particularly through the use of the Internet, are facilitating fairly inexpensive, simple-to-implement solutions to problems which previously would have required massive investments of time and money.

The implementation of advanced IT solutions typically requires changes in organizational structure, as well as in employee job descriptions and behavior. Although these issues are not the focus of this chapter, they need to be kept in mind; for a discussion of these issues, see [102].

Specifically, in this chapter we will discuss the following questions:

- What are the goals of IT from the perspective of supply chain management?
- What IT components are needed to achieve the goals of supply chain management?
- What are the supply chain component systems and how should they be approached?

- What are the trends in IT and how do they affect supply chain management?
- What are the stages in the development of enterprise IT?

10.2 Goals of Supply Chain Information Technology

In this section, we consider some of the ultimate goals of IT as it relates to the supply chain. Some companies and industries are currently far from achieving these goals, while others are well on their way to accomplishing many of them.

To utilize information, we need to collect it, access it, and analyze it. Supply chain management system goals in these areas are:

- Collect information on each product from production to delivery or purchase point, and provide complete visibility for all parties involved.
- Access any data in the system from a *single-point-of-contact*.
- Analyze, plan activities, and make trade-offs based on information from the entire supply chain.

The primary goal of IT in the supply chain is to link the point of production seamlessly with the point of delivery or purchase. The idea is to have an information trail that follows the product's physical trail. This allows planning, tracking, and estimating lead times based on real data. Any party that has an interest in the whereabouts of the product should be able to have access to this information. As we can see in Figure 10.1, information and products flow from the supplier to the manufacturer, internally through the manufacturer's distribution system, and then on to the retailers.

Evidently, the retailer needs to know the status of its orders and the suppliers need to be able to anticipate an incoming order from the

FIGURE 10.1

Flow of information and goods in the supply chain

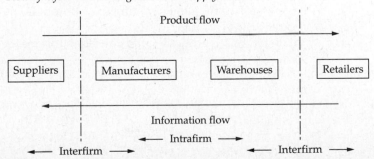

manufacturer. This entails access to data that reside in other companies' information systems as well as across functions and geographic locations inside a company. Furthermore, the participants need to see data in their own terms; that is, if suppliers of cotton are looking at the demand for Q-Tips, they need it translated into pounds of cotton consumed. Therefore, translation tables, such as bills of material, are required throughout the system.

The availability of information regarding the status of products and material is the basis on which intelligent supply chain decisions can be made. Furthermore, it is not sufficient to simply track products across the supply chain; there is also a need to alert diverse systems to the implications of this movement. If there is a delay in a delivery that will affect production schedules, the appropriate systems need to be notified so they can make the proper adjustments by either delaying the schedules or seeking alternative sources. This goal requires standardization of product identification (e.g., bar coding) across companies and industries. For example, Federal Express has implemented a tracking system that provides ongoing information on the whereabouts of any package handled by the company, and makes this information available internally as well as to customers.

Related to this is the important goal of having a single-point-of-contact for all of the available information, so that information provided to a customer or required internally can be accessed in one stop and be the same, regardless of the mode of inquiry used (e.g., phone, fax, Internet, kiosk) or who is making the inquiry. This requirement is complicated by the fact that to satisfy a customer's query, information may be required that resides in various locations within one company and, in some cases, across several companies.

In many companies, information systems tend to be islands, depending on their functions within the company. Customer service will work with one system, accounting with another, and the manufacturing and distribution systems are completely separate (see Figure 10.2). Occasionally there may be a transfer of some crucial information that needs to be accessed across systems, but if the transfer is not done in real time, then the systems never have exactly the same data. The customer service representative receiving an order may not be able to provide shipping status information, and the plant may not be able to inquire about current outstanding orders. Ideally, everyone who needs to use certain data should have access to the same real-time data through any interface device (see Figure 10.3).

Banking applications are advanced in this respect—you can access the same account information the bank tellers use, from almost anywhere over the telephone, computer, or ATM machine. Nevertheless, these systems may still be weak at linking all of a customer's accounts into a single point of inquiry—for example, accessing mortgage information at the same time as a bank account.

FIGURE 10.2

Current information systems

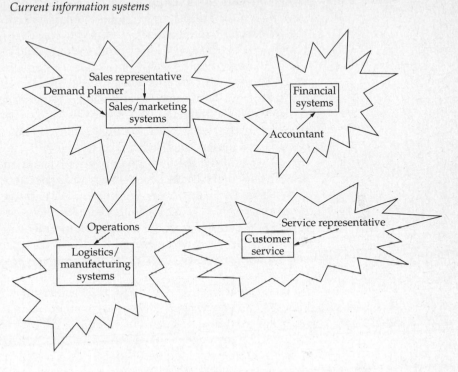

FIGURE 10.3

New generation of information systems

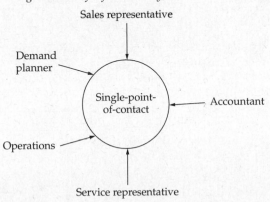

The third goal is related to analyzing the data, especially in a way that takes into account the global supply chain picture. In addition, the information system must be utilized to find the most efficient ways to produce, assemble, warehouse, and distribute products—in other words, the best way to operate the supply chain. As we have seen, this entails various levels of decision making—from operational decisions involving the way to fulfill a customer order, to tactical decisions related to which warehouse to stock with what product, or what the production plan for the next three months should be, to strategic decisions about where to locate the warehouse, and what products to develop and produce. To facilitate this, systems need to be flexible enough to accommodate changes in supply chain strategies. To achieve this kind of flexibility, systems need to be highly configurable, and new standards need to be developed. We will discuss these issues in detail below.

As we will see, the three goals of supply chain management do not all have to be achieved at the same time, and are not necessarily dependent on each other. They can be targeted in parallel, with the order of importance depending on the industry, company size, internal priorities, and return on investment considerations. For instance, a bank could not survive without single-point-of-contact capability, a delivery company without a sophisticated tracking system, and a high-tech manufacturer without a production planning system.

To achieve these goals and to master the decisions and problems that arise when considering how to address them, it is helpful to understand many of the major issues in IT development, particularly as they relate to supply chain management. As we see in Figure 10.4, the following are the means toward achieving these goals.

FIGURE 10.4

Goals and means of supply chain management

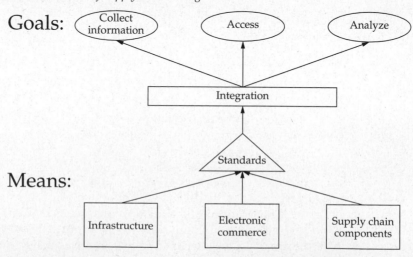

- *Standardization*—IT standards are what allow systems to work together. They drive the cost and sometimes the feasibility of implementation.
- *IT infrastructure*—the IT infrastructure, whether internal or external to a company, is a basic component of system capabilities. Without the communications and database capabilities, some of the goals outlined cannot be achieved.
- *Electronic commerce*—the emerging field of EC is attracting much attention. What does it mean and what level is achievable and cost-effective?
- *Supply chain system components*—the various systems that are involved directly in supply chain planning. These are typically systems that combine short-term and long-term DSS elements.
- *Integration-related issues*—How should priorities be set in order to achieve the goals discussed above? What kind of investments should be made in the short term and in the long term?

10.3   Standardization

Although it is hard to predict in an ever-changing field such as information technology (IT), some trends and practices are evident. Primary among these is the push toward IT standards. Although some issues are specific to logistics and supply chain management, most developments are occurring across industries and application areas. The IT field is evolving to a high level of standardization for the following reasons:

- *Market forces*—corporate users need standards in order to reduce the cost of system maintenance.
- *Interconnectivity*—the need to connect different systems and work across networks has pushed the development of standards.
- *Reduced costs in software* purchase, development, and deployment.
- *Economies of scale*—standards reduce the price of system components, development, integration, and maintenance.

The trend toward standardization has produced PC software and hardware that is increasingly affordable and easy to use. The Internet has allowed almost everyone to benefit from an international network of computers for commercial and private use. In the process, standards for communication and display of data that can be used on any network have been introduced.

More important, standards have enabled forms of communication, which heretofore existed internally in many companies, to work across companies and to become as ubiquitous as phone calls. The most obvious example is electronic mail (e-mail), but this is by no means the only form. File and information transfer between individuals and companies is greatly simplified by the Internet, which can encompass anything from online order forms to documents and electronic payments. The Internet has enabled and accelerated many existing IT trends, and has created new ones.[1]

Electronic data interchange (EDI) is a good example of the advantages of standardization. The common transaction formats that comprise the basis for EDI allow companies to electronically transmit data that used to be handled in paper forms and by data entry. We will expand on the topic of EDI in Section 10.5, "Electronic Commerce."

A major detriment to supply chain IT standardization is a lack of common terminology. This is being addressed by an IT industry consortium called RosettaNet (see *www.rosettanet.com*). It has developed an electronic technical dictionary that provides a common business language about supply chain processes.

The expensive process of software development is one of the last frontiers in the standardization battle, but it is also benefiting from standards.

Open interfaces allow external access to the functionality of systems. Windows Application Programming Interface (API), for example, enables the creation of applications for Microsoft's Windows operating systems. Similarly, open interfaces for database applications, such as the Open Database Communication (ODBC) standard, allow developers to easily write applications that can access data stored in various database management systems. File standards such as dBase, Excel, Lotus, Word, and Word-Perfect, and reporting standards such as the Structured Query Language (SQL) can also be considered part of the trend toward open standards. Not long ago, companies would use file formats that were proprietary and could not be used with other systems (e.g., until recently, in Geographic Information Systems).

Open interfaces are also being defined for enterprisewide systems. The Open Application Group (OAG) is developing a set of application interface definitions to facilitate the sharing of data between business software modules (e.g., manufacturing management modules, human resources modules, and accounting modules) of different software vendors. The ultimate goal is to enable different modules and systems to interact at a higher level than file exchanges. This is one of the missing pieces that will allow high-level process sharing (see Section 10.5).

Many companies are in the process of implementing *enterprise resource planning (ERP)* systems, which create an enterprisewide transaction backbone and integrate manufacturing, financial, and other systems. Although there is no standard *across* ERP systems, the introduction of any one of these systems provides a standard to which the implementing company must conform. Major ERP vendors are developing interfaces that will al-

---

[1]See James Martin's "Cybercorp" [75] for an interesting discussion of these issues.

low other applications to access data stored within the ERP system. This will make their products easier to interact with, and will encourage developers to produce compatible software. Of course, every one of the major ERP vendors would like its platform to become the standard. One way to achieve this is to demonstrate the availability of many third-party applications that do not require complex integration for the ERP vendor's platform.

For all the obvious advantages of standardization, we should mention a few of its drawbacks. Problems surround the cost of creating a standard and the power of those who hold standards, especially if these standards are proprietary. Proprietary standards are problematic because they may not necessarily be the "best" standards, just those belonging to the most powerful company. This happened in the video battle of Beta versus VHS and in the PC operating system battle of IBM versus Apple versus Microsoft. Proprietary standards limit competition and therefore selection and advances in products beyond what the company owning the standard is willing to offer. Even Open Group standards, such as EDI, may sometimes limit growth because of (1) the difficulty of making changes acceptable to a committee and (2) producing timely improvements. There are even security issues that arise when everyone is running the same software—if someone finds a problem or takes advantage of a security flaw, he or she can access or bring down every system of the same type.

10.4 Information Technology Infrastructure

The information technology (IT) infrastructure is a critical factor in the success or failure of any system implementation. The infrastructure forms the base for data collection, transactions, system access, and communications.

IT infrastructure typically consists of the following components:

- Interface/presentation devices
- Communications
- Databases
- System architecture

10.4.1 Interface Devices

Personal computers, voice mail, terminals, Internet devices, bar-code scanners, and personal digital assistants (PDAs) are some of the interface devices most commonly utilized. A key trend in IT is toward uniform access capability anytime and anywhere, and interface devices clearly play a major role in this area. In addition, graphical display of data and information is becoming prevalent. There are two standards competing with, or complementing, each other that are shaping this trend. One is the so-called

Wintel standard—the Windows interface on Intel-based computers—and the other is the web browser and Java standards. While the two standards now exist alongside each other, it is not clear which one will prevail in the long run or whether some new devices (e.g., PalmPilot) will create yet another standard.

This trend toward enhanced graphics will continue with more seamless integration of systems such as Geographic Information Technology and three-dimensional graphics, which may soon be a standard part of spreadsheets and other analytical processing systems. Automatic data capture interfaces, such as bar-code readers and radio frequency (RF) tags, are also becoming standardized and commonly used. In supply chain management, product tracking is critical, and there are a few standard ways to do this. The first is to include bar-coded information on all products and record the transactions. Equipment that records point-of-sale information is extremely important, especially if these data are accessible by the supplier, as in vendor managed systems. In addition, RF tags on items can be used to locate the items, particularly in large warehouses. Wireless communication devices and GPS capabilities enable tracking of tagged cargo while in shipment.

10.4.2   Communications

Interface devices are connected to either an internal system (e.g., LAN, mainframe, intranet) or an external network—either a private company network (e.g., IBM's Advantis) or to the Internet. Sometimes direct links to another company's system are utilized for efficiency and security. There are two major trends in communications: the first is wireless communications, which is replacing the hard-wired phone links most of us use today; the second is the single-point-of-contact for communications. In other words, we may eventually use a personal phone where we can be called wherever we are and also pick up other forms of communication such as e-mail.

Advanced communications capabilities enable many applications, including:

Electronic mail (e-mail) can be internal to a company or external. The Internet provides for simple cross-company interaction that was unavailable until recently because every company had its own internal system. E-mail allows for communication across time zones and transfer of information and data.

Electronic data interchange (EDI), electronic transactions between trading partners such as shipping, is enabled through some communications link between two parties and a standard protocol. Most current applications involve private secure lines, but EDI is migrating to the Internet, which provides a simple way to allow for communication between companies or with customers, yet requires a relatively small investment.

Groupware enables group work by allowing shared access to information and specialized software so that knowledge can be shared throughout the company. There are also applications that allow sharing of electronic whiteboards and work on joint documents.

Location tracking is the ability to locate a truck or cargo at any time during distribution. This technology requires a combination of the Global Positioning System (GPS) and wireless communications.

10.4.3   Databases

Data need to be organized in some form of a database, including transaction information, status information, general information (prices and so on), forms, and group work. Organizing these data is an extremely challenging activity and may require specialized databases, depending on the type of data. Some types of databases are described below:

Legacy databases. These systems are usually built around a hierarchical or network database. These databases can store large amounts of data, typically transaction data, and perform extensive processing. They typically have an online and batch component. Programs are written in COBOL (*common business oriented language*) and reporting tools are somewhat cumbersome to use.

Relational databases. These databases allow the storage of related data in such a way that standardized reporting and querying of related data is facilitated. For example, Structured Query Language (SQL) is designed only for relational databases. Relational databases may be centralized on a mainframe computer or server, or they may be distributed across a network of personal or minicomputers.

Object databases. These can hold not only numeric and character data but more sophisticated objects such as pictures or graphic structures. Object databases are used to store different kinds of information in a way that relates them to database operations. These databases already exist for some applications but are not yet standard and are costly to maintain. Storing graphic and other nonstandard data requires considerably more storage space than text/numeric data and is more complicated to manipulate.

Data warehouses. These databases combine data from other system databases to allow query by sophisticated analysis tools. Data warehouses usually involve enterprise data and hold extremely large amounts of data.

Datamarts. Datamarts are smaller versions of data warehouses, and usually store a smaller set of data and are more departmental in scope.

Groupware databases. These are specialized databases designed to accommodate group functions, such as keeping track of updates, allowing multiple user access, and so forth. Group databases are also important in the age of telecommuting and virtual companies, where keeping everyone up-to-date with relevant data is impossible without a shared database.

10.4.4   System Architecture

System architecture is the way the components—databases, interface devices, and communications—are configured. We have added this topic to the section on information technology infrastructure because the design of the communications networks and choice of systems depends on the implementation of these systems.

Legacy systems evolved as departmental solutions using mainframe or minicomputers which were accessed through "dumb" terminals (see Figure 10.5). The PC was initially used apart from a company's main systems for special applications such as word processing or spreadsheets. Eventually the PCs in an office were connected by means of local area networks (LANs) so users could share files, e-mail, and other applications. These networks were then extended across companies with wide area networks (WANs) that connected the dispersed offices of a company. Finally, new systems were developed to take advantage of the PC's computing power and friendly graphic interface. In these systems, the PC is typically called the "client" and the main processor is the "server." *Client/server computing* is a form of distributed processing whereby some processes are performed centrally for many users while others are performed locally on a user's PC.

Most current system design involves client/server structure (see Figure 10.6), although the sophistication and price of the client, the number and type of servers, and various other design parameters vary greatly from system to system. Examples of servers include database servers that allow Structured Query Language (SQL) requests from users, transaction-

FIGURE 10.5

Legacy system architecture

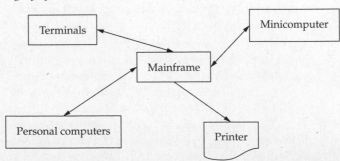

FIGURE 10.6

Client/server system architecture

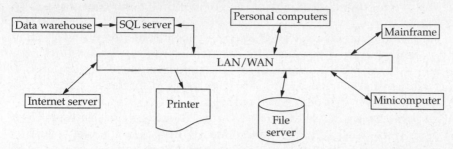

processing monitors, directory/security servers, and communications servers. See [42] for an introduction to client/server concepts.

The Internet is a form of client/server where the local PC browser processes the HTML (hyper text markup language) pages and Java applets (i.e., small applications) that are retrieved from servers—in this case from all over the world. The client/server model is now evolving towards a webcentric model where the client is a web browser connected to a web server. The computer industry, coming back in full circle to the dumb terminal, has arrived at the concept of the network PC or thin client, which is a web browser that can download any necessary applications and will be cheaper to support than a PC. The problem seems to be that this concept will shift more computing onto the server and more traffic onto the network, so it is not clear how this idea will be implemented in practice.

The power of the client/server concept is in distributing functions among specialist servers that perform them efficiently; it is also easier to add new modules and functions. The disadvantage is the added complexity of navigating between these servers and making sure that data are processed correctly and updated across the network. The implementation of client/server systems has also given impetus to the trend toward standardization because each server needs to be able to communicate tasks and processes across the network. This feature is called *interoperability*, which means two systems are capable of interacting in a sophisticated way that is a built-in feature of their design. Many interfaces between systems are created through file transfers or other temporary schemes as we will see in the Aerostructures case in Chapter 11, because the systems use different file formats and communications schemes. When standards for intrasystem operation become common, tools will be available to perform these interfaces and provide full data and process sharing interface mechanisms.

The applications that reside between the server and the client are collectively called *middleware*, literally the slash (/) in the term *client/server*. These are typically tools that facilitate communication between different system architectures, communication protocols, hardware architectures, and so forth. The parts of an application that reside on a server, client, or as middleware depend on specific implementations. This is part of the three-tiered architecture model now favored by many client/server designers.

Middleware can be important in the implementation of supply chain systems since, in many cases, the information for the planning tool exists in a number of locations and forms across the company. The appropriate middleware can be used to collect the data and format it in a way that can be used by various planning tools. That is how many supply chain applications are currently implemented. For instance, a telecommunications company may have billing information for the company's various services, such as long distance and wireless, stored on different systems. A customer service representative might have to search multiple locations for a customer's bills, if the customer purchased more than one service. Middleware would perform the function of looking through the databases and combining the information.

The system architecture of the future will need to support a high level of flexibility and frequent changes in the way supply chains and other business processes are run. This requires highly configurable systems that can be easily transformed in response to changed processes and business requirements. Furthermore, systems need to be highly interoperable so they can interact as well as support internal and external communications.

10.5   Electronic Commerce

Electronic commerce (e-commerce) refers to the replacement of physical processes with electronic ones and the creation of new models for collaboration with customers and suppliers. E-commerce applies to the interaction between different companies as well as to the interaction of individuals with companies. Examples are purchasing over the Internet, EDI, mail tracking, and e-mail.

E-commerce has been in existence for many years, using private networks for corporations (e.g., WANs) and public ones at universities and government agencies. The acceptance of Internet standards has accelerated the adoption of e-commerce, especially between individual buyers and companies but also between companies. The initial use of the Internet, showcasing marketing material, has expanded to allow user status and tracking inquiries as well as product purchases. Companies allow users to access their databases to troubleshoot product problems, thus saving the company money in support calls.

Companies use Internet standards internally—*intranets*—as well as externally—*extranets*. The difference between Internets, intranets, and extranets is explained mostly by who is allowed access to the system. Intranets allow companies to implement internal applications without having to develop custom interfaces and avoid incompatible types of hardware and special dial-in procedures. Internet applications typically allow unlimited access, but extranets allow limited access by restricted partners and customers from outside the company to certain applications and data.

The advantages of e-commerce are numerous:

- Companies and publishers have a global presence and the customer has global choices and easy access to information.
- Companies can improve competitiveness and quality of service by allowing access to their services any place, any time. Companies also have the ability to monitor customers' choices and requests electronically.
- Companies can analyze the interest in various products based on the number of hits and requests for information.
- Companies can collect detailed information about clients' preferences, which enables mass customization and personalized products. An example is the purchase of PCs over the web, where the buyer specifies the final configuration.
- Supply chain response times are shortened. The biggest impact is on products that can be delivered directly on the web, such as forms of publishing and software distribution.
- The roles of the intermediary and sometimes the traditional retailer or service provider are reduced or eliminated entirely in a process called *disintermediation*. This process reduces costs and adds alternative purchasing options.
- Substantial cost savings and substantial price reductions related to the reduction of transaction costs can be realized. Companies that provide purchasing and support through the web can save significant personnel costs.
- E-commerce allows the creation of virtual companies that distribute only through the web, thus reducing costs. Amazon.com and other net vendors can afford to sell for a lower price because they do not need to maintain retail stores and, in many cases, warehouse space.
- The playing field is leveled for small companies which lack significant resources to invest in infrastructure and marketing.

Example 10.5.1 | Dell Computer Corporation is the first company to move the direct-sell model to the Internet. Its web site allows customers to configure a PC system with the desired features, order, and track the order status. Specifically, Dell's order-tracking feature allows customers to follow their purchases in real time from order to delivery. Customers can also register to be notified by e-mail as soon as their order is shipped. In addition, Dell has created secure private sites for its corporate and public-sector customers. Such premier pages provide one-stop access to service and support information customized to the customer's products, flexible reporting tools, manufacturing status for systems, and listings of approved configurations. Another feature of the web site is the Internet service feature, which provides customers with online access to much of the same technical reference materials used by Dell telephone support personnel. Dell expects the enhanced services to prove more convenient for home PC users, and to provide businesses with another tool to help lower the total cost related to PC service and support. Dell Computer's new self-diagnostic tools shown on the Internet include more than 100 symptom-specific troubleshooting modules that walk customers interactively through common system problems.

There are some difficulties associated with electronic commerce, most importantly security issues associated with the transfer of private and financial information over public communications lines and the ability of unauthorized users to access servers and other computers connected to the Internet. Other issues include the slow development of the required infrastructure and cheap, easy-to-use devices to make e-commerce more accessible.

10.5.1 Electronic Commerce Levels

There are various levels of e-commerce depending on the sophistication of the transaction and the level of data interchange. Table 10.2 illustrates the four levels of e-commerce based on the type of exchange and data and process sharing.

We proceed to describe the various levels in more detail and provide additional information about each example.

Level 1—One-way communication. This level has only one-way communication—the other party does not need to respond, as in the case of e-mail file transfer or web browsing, or at least does not need to respond in real time. The browser or file data is usually for general use, through hypertext links, and cannot be accessed on the basis of any input data. This form of e-commerce has been around for more than 10 years, when Gopher and similar systems provided the

TABLE 10.2   Summary of Electronic Commerce Levels

Level Number	Description	Example
1	One-way communication	E-mail, FTP, browsing
2	Database access	Inquiries, forms, purchases, tracking
3	Data exchange	EDI, clearinghouse
4	Sharing processes	CPFR, business communities, VCI

browsing options before *World Wide Web* standards, developed at CERN,[2] became widely used.

Level 2—Database access. At this level the user of e-commerce is accessing a database for personal or tailored information by entering data through data-entry forms. In addition, the user can make personalized requests and orders, such as status inquiries and purchases over the Internet. The database access level also includes searches in company knowledge bases for obscure error messages and problem reports as well as use of vendor catalogs. Individual purchases can be made on the Internet using credit cards. This has raised some security issues, but it is no less safe than making a store purchase with a credit card. Business purchasing is typically more complex because there are restrictions concerning who can order and what configurations are acceptable. For that reason, Dell Computer, in the example above, created custom pages for businesses.

A more advanced application at this level is the creation of Internet sites that match buyers and sellers. These include electronic stock markets such as E*TRADE (www.etrade.com), transportation exchanges such as the National Transportation Exchange (www.nte.net) and auction and trading sites such as ebay (www.ebay.com).

These sites enable individuals and companies to either cut out the intermediary (in stock transactions), utilize available capacity more efficiently (as in the transportation exchange), or enlarge the market for commodities that are difficult to trade in a small market.

Level 3—Data exchange. This level applies mainly to business-to-business transactions and requires computers on both ends to exchange information typically using *electronic data interchange (EDI)*. EDI is a set of standards for different transactions between trading partners which has been set by the American National Standards Institute (ANSI) and by the International Standard Organization (ISO) in its Electronic Data Interchange for Administration, Commerce and Transport (EDIFACT) standard. Data exchange allows trading partners to ship electronic transactions instead of paper when performing purchasing, shipping, and other transactions. The time and money involved in implementing an EDI system implies that EDI becomes more economical as the number of trading partners with access to the system increases. In recent years communication costs have been going down thanks to Internet EDI applications; these developments increase the cost effectiveness of EDI. See [48].

---

[2]Conseil Européen pour la Recherche Nucleaire (the European Laboratory for Nuclear Research) in Geneva, Switzerland.

Another form of data exchange is the automated clearinghouse, which enables an industry to consolidate data and allow inquiries by all parties. This approach is used in the banking industry for instance, to process student loans, and in healthcare to process claims.

The data exchange level of application will soon be applied more extensively to individual transactions; for instance, filing International Revenue Service forms and receiving confirmation and corrections electronically. There are still many security issues, such as the use of digital signatures and authentication schemes, that need to be agreed upon to make this effective. Another development that will allow individuals to participate at this level is the application of electronic cash. This will allow charging small amounts for various electronic transactions and will make it easier to use networks for low-cost transactions such as phone calls, reading an article, software use, and many others. Finally, because of the global reach of the Internet, issues such as taxes, tariffs, and exchange rates need to be resolved before the full global potential is unleashed.

Level 4—Sharing processes. The final level, still primarily in development, will occur when different entities share processes, not just data, electronically. For this to happen, standards need to be agreed upon for applications to communicate with each other and for companies to share processes.

A few industry consortiums are working on e-commerce process-sharing standards. Microsoft is trying to impact the supply chain e-commerce market with the value chain initiative (VCI) whose goal is "to deliver a dynamic data stream that connects trading partners around the world from the largest to the smallest with real-time data." The idea behind VCI is to enable the single-point-of-contact concept through the Internet as well as to evolve the enterprise system of the future; see [80]. A VCI-enabled application has standard software embedded that allows it to interact with other such applications. The application will communicate between them to complete an interaction. For instance, if a user places an order the warehouse management system will be notified by the order system. This system will trigger a fleet-management system that will take care of allocating transportation or, in case the order cannot be filled, issue instructions to a manufacturing system on how to build the product. The manufacturing system will allocate the resources for the job, locate the raw material, and so on.

Another attempt at standardizing processes for e-commerce is the Supply Chain Operations Reference Model (SCOR) developed by the Supply Chain Council, which is an attempt by several software vendors to define standard processes for supply chain management [107]. The focus of SCOR is to provide a language that can describe, measure, and compare supply chain operations. The language is meant to provide a common reference for communications between intracompany functions and intercompany supply chain partners.

A more concrete example is Collaborative Planning, Forecasting and Replenishment (CPFR), a web-based standard that enhances vendor managed inventory and continuous replenishment by incorporating joint forecasting. With CPFR, parties exchange electronically a series of written comments and supporting data which includes past sales trends, scheduled promotions, and forecasts. This allows the participants to coordinate joint forecasts by concentrating on differences in forecast numbers. The parties try to find the cause of the differences and come up with joint and improved figures. As we emphasized in Chapter 4, the results of multiple forecasts can be very expensive over the supply chain. Indeed, sharing forecasts with distributors and other parties will result in a significant decrease in inventory levels since it tends to reduce the bullwhip effect (see Chapter 4). To do this, systems need to be designed to allow data verification and ensure standard practices of coordination.

The first application of CPFR was completed by American Software Inc. The Atlanta software company completed its first installation of CPFR-based software at Heineken USA. The system has reduced the delivery lag from eight weeks to four weeks. See [18] for more information. Wal-Mart and Warner-Lambert are using Listerine to test CPFR concepts and software, which they developed with Benchmarking Consultants and major supply chain and ERP software companies. An important element of this process is the ability to collaborate and allow for some risk sharing between the partners in the process. In this case, Wal-Mart agreed to extend its order cycle from nine days to six weeks, which is the manufacturing time for Listerine [57].

Reaching this level of e-commerce is the next challenge and, considering that EDI evolved over the last 15 years and this level involves only transactions, this is not a simple effort. Many interactions between companies involve a variety of sophisticated processes and data structures that will not be easy to translate into universal standards. Furthermore, the amount of information and communication capabilities required to provide real-time data is extensive and the current Internet infrastructure is unable to handle huge amounts of data well.

10.6 Supply Chain Management System Components

In the previous section, we covered developments in information technology without focusing on supply chain management. The infrastructure issues, which ERP systems attempt to resolve, bring all business functions together and make an enterprise more efficient. They do not, however, help answer the fundamental questions of what should be made, where, when, and for whom. This is the role played by human planners with the aid of various analytical tools such as decision-support systems (DSSs), as discussed in Chapter 11.

As we saw in Section 10.2 where we analyze the goals of IT, the first two goals, collecting and accessing data, require enterprise as well as interenterprise systems, which are not yet available in many industries. The third supply chain management goal of data analysis may be the most achievable and the one with the highest and most immediate *return on investment (ROI)*. Such systems are much faster to implement and cause little disruption across the company—few people need to be trained to use a dedicated DSS.

The DSS that various companies and industries employ depends, among other things, on manufacturing characteristics, demand fluctuation, transportation costs, and inventory costs. For instance, if a company's predominant cost is transportation, the first DSS implementation would be a fleet routing system or a network design project. On the other hand, if there is a high variability in demand and complex manufacturing processes requiring setups when switching between products, a demand planning system may be the most urgent.

As we will discuss in more detail in Chapter 11, these systems typically support the strategic, tactical, and operational levels. Some of the supply chain components predominantly support one level while others may support more than one, depending on how they are defined and utilized. The case study example at the beginning of this chapter illustrates a typical application of supply chain optimization.

We will describe some sample supply chain DSSs in applications in Chapter 11. These include:

- Logistics network design
- Inventory deployment
- Sales and marketing region assignments
- Distribution management
- Inventory management
- Fleet planning
- Production location assignment/facility deployment
- Lead time quotation
- Production scheduling
- Workforce scheduling

We will add three more examples here:

1. Demand planning. As we have seen, demand forecasts play an important role in many supply chain decisions. Typically, forecasts are made using various statistical techniques which take into account the history of the item, stability of demand, completeness of information about promotion expectations, and other product-specific data. The demand planning process is particularly difficult because so many of the departments involved in the supply chain play a role in determining forecasts, as well as in determining final sales. For instance, the sales group typically builds business plans to hit geographic quotas. Similarly, marketing works to meet specific market-share goals, and operations coordinates the production and distribution of products. Each of these areas utilizes different levels of detail and relies on unique pockets of information to make decisions.

These kinds of decisions all affect final sales, but they are often made independently of each other. Clearly, to achieve feasible demand plans effectively, each area must have real-time visibility into both the information driving these decisions and the actual decisions made by the other groups. Indeed, to truly make decisions that benefit the entire supply chain, a collaborative process in which each group contributes information to the ultimate demand plan is needed. In this way, the separate business functions can agree to a demand plan that reflects all of the available information and meets all of their needs.

In addition, demand planning can go beyond a single enterprise to a collaborative effort among different companies. CPFR and other e-commerce initiatives for sharing information will be a major factor in how these systems are developed.

2. Capacity or supply planning. Determining how much to produce and where to produce it is similarly critical. Capacity and supply planning is a complex task, requiring strategic, tactical, and operational planning. Although these planning levels focus on distinct time horizons—days, weeks, months, and years—each decision level depends on all the others, making effective plans difficult to produce. In addition, as in the case of demand planning, information is required from many different supply chain locations to make effective supply plans, and these plans in turn affect many different parts of the supply chain.

There are many different types of systems for capacity or supply planning, depending on the particular planning level or levels being considered. At one extreme, strategic decision support systems use long-term forecasts to make capacity expansion decisions. At the other extreme, operational online systems allow service representatives to estimate delivery time and manufacturing locations for their potential customers.

3. Procurement/purchasing. Procurement is a significant activity for many companies. It is not uncommon to find firms who spend more than half of the value of their shipments on purchased materials and equipment. Effective procurement management involves managing supplier databases, sending bid requests, and tracking information about order and shipment status. Also, in many cases (e.g., the automotive industry) the purchasing company needs to redesign its inbound logistics network. For instance, the purchasing company may need to locate cross-docking facilities so that consolidation from different suppliers is possible.

10.7 Integrating Supply Chain Information Technology

How do all the elements of information technology (IT) come together? Supply chain management is extremely complex, so there is no simple or cheap solution to the issues we have raised. Many companies do not think it is cost effective to introduce certain IT innovations because they are not sure there will be a significant return on investment. Trucking companies do not purchase sophisticated tracking systems because few clients would actually want to receive such detailed information. Warehouse managers do not invest in radio frequency (RF) technology because it is too expensive.

The important element is to analyze what each component can contribute to the enterprise and then plan the investment according to the specific needs of the company and the demands of the industry. It should be noted, however, that the holistic solution is frequently greater than the arithmetic sum of the parts—that is, installation of a warehouse control system and a transportation management system can do wonders for customer service performance.

Companies need to decide whether to automate their internal processes or agree to some industry conventions—which usually happens when investing in an enterprise resource planning (ERP) system from one of the major vendors (e.g., SAP, PeopleSoft, Oracle, Baan). As more and more companies share information such as order entry, requisition, bills of material, and so forth and take part in joint planning, one can expect standard approaches to sharing this information will lower everyone's cost of doing business. In supply chain management, no single standard has yet emerged, as each ERP vendor continues to set its own de facto standards.

Due to the lack of standards, it is quite likely that in the near future middleware in the form of message brokers whose objective is to mediate between different systems and different standards will be developed. Eventually supply chain standards will become part of the basic systems that constitute the infrastructure.

In the following sections, we will review some important aspects of supply chain system integration. First, we review Manugistics' Supply Chain Compass Model for evaluating a company's stage of development in IT for supply chain management. As a major vendor of supply chain systems, Manugistics helps clients pinpoint their current state of development as well as point them toward goals for the future. In the next section, we discuss implementation of ERP and DSS. What are the priorities in implementation? What should a company invest in first? Finally, we will review the "best-of-breed" compared with the single-vendor package dilemma and illustrate the dilemma with an example of two companies engaged in the same business that are taking divergent routes.

10.7.1 Stages of Development

Manugistics has developed a five-stage business model called the Supply Chain Compass Model to evaluate a company's development in the application of IT for supply chain management [73]. Note that, at any point in time, different parts of a company's business may be in different stages of development. The model defines the goals, structure, and IT of an organization in each stage. Thus, the Compass model is useful in evaluating current development and identifying where other companies are heading and future competitive advantages lie.

Stage I: The Fundamentals—Focus on quality. The driving goal of the organization in this stage is to produce dependable, consistent, quality products at the lowest possible cost. To accomplish this goal, companies in Stage I typically focus on automating existing functions and tasks. Departments function as independent units, and systems reflect this structure. Planning tools are chiefly spreadsheets.

Stage II: Cross-Functional Teams—Serve our customers. Companies moving toward Stage II concentrate on serving the customer, specifically focusing on order fulfillment. Companies in this stage are beginning to consolidate their supply chains in some areas, such as combining distribution and transportation into logistics, and manufacturing and purchasing into operations, with the ultimate goal of better meeting customer demand. Information technology in this stage is typically packages that provide functionality in certain areas. Planning is performed using point tools.

Stage III: Integrated Enterprise—Drive business efficiency. Companies in Stage III focus mostly on efficiency. The driving goal is to be highly customer responsive, leveraging the ability to quickly deliver high-quality products and services at the lowest total delivered cost. Stage III companies become highly responsive by investing in operational flexibility and integrating their internal supply chains, from the acquisition of raw materials to the delivery of products to the customer. IT is integrated at this point with enterprise supply chain planning systems.

Stage IV: Extended Supply Chain—Create market value. As companies move into Stage IV, creating market value becomes increasingly important. Companies implement a strategy of increasing market share by achieving "preferred partner" status with key customers. The driving goal is profitable growth, which they accomplish by providing customer-tailored products, services, and value-added information which differentiate them from competitors. IT is interoperable internally and with certain customers. Point-of-sale information is employed in planning through data warehouse and DSS tools.

Stage V: Supply Chain Communities—Be a market leader. This stage focuses on market leadership. Companies consolidate into true supply chain communities whose members share common goals and objectives across and among enterprises, using forward-looking technologies such as the Internet. Stage V companies are able to streamline their business transactions with their partners to maximize growth and profit. IT is fully networked with partners outside the company, which allows synchronized supply chain planning.

Table 10.3 presents a summary and a comparison of the different stages of IT development.

As we have mentioned before, the ultimate goal is to standardize processes across an industry so companies can collaborate and cut costs. The ability to interact with as many business partners as possible in e-commerce projects makes this goal attractive. However, many companies report that the success of an application such as EDI requires that a large number of suppliers and customers utilize the system, a "critical mass"; otherwise the expected cost savings cannot be achieved and the system is not cost effective.

TABLE 10.3   Manugistics Supply Chain Compass

Stage	Name	Goal	Organization	IT	Planning
I	Fundamentals	Quality and cost	Independent departments	Automated—MRP and other applications	Spreadsheets
II	Cross-functional teams	Customer service	Consolidated operations	Packaged-MRPII	Point tools
III	Integrated enterprise	Profitable customer responsiveness	Integrated internal supply chain	Integrated ERP	Enterprise supply chain planning
IV	Extended supply chain	Profitable growth	Integrated external supply chains	Interoperable customer management systems	POS supply chain planning
V	Supply chain communities	Market leadership	Rapidly reconfigurable	Networked, networkcentric commerce	Synchronized supply chain planning

10.7.2   Implementation of ERP and DSS

Implementation of a system that supports supply chain integration involves infrastructure and decision-support systems. The ERP systems that are typically part of the infrastructure are different in many ways from the supply chain DSS. Table 10.4 compares enterprise resource planning (ERP) and decision-support systems based on various implementation issues.

The question is what strategy should a company use in deciding what system to implement and when. IT goals (see Section 10.2) suggest that a company first must install an ERP system so that the data will be accessible and complete. Only then can it start analysis of its entire supply chain processes using various DSS tools. This may be the ideal, but in reality the data needed to achieve supply chain efficiencies already exist—maybe not in a single easy-to-access database, but it is worth the time it takes to assemble the database compared to the cost of waiting for installation of the ERP system.

These issues are illustrated in Table 10.4. The length of an ERP implementation compared to a typical DSS is much longer. The value of an ERP system to the enterprise involves the first two goals—visibility and single-point-of-contact—and, while these can imply improved operations, DSSs impact the ability to perform strategic and tactical planning as well. This means that DSS projects have a much better ROI. Finally, DSS installations are typically cheaper and easier to implement and they affect a smaller number of highly trained users compared with those of an ERP system, which has a large number of users who require less extensive training.

Indeed, as we saw in the Starbucks case study at the beginning of this chapter, companies do not necessarily wait for an ERP implementation to proceed with DSS projects. Indeed, in many cases it makes sense to first implement DSS projects which provide a more immediate and observable return. Of course, companies examine their financial and human resources

TABLE 10.4   ERP and DSS for Supply Chain Management

Implementation Issue	ERP	DSS
Length	18–48 months	6–12 months
Value	Operational	Strategic, tactical, operational
ROI	2–5 year payback	1–year payback
Users	All end users	Small group
Training	Simple	Complex

TABLE 10.5   Priorities when Implementing DSS

Industry	DSS
Soft drink distributor	Network and transportation
Computer manufacturer	Demand and manufacturing
Consumer products	Demand and distribution
Apparel	Demand and capacity and distribution

before they decide on the order and number of projects they will tackle at a time.

The type of DSS implemented depends on the industry and the potential impact on the business. Table 10.5 includes some examples from various industries. In the soft drink industry, where distribution is a major cost factor, priorities are different than those of a computer manufacturer which has a complex manufacturing process with many different products and whose distribution cost is only a fraction of product cost. Thus, in the latter case, the manufacturer can utilize expensive shipping solutions.

10.7.3   "Best-of-Breed" versus Single Vendor ERP Solutions

Supply chain IT solutions consist of many pieces that need to be assembled in order to achieve a competitive edge. They include infrastructure (ERP) and various systems to support decision making (DSS). Two extreme approaches can be taken: The first is to purchase the ERP and supply chain DSS as a total solution from one vendor; the second is to build a "best-of-breed" solution which purchases the best-fit solution in each category from a different vendor, thus producing a system that better fits each function in the company. While the best-of-breed solution is more complex and takes longer to implement, it may be an investment that provides greater long-term flexibility and better solutions to the company's problems. Of course, the long period of implementation can also cause the solution to be less useful at the end and cause difficulty maintaining IT staff and enthusiasm for the project. Many companies choose an interim approach which has a dominant ERP provider; the functionality that cannot be provided by the vendor, or does not suit the company, is provided through best-of-breed or in-house systems. Finally, there are companies, (e.g., Wal-Mart) that still prefer in-house, proprietary software development [17]. This probably makes sense for extremely large companies with expert IT departments and systems that already serve the company well. Table 10.6 summarizes the pros and cons of these approaches:

TABLE 10.6 **"Best of Breed" versus Single-Vendor and Proprietary**

Implementation Issue	Best of Breed	Single Vendor	Proprietary
Length	2–4 years	12–24 months	Not known
Cost	Higher	Lower	Depends on expertise
Flexibility	Higher	Lower	Highest
Complexity	Higher	Lower	Highest
Quality of solution	Higher	Lower	Not sure
Fit to enterprise	Higher	Lower	Highest
Staff training	Longer	Shorter	Shortest

In the introductory case study to this chapter, we introduced two coffee producers who chose completely different routes to implement their systems. Starbucks is implementing "best-of-breed" enterprise resource planning and decision-support systems while Green Mountain Coffee is implementing a one-vendor ERP solution. Note how the points mentioned in Table 10.6 come to play in the implementation experiences of the two companies.

SUMMARY

What does all this mean to the logistics manager? How are the goals identified in the first section achievable? How will the three major goals below be achieved?

- Information availability on each product from production to delivery point.
- Single-point-of-contact.
- Decision making based on total supply chain information.

The major trends in information technology, as we have seen throughout this chapter, will make it possible to achieve the first two goals.

Standardization of processes, communications, data, and interfaces will bring about cheaper and easier methods to implement the basic infrastructure. IT infrastructure will become more accessible to companies of any size and will work across companies in an almost seamless way. This will allow access to IT and integration of the systems at every level of the supply chain—therefore, there will be more information and tracking of products at each level. Products will be tagged and tracked through the supply chain and will be as easy to locate as a Federal Express package.

Data display and access in various forms will become integrated in systems and will not require any specialized knowledge. This will make system interfaces more intuitive and relevant to the task at hand.

The various systems will interact in a way that blurs the current boundaries. Systems purchased as "best of breed" by different people at various levels in the organization will become better integrated and use common interfaces. There will be a proliferation of applications that can plug into a company's enterprise system to provide specialized functionality. The third goal will be achieved through development of decision-support systems and intelligent agents who are more sophisticated, rely on real data, and are interoperable—they will be the instruments of competitive advantage.

Finally, electronic commerce will change the way we work, interact, and do business. E-commerce will provide an interface to businesses and government that allows meaningful product data and comparison, and transactions that follow through with error checking and correction capability. It will enable access to data that exist in government, educational, and private databases and the ability to modify or correct these data. Businesses will be able to expand their intercompany transactions into more sophisticated applications that can perform some basic processes and pass the information on to other applications. In a process as complicated as supply chain management, systems that not only perform their own function but also alert others in the system will be especially beneficial to fulfill the three goals we have outlined.

CHAPTER 11

Decision-Support Systems for Supply Chain Management

CASE: SUPPLY CHAIN MANAGEMENT SMOOTHS PRODUCTION FLOW

As a manufacturer of wings and wing components for commercial and military aircraft, the Aerostructures Corp.'s build-to-order machine shops used to run into a lot of turbulence trying to move components through its fabrication processes.

Thanks to its recent use of Rhythm—a supply-chain management system from i2 Technologies, Inc. in Irving, Texas—Aerostructures has leveled out its work flow and has knocked $500,000 off its inventory costs.

In the past, when the Nashville-based company accepted a large order to build 50 "stringers," the stringers might get fitted for material one day and then sit idle for a few days before being heat-treated and contoured in a stringer oven. Stringers are pieces of contoured metal used to connect the top of a wing with a support structure and are up to 50 feet long.

The old setup wasted time. The stringer ovens and other manufacturing equipment often weren't being used efficiently because Aerostructures couldn't schedule any smaller jobs around lapses in production. The company's antiquated manufacturing resource planning (MRP) system wasn't designed to pinpoint work schedules for manufacturing equipment.

And because Aerostructures' custom-made products typically move through 220 operations before they are completed, the company couldn't afford to let its unfinished products sit around for too long.

"If an order was due tomorrow, the system could recognize that, but it couldn't tell you that you could run two smaller jobs in the same amount of time," said Julie Peeler, corporate vice president of manufacturing and information systems.

Source: Thomas Hoffman, *ComputerWorld*, December 10, 1997. Copied with permission.

249

Aerostructures uses a 10-year-old MRP-II system from McCormack & Dodge called Production Inventory Optimization System (PIOS) running on an IBM S/390 MVS mainframe.

Aerostructures' legacy setup also threw its build-to-order inventory management out of whack because the MRP system was backing up the company's lead times on production runs. That made it difficult for Aerostructures to order aluminum, titanium, and other materials.

Rhythm, which has been up and running since the middle of last year, has helped Aerostructures schedule jobs more effectively. The PIOS system feeds planning information into the IBM RS/6000-based Rhythm system at night, using its Computer Associates International, Inc. CA-IDMS database as a gateway.

Rhythm then calculates how work orders should be prioritized and uploads that information back to the PIOS system before the next morning's MRP run, Peeler said.

Aerostructures has invested $650,000 in hardware, software, and support.

Aerostructures' use of Rhythm reflects just how hot these manufacturing optimization systems are right now, analysts said. "The win for a company like Aerostructures is being able to smooth out their interenterprise supply-chain operations," said Dennis Byron, an analyst at International Data Corp. in Framingham, Massachusetts.

Still, installing such a system is half the battle, said Barry Wilderman, an analyst at Meta Group, Inc., in Stamford, Connecticut. That's because systems such as Rhythm or manufacturing scheduling software from Rockville, Maryland-based Manugistics, Inc. are so complex.

Peeler agreed.

She said it took i2 most of the summer of 1996 to refine the system to meet Aerostructures' specs. "If optimization was easy, lots of people would do it," she said.

Aerostructures is midway through replacing its McCormack & Dodge MRP system with the Baan Co.'s enterprise resource planning (ERP) system.

Peeler said it isn't clear if Aerostructures will keep the i2 system, because Rhythm can be interfaced to, but not integrated with, the Baan ERP system.

By the end of this chapter, you should be able to answer the following questions:

- What are the goals of a software installation like the one described at Aerostructures?
- What type of decision support tools were selected for the system and why?
- What is the relationship between Aerostructures' systems and its Rhythm supply chain optimization software?
- How will current trends in the information technology area effect Aerostructures' decision support systems implementation?

11.1 Introduction

Many of the advances in the control and management of supply chains are driven by advancing computer technology. In Chapter 10, we considered this *information technology* and all of its many facets. In the current chapter, we focus in particular on *decision-support systems (DSS)*.

Like many complex business systems, supply chain management problems are not so rigid and well defined that they can be delegated entirely to computers. Instead, in almost every case, the flexibility, intuition, and wisdom that is a unique characteristic of humans is essential to manage the systems effectively. However, there are many aspects of these systems that can only be analyzed and understood effectively with the aid of a computer. It is exactly this type of assistance which decision-support systems are designed to provide. As the name implies, these systems do not make decisions. Instead, they assist and support the human decision maker in his or her decision-making process.

Decision-support systems range from spreadsheets, in which users perform their own analysis, to expert systems, which attempt to incorporate the knowledge of experts in various fields and suggest possible alternatives. The appropriate DSS for a particular situation depends on the nature of the problem, the planning horizon, and the type of decisions that need to be made. In addition, there is frequently a trade-off between generic tools that are not problem-specific and allow analysis of many different kinds of data, and often more expensive systems that are tailored to a specific application.

Within the various disciplines that make up supply chain management, DSSs are used to address various problems, from strategic problems such as logistics network design to tactical problems such as the assignment of products to warehouses and manufacturing facilities, all the way through to day-to-day operational problems like production scheduling, delivery mode selection, and vehicle routing. The inherent size and complexity of many of these systems make DSSs essential for effective decision making. DSS in supply chain management are often called **Advanced Planning and Scheduling** (APS) systems. These systems typically cover the following areas:

- *Demand planning*—determine accurate forecasts based on historical data, understanding of customers' buying patterns. Recently this process also involves collaboration with buyers and suppliers.
- *Supply planning*—efficient allocation of logistics resources to meet demand. This includes strategic supply chain planning, inventory planning, distribution planning, collaborative procurement & transportation planning. These systems are sometimes called **Distribution Resource Planning** systems (DRP).

- *Manufacturing planning and scheduling*—efficient allocation of manufacturing resources to meet demand. This includes the traditional Material Requirements Planning (MRP) systems which schedule and maintain priorities and order for purchased and manufactured parts. It also includes systems for quoting lead times to customers.

Typically, decision-support systems use the quantifiable information available to illustrate various possible solutions, and allow the decision maker to decide which one is most appropriate, based on other, possibly nonquantifiable, factors. Often, DSSs allow the decision maker to analyze the consequences of decisions, depending on different possible scenarios. This kind of what-if analysis can help avoid problems before they occur.

Many decision-support systems use mathematical tools to assist in the decision-making process. These tools, often from the mathematical discipline of *operations research*, were first developed to assist the armed forces with the enormous logistical challenges of World War II. Since then, improvements in these techniques, as well as ever-increasing computer power, have helped to improve these tools and make them more accessible to others.

The tools of artificial intelligence (AI) are also employed in the design of decision-support systems. *Intelligent agents* use AI to assist in decision making, especially in real-time decisions, such as determining how to supply a customer in the shortest possible time or to quote a delivery lead time as the customer waits on the phone. Following Fox, Chionglo, and Barbuceanu [39], we define an *agent* as a software process whose goal is to communicate and interact with other agents, so that decisions affecting the entire supply chain can be made on a global level. For example, the intelligent agent that assists the customer service rep in determining the appropriate lead time could interact with the intelligent agent that schedules production to help ensure that the lead time is met. Red Pepper Software's ResponseAgent is an example of such a planning and scheduling agent; it works as an intelligent assistant to planners and schedulers [113].

Expert systems also fall under the umbrella of artificial intelligence. These systems capture an expert's knowledge in a database and use it to solve problems. Expert systems rely on an extensive database of knowledge, usually expressed as a set of rules. Solving a problem involves applying the rules in the knowledge base and producing a conclusion that has the ability to explain how it was reached. Within the context of a decision-support system, this kind of expert system might suggest alternative solutions for which the human decision maker has neither the time nor expertise to recognize. Although not extensively used in logistics practice, these systems have an important role because of their capability to capture and explain expert reasoning.

As massive *data warehouses* that integrate the databases of entire firms become more popular, decision-support systems are performing analyses of these databases to assist with decision making. These DSSs employ sophisticated statistical tools to analyze data warehouse information. Recently, the tools of *data mining*, which comb through data in an attempt to find patterns and relationships in unexpected places, are proving increasingly valuable. These tools are currently used to find unexpected marketing relationships, but they could also be utilized to analyze supply chain relationships such as those existing between transportation and inventory (see Chapter 3).

11.2   Understanding Decision-Support Systems

To effectively select and use decision-support systems, it helps to understand the essential pieces of a properly configured system. The three major components of a DSS are the input databases and parameters, the analytical tools, and the presentation mechanism.

• The *input data* is a form of database with the basic information needed for decision making. This can be a PC-based database extract designed for the specific problem, a data warehouse with an accumulation of a company's transactions, or distributed databases accessed through a network. This database can also include certain parameters and rules, such as the desired service level, hard-coded restrictions, and various other constraints.

• The data analysis usually involves embedded knowledge of the problem while also allowing the user to fine-tune certain parameters. The *analytical tools* employed are operations research and artificial intelligence-based algorithms, cost calculators, simulation, flow analysis, and other embedded logic procedures. This component is the most complex, because there are few off-the-shelf solvers that can deal with the huge variety of problems that companies face.

• Various database and spreadsheet *presentation tools* can be used to display the results of DSS analysis. Often, however, the output contains too much information, such as lists and tables, which may be too difficult for the decision maker to absorb. Therefore, various *data visualization techniques* are employed to enable the user to comprehend the vast quantity of output data. For example, location, routing, and sales DSSs use geographic information systems (GISs) to display complex geographic data in problems such as site location, routing, and supply chain analysis. Similarly, scheduling systems use Gantt charts to display factory schedules, and simulations use animation to illustrate the relationships in the model.

All of these components are markedly affected by the planning horizon of the problem being considered. As we have seen, strategic decisions typically require long-term planning and may involve the aggregation of historical data and forecasting considerations, while their analysis and presentation does not need to be particularly rapid because immediate response is not an issue. In contrast, operational decisions typically involve short-term planning, require current data, and demand fast response from the DSS.

11.2.1 Input Data

As in all kinds of analyses, the data used as input to the DSS are critical to the quality of the analysis. Until fairly recently, acquiring the appropriate information was a complicated feat in itself. By and large, the information collection battle has now been won in corporate America. Extensive deployment of information technology such as ERP, bar coding, point-of-sale, and electronic commerce has provided companies with large business databases. These are now often collected into huge data warehouses or smaller data marts which, along with the appropriate tools, facilitate the analysis of the data. In addition, the proliferation of networks and network access tools means that accessing various geographically distributed databases is now feasible.

Depending on the type of analysis, a DSS may require collecting information from various parts of a company. For example, supply chain network design requires both static and dynamic information from different parts of a company. The static data include plant production rates, plant locations, warehouses, and customers as well as warehousing and transportation costs. The dynamic data involve forecasts, orders, and current deliveries. This type of information will not usually be found in one database or one department in a company.

To evaluate the quality of the data and the quality of the models built into the system, it may be possible to load the current data and models into the system to see whether these correspond to reality. For example, consider a truck routing decision-support system. Ultimately, the goal of such a system is to provide routes that enable the trucks to make deliveries and pickups efficiently at the required times. However, the model can be tested by loading the current truck routes into the system, and observing if travel times, for example, are the same as the travel times actually experienced by the truck drivers. Similarly, projected costs from the model can be compared with actual financial and accounting records. This process, typically known as *model and data validation*, is essential to ensure that the model and data are *accurate enough*. Of course, the meaning of "accurate enough" depends on the decisions being made. For more information on this issue, see Chapter 2, Section 2.3.

In addition, the decision planning horizon affects the detail of the data required. For strategic planning, it often makes sense to aggregate yearly data while recent raw daily or weekly data may be best for short-term planning. The accuracy of the solution depends on the input data—therefore, the quality of the input data will determine to some extent the tools needed for the analysis.

Example 11.2.1

A DSS is often used at the strategic level to help with logistics network design. The DSS assists in deciding on the number of warehouses required, their size, and the customer allocation to each warehouse. The DSS uses information about the distribution system to calculate the various costs related to site selection and customer allocation. The data required for this problem involve the manufacturers, warehouses, customers, and the transportation between them. Since this is a long-term planning tool, yearly demand data and costs are typically used, but sometimes the user may need to determine how to account for seasonality. In addition, for this kind of DSS to be utilized successfully, the user needs to break the products into product families and to specify inventory policies. This will allow calculations of the warehouse sizes and frequency of deliveries. Some of the required input data is summarized in Table 11.1.

TABLE 11.1   Input Data for Logistics Network Design

Component	Data
Manufacturer	Location Production capacity and cost Transportation costs to warehouses
Warehouse	Location Fixed costs Variable costs (labor, utilities) Inventory turnover Transportation costs to retailers
Retailer	Location Annual demand by product
Product	Volume Weight Holding cost

This type of data may not be readily available in the company database. Even if the data are accessible, they may not be in the required format, particularly if the DSS involves geographic display and analysis. As one might expect, collecting, tabulating, and verifying the data can take considerable time.

11.2.2   Analytical Tools

Another DSS issue that needs to be established is the measures to evaluate the various solutions. Reducing total cost may be a goal, but in some cases improving customer service level may be more pertinent. DSS interfaces usually allow setting these parameters and indicating the balance required by the user.

Once data have been collected, they must be analyzed and presented. Depending on the DSS and the particular decision being made, there are many different ways to analyze the data. It is important for the decision makers to *understand* how the DSS analyzes the data in order to assess the validity and accuracy of the decision-support system's recommendations. Of course, depending on the analysis, statistics can tell many different stories; see [105] for an interesting discussion of these issues. It is up to the decision maker to determine which analysis is most appropriate.

In Section 11.3, we discuss different decisions related to supply chain management and the tools that a DSS typically uses to analyze the appropriate data. Here, we examine common DSS analysis tools and techniques in general.

Queries. Often vast quantities of data make manual analysis difficult. Decisions are often facilitated by simply allowing decision makers to ask specific questions about the data, such as "How many clients do we service in California?" and "How many clients purchased over $3,000 of a certain product by state?"

Statistical analysis. Sometimes asking questions is not enough. In this case, statistical techniques can sometimes be used to determine trends and patterns in the data. For example, statistical data like the average inventory in a warehouse, the average number of stops and length of a route, and the variability of customer demand, can often be useful to decision makers.

Data mining. Recently, as corporate databases have become larger and more all-encompassing, new tools have been developed to look for "hidden" patterns, trends, and relationships in the data. Data mining, for example, produced the marketing gem that men purchase beer and diapers on Friday afternoon.

Online analytical processing (OLAP) tools. Online analytical processing tools provide an intuitive way to view corporate data, typically stored in data warehouses. OLAP tools aggregate data along common business dimensions and let users navigate through the hierarchies and dimensions by drilling down, up, or across levels. OLAP tools also provide sophisticated statistical tools to analyze these data and tools to present them. Mostly they are generic tools—more sophisticated than spreadsheets and easier to use than database tools—for the analysis of large amounts of data.

Calculators. Simple decision-support tools can facilitate specialized calculations such as accounting costs. In many cases, more than simple calculations may not be warranted, especially if the changes are predictable and easy to evaluate. This may be the case for forecasting or inventory management, for some product types, while others may need more sophisticated tools.

Simulation. All business processes have random components. Sales may take one value or another. A machine may or may not fail. Often these random, or stochastic, elements of a problem make analyzing it very difficult. In these cases, *simulation* is frequently an effective tool to help in decision making. In simulation, a model of the process is created on a computer. Each of the random elements of the model (e.g., sales, failures) is specified with a probability distribution. When the model is "run," the computer simulates carrying out the process. Each time a random event occurs, the computer uses the specified probability distribution to randomly "decide" what happens.

Consider, for example, a simulation model of a production line. As the computer runs the model, a series of decisions is made. How long does a job take on machine 1? On machine 2? Does machine 3 break while job 4 is being processed on it? As the model runs, statistical data (e.g., utilization rates, completion times) are collected and analyzed. Since this is a random model, each time the model is run, the results may be different. Statistical techniques are used to determine the model's average outcome and the variability of this outcome. Also, by varying input parameters, different models and decisions can be compared. For example, different distribution systems can be compared, utilizing the same simulated customer demand. Simulation is often a useful tool to understand very complex systems which are difficult to analyze analytically.

Artificial intelligence. As we discussed in Section 11.1, artificial intelligence tools may be employed in the analysis of DSS input data. These may be databases of rules collected from experts that can be applied to specific problems, or online intelligent agents. The former systems are often used to solve technical problems, such as troubleshooting a computer failure or a complex chemical procedure, while the latter are more appropriate for managing different components in the supply chain. Indeed, a number of DSSs for supply chain management can be viewed as using intelligent agents to plan and execute different activities in the supply chain. These systems are characterized by the following interrelated issues [39]:

- The activities allocated to each intelligent agent (i.e., software processor).

- The level and nature of interactions between the different agents.
- The level of knowledge embedded within each agent.

For instance, a real-time supply chain planning tool involves the following components: intelligent agents that are located at each facility and collect information and enable planning and scheduling for the facility. In this case, facilities include manufacturing plants and distribution centers. Each agent interacts with other agents so that they can balance excess capacity at different plants, find missing parts, or coordinate production and distribution. A central planning agent communicates with agents that are located at each facility to collect status information and relate central planning decisions. The type and level of decisions made by the agents—as opposed to human operators—and the frequency and level of communications between agents depend on the specific implementation.

Mathematical models and algorithms. As we discussed in Section 11.1, mathematical tools, often from the discipline of operations research, can be applied to the data to determine potential solutions to problems. For example, these tools may generate the best set of locations for new warehouses, an efficient route for a truck to take, or an effective inventory policy for a retail store. These algorithms fall into two categories:

- *Exact algorithms.* Given a particular problem, these algorithms will find a solution that is mathematically the "best possible solution." In general, these kinds of algorithms may take a long time to run, especially if a problem is complex. In many cases, it is impossible to find the optimal, or very best, solution. In other cases, it may be possible but not worth the effort. This happens because the input data to these algorithms are often approximated or aggregated, so *exact solutions to approximate problems may be worth no more than approximate solutions to approximated problems.*
- *Heuristics.* These are algorithms that provide good, but not necessarily optimal, solutions to problems. Heuristics typically run much faster than optimal algorithms. Most DSSs that use mathematical algorithms employ heuristics. A good heuristic will rapidly give a solution that is very close to the optimal solution. Heuristic design often involves a trade-off between the quality of a solution and speed. It is often useful if in addition to the solution, the heuristic provides an estimate of *how far the heuristic solution is from the optimal solution.*

See Chapter 2 for additional discussion on exact and heuristic algorithms.

The analytical tools used in practice are typically a hybrid of many of the tools described above. Almost all decision-support systems will offer a combination of tools, and many will allow further analysis using generic tools such as spreadsheets. Note that some of the tools listed above may be embedded in generic tools (e.g., spreadsheets).

Most DSSs employ analytical tools that have some specific embedded knowledge of the problem being solved. Since these problems are usually complex, the DSS employs its problem knowledge to find efficient solutions. These are solutions that minimize cost and satisfy service-level requirements.

There are many factors that dictate the appropriate analytical tools to use for a particular decision-support system. These include:

- The type of problem being considered.
- The required accuracy of the solution—there may be no need to find the optimal solution.
- Problem complexity—some tools may not be appropriate for very complex problems.
- The number and type of quantifiable output measures.
- The required speed of the DSS. For operational systems such as lead-time quotation and vehicle routing, speed may be essential.
- The number of objectives or goals of the decision maker. For example, a DSS for truck routing may need to find a solution with the minimum number of vehicles and the least total distance traveled.

Table 11.2 shows a number of problems and the analytical tools that are appropriate for them.

TABLE 11.2   Applications and Analytical Tools

Problem	Tools Used
Marketing	Query, statistics, data mining
Routing	Heuristics, exact algorithms
Production scheduling	Simulation, heuristics dispatch rules
Logistics network configuration	Simulation, heuristics, exact algorithms
Mode selection	Heuristics, exact algorithms

Example 11.2.2   Consider the logistics network design problem described in Example 11.2.1. For this problem, heuristic approaches and optimization-based techniques have been

developed in the past few years. The choice between heuristics and optimization depends on the complexity of the specific problem and on the various modeling issues (e.g., service level) that the user wishes to consider. For instance, optimization-based techniques may be limited in the size of problem they can handle and in the number of parameters and special cases they can consider. Finally, some solvers also combine heuristics and optimization.

11.2.3   Presentation Tools

These tools are used to display the data to the decision maker. There are a varied number of formats including:

- Reports
- Charts
- Spreadsheet tables
- Animation
- Specialized graphic formats, such as a layout of a floor plan.
- Geographic Information Systems

The reader is likely to be familiar with most of these items—reports, charts, and tables are very common. Animation is often used as a tool to present output of the simulation models described above; this helps the user verify the validity of the simulation model and understand the simulation results. Specialized graphic formats are extremely dependent on the nature of the problem being solved. For example, a facility layout DSS may present a suggested floor plan for a new facility.

In supply chain management, much of the output of a DSS is geographic in nature. For example, Logistics Network Design, Sales Territory Analysis, and Truck Routing Software all include geography-related output. In the last few years, the *geographic information system* (GIS) has become more common as the presentation vehicle of choice for many supply chain management decision-support systems. In the following paragraphs, we describe the GIS system in more detail.

Geographic Information Systems
A geographic information system (GIS) is an integrated computer mapping and spatial database management system that provides a broad array of functions for the storage, retrieval, management, analysis, and display of geographically referenced data.

Typical GIS capabilities include:

- Mapping and thematic mapping
- Database management
- Interactive data query

- Spatial data retrieval
- Geographic data manipulation
- Spatial data analysis
- Geocoding
- Geographic data import/export
- Buffering/polygon overlay

The advantage of using a GIS platform is that it combines database, query, and reporting tools in addition to geographic display and analysis. In logistics modeling, GIS has the further advantage of allowing automated distance and travel time calculations. Some limited forms of GIS are now included in spreadsheets (Excel 7.0) but are not as extensive as the full-blown packages. These systems originally existed only on high-end UNIX workstations, but there are now many excellent, relatively inexpensive systems that run on PC platforms and networks. A major issue in deploying GIS is the availability and quality of the geographic data. Excellent data, with information about the geography, street networks, and demography are available for the United States at a very low price. In other countries, however, the data may not exist or may be tightly held so that their use can be a major expense and deterrent to the effective use of GIS. Even in the United States, these data may not be perfect for every application, or they may be outdated and need to be constantly upgraded to be of any use.

Originally, GIS was extensively used in applications such as:

- Market analysis
- Census and demographic data analysis
- Real estate
- Geology
- Forestry

More recently, however, GIS has found application in areas of potentially more interest to the supply chain manager, such as:

- Network analysis—transportation, telecommunications
- Site selection
- Routing
- Supply chain management

Figure 11.1 presents a typical GIS interface for supply chain management. The screen includes information about suppliers' warehouses, customers, and the flow of material throughout the logistics network.

Not surprisingly, there are special considerations in the use of GIS for logistics modeling. Often, time must be spent *geocoding* and *estimating travel time*. Geocoding is the translation of addresses into geographic coordinates. Geocoding requires databases that can assist in the translation.

FIGURE 11.1

A typical GIS interface for supply chain management

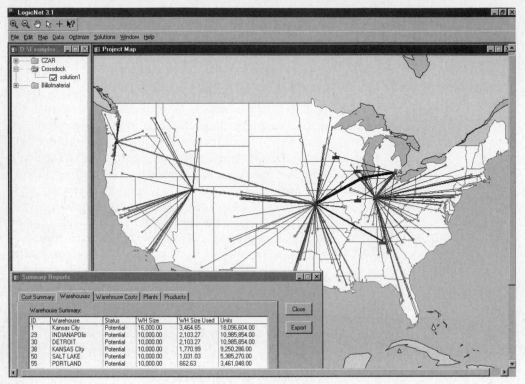

Although widely available in the United States, these data may be hard to come by in other countries. To prepare customer data for use by a DSS, this step is required and may be lengthy, depending on the quality of the address data.

In most logistics applications, it is necessary to use the distance between two locations in order to estimate travel time and transportation costs. This can be done in several ways. One is to calculate the straight-line distance between the two coordinates and multiply it by a factor that estimates the circuity of the roads between the two points. This of course is a very simplistic approach and it does not require more information than the coordinates. In this case, the DSS typically applies different factors for different zones. Another way to calculate travel distance is to use the actual road network, identify the best route, and determine the distance. This requires extensive and accurate information about the road network, including one-way streets and other details of this nature. It is also an extremely time-consuming process to calculate the network even

TABLE 11.3   Road and Estimated Distance

Item	Estimated Distance	Road Distance
Data	Cheap	Expensive
Complexity	Low	High
Accuracy	Medium	High
Speed	High	Low

for a moderate-sized problem. Table 11.3 compares the two alternatives. More on these two techniques can be found in Chapter 2.

In both types of calculations, assumptions need to be made about the speed of travel in order to estimate travel time. It is always possible to let the user enter the travel time between each pair of locations in the model, but this is usually impractical in large problems.

Although users of routing systems may demand a road network because it seems to provide a more accurate solution, experience has shown that this approach may not produce significantly better results than an approach that uses estimates of the distance. This is true even in short-haul distances and inner-city routing, such as school bus routing.

DSS may come with an embedded GIS or use a commercial GIS as a platform or server for presentation of geographic data. Geographic data available for the United States are mostly based on TIGER/Line files. The acronym TIGER stands for *Topologically Integrated Geographic Encoding and Referencing*, which is the name for the system and digital database developed at the U.S. Census Bureau to support its mapping needs for the decennial census and other bureau programs. The TIGER/Line files are extracts from the TIGER database and are available to the public. Most GIS vendors allow the user to load these files or distribute their own versions and formats based on these data. Otherwise there are no agreed-upon standards for geographic data representation apart from the leading vendors' formats, which can usually be converted from one system to another.

Integrating Algorithms and GIS

As mentioned earlier, GIS has found application in areas important to supply chain management. These include logistics network design, routing, mode selection, and so forth. The idea in all these applications is to integrate the GIS with mathematical models and algorithms. Figure 11.2 provides a schematic representation of such a system.

In such a system, geographic data are provided by the GIS while attribute data, including demand information, costs, production, and storage capacities, are downloaded from standard databases. These data are sent

FIGURE 11.2

A general framework for integrating algorithms and GIS

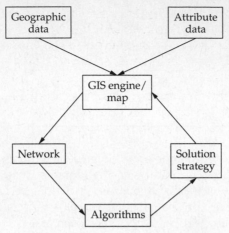

to the GIS engine that is the heart of the system. The engine constructs a *symbolic network* that represents the various relationships between the components of the supply chain. The network is then used by a collection of exact and heuristic algorithms to generate a number of solutions or strategies that minimize various objectives and satisfy the constraints in the system. These solutions can be viewed, modified, and analyzed by the user in order to implement the most appropriate one.

What are the advantages of integrating GIS and mathematical models and algorithms? The system

1. Allows the user to visualize the data and the model to verify that they truly represent the supply chain environment.
2. Provides an accurate street-level database (if needed), including one-way streets and turn difficulties.
3. Allows the user to visualize the solution and strategies generated by the system.
4. Allows for sensitivity (i.e., what-if) analysis.

11.3   Supply Chain Decision-Support Systems

As we have seen in Chapter 1, supply chain management encompasses a large variety of decisions. In the following paragraphs, we examine some of these decisions, and try to point out how DSSs can help in the decision-making process. This list is arranged roughly from strategic to operational decisions.

Demand planning. Developing accurate demand forecasts is critical for the efficiency of the entire supply chain. Therefore forecasting has become an important DSS area, and collaborative tools and standards as well as other more classical statistical tools are being developed to assist the process.

Logistics network design. We have already discussed logistics network design in previous examples. Network design involves the determination of warehouse and factory locations, and the assignment of retailers or customers to warehouses. Typical input data include candidate locations, transportation costs, aggregate demand forecasts, and so on. Heuristic or optimal algorithms are used to suggest network designs. Not all criteria can be quantified, so the decision maker must ultimately use his or her judgment.

Example 11.3.1	The mid-Atlantic region of the American Red Cross, see [52], utilized a decision-support system based on optimization models to determine the effect of a proposed relocation on blood distribution and collection. Initially, the mid-Atlantic region had three sites for blood processing, two of which collected and distributed blood, and one of which collected blood only. A new facility was being considered and several scenarios, some of which involved closing an old facility and others reallocating resources, were considered. Mathematical models were used to support this decision by determining the effects of labor and transportation costs in each of the alternatives. In the end, the new facility was not built because, by more efficiently utilizing the currently existing facilities, the mid-Atlantic region was able to meet its goals without the capital expense of building a new facility.

Example 11.3.2	In 1993 Procter & Gamble (P&G), see [52], began a program of redesigning its entire supply chain. For various reasons, P&G concluded that it could reduce the number of plants needed, which would lead to lower costs. As is typical at P&G, teams were organized along product lines to analyze the manufacturing situation. In addition, separate teams were organized to analyze the disribution center (DC) locations and suggest alternatives for assigning customers to the DCs.

Working with faculty from the University of Cincinnati, P&G engineers developed a DSS to aid the teams involved with these decisions. To help with DC location and customer assignment, mathematical techniques were used to determine a family of good solutions to the problem. To optimize product sourcing decisions, mathematical techniques were developed and combined with a geographic information system (GIS). The GIS allowed the product sourcing teams to visualize potential solutions generated by the system, which helped the teams better understand the interaction between the various cost drivers in the system.

Indeed, the insights provided by this kind of understanding often led to new and better solutions. In addition, visualizing data and solutions helped the team to see input database errors that might otherwise have gone undetected.

The entire redesign of the North American manufacturing and distribution system led to cost savings of over $250 million annually at Procter & Gamble. Although it is difficult to quantify how much of this was a direct result of the DSS, P&G internally credits the system with leading to at least 10 percent of the savings.

Inventory deployment. Even when the firm does not wish to modify its logistics network, decisions must be made about what inventory to keep in which warehouses and at what times. This is the inventory deployment decision. Here, transportation costs, demand forecasts, and inventory holding are used to determine the levels of inventory to keep in each location in each period. Once again, the DSS may use optimal or heuristic algorithms to generate suggested policies.

| Example 11.3.3 | Amoco Chemical Corporation, see [31], was confronted with a set of common inventory management challenges: |

1. Identifying appropriate inventory levels at different echelons in the supply chain.
2. Dealing with capacity constraints of capital, equipment, and people.
3. Conflicting organizational objectives between sales, production, and inventory managers. These objectives include:

- Relocate working capital to fund growth.
- Maintain or improve customer service levels.
- Improve operational efficiency.
- Push to be the best in industry.

Together with Mercer Management Consulting Inc., Amoco developed a custom DSS to address these issues. The system models Amoco's multiechelon logistics network, costs, and objectives. It uses both optimization and simulation techniques in the analysis. Optimization is used to determine inventory targets. Once inventory targets are determined, simulation is applied to test the stocking policy, associated cost, and customer service. According to Amoco, implementation of the system has provided the following benefits:

- Understanding of inventory costs, including shortage cost.
- Inefficient practices cannot be covered up with excess inventory.
- Better planning, coordination, and communication.

Sales and marketing region assignment. Sales regions need to be assigned in a way that keeps both the customers and the sales representatives happy while sales are maximized. A DSS for sales region assignment typically uses customer location and demand forecasts as input, and designs sales regions according to a series of objectives (e.g., distance traveled, sales potential) selected by the decision maker.

Distribution resource planning (DRP). These models determine the appropriate routes and inventory policies for a set of warehouses and retailers. Given warehouse and retailer locations, inventory and transportation costs, and demand forecasts for each retail outlet, these DSSs utilize analytical techniques to determine policies that will achieve high levels of customer service at minimal cost.

Material requirements planning (MRP). MRP systems use a product's bill of materials and component lead times to plan when manufacturing of a particular product should begin. Although these DSSs typically do not use sophisticated mathematical approaches, they are very popular in industry. These DSSs can serve as a good example of why the decision maker should use only the output of a DSS as a possible problem solution. Often MRP systems propose *impossible* schedules because they typically do not take production capacities into account. It is up to the decision maker to modify the plan in such a way that it becomes a feasible schedule without becoming too expensive.

Example 11.3.4 | Tanner Companies, Inc., see [12], is a manufacturer of quality women's clothing. In the early 1990s, the company had problems with poor on-time delivery rates (around 74 percent) and high levels of work in process. To address these issues, the company turned to a scheduling decision-support system. The system takes input from a database that describes in detail the material and labor requirements for each of the many hundreds of items that Tanner manufactures. One of the most time-consuming parts of the implementation involved assembling this database, because the information was not readily available.

Based on the input data as well as incoming orders, the system generates manufacturing schedules. In particular, the system generates schedules that minimize shortages and finished goods inventory within the given production and demand constraints. Since these are conflicting objectives, there may be many schedules that reduce shortages, for example, but raise the level of finished goods inventory. Thus, the system generates a set of potential nondominated schedules, or schedules in which the performance based on one objective cannot be improved except by hurting the performance based on the others. Given this set of schedules, management must ultimately decide which schedule to use. Initially prototypes used mathematical programming techniques, but ultimately heuristics had to be used because of the magnitude of the problem.

The system utilized an intuitive menu-driven interface, so training time was minimal, and user confidence was high from the beginning. By the end of the one-year period in which the system was developed, revised, and implemented, on-time deliveries increased to 90 percent and work-in-process inventory was reduced by more than $200,000. Also, the scheduler was freed from mundane and repetitive scheduling tasks, and was able to focus more on planning issues.

Inventory management. When a facility holds many different items in inventory, managing that inventory can be extremely difficult. An inventory management DSS uses transportation and holding cost information, along with lead times and projected demand, to propose inventory policies that help the decision maker achieve some combination of low cost and high customer service.

Production location assignment/facility deployment. Many manufacturers have a network of production facilities, each of which can manufacture a particular product or components of a particular product. A facility deployment DSS takes production costs, lead times, transportation costs, and demand forecasts as input, and suggests possible assignments of products or components to manufacturing facilities. These DSSs often use some combination of artificial intelligence and mathematically based techniques.

Fleet planning. Fleet planning typically involves not only the dispatching of a company's own fleet but also decisions regarding selection of a commercial carrier on certain routes. Since rate structures can often be very complex, and speed and reliability may vary from carrier to carrier, transportation *mode selection* is frequently a difficult problem. In addition, input data such as rate structures need to be frequently updated.

An important component in fleet planning is fleet routing. Here we distinguish between two systems: static and dynamic. In static systems, daily routes are typically planned in the morning and weekly routes are drawn up at the beginning of the week. These routes are not changed during the day or the week. In dynamic systems, routes are updated during the planning horizon (i.e., day or week). For example, consider telephone repair crews. Calls may come in during the day, and work can be assigned as they come in. These systems are more complex then their static counterparts, since the DSS has to try to minimize operating costs on the fly; that is, without knowing the entire set of repair locations at any time.

| Example 11.3.5 | Mobil Oil Corporation, see [8], uses a decision-support system to consolidate and dispatch shipments of lubricant products. Mobil has 10 plants and receives hun- |

dreds of orders every day. These orders are filled using either a vehicle from Mobil's dedicated fleet of trucks, or a dedicated truck from one of Mobil's suppliers.

Mobil's dispatchers had to address many issues, including the selection and dispatching of private vehicles instead of contract carriers, the consolidation of orders, and when to ship orders early to take advantage of consolidated resources.

To address these issues, Mobil collaborated with Insight, Inc., and developed the heavy-products computer-assisted dispatch (HPCAD) system. This system takes order, distance, and trucking rate information, and prepares a set of feasible work schedules. The system calculates costs for each of these schedules. Then an optimization module uses this information to determine a detailed, cost-effective dispatch plan. The DSS is designed so that the dispatcher can interact with the system in developing the dispatch plan.

Mobil's internal audits have concluded that by utilizing delivery resources more effectively, the HPCAD system saves the company over $1 million annually. The company estimates that 77 percent of dispatches generated by means of HPCAD are different than the dispatches would have been employing a completely manual system.

Example 11.3.6	CSX Transportation, see [51], one of the largest railroads in the world, developed a DSS called CARS (Computer Aided Routing and Scheduling) to explore the strategic relationship between routing and scheduling within the CSX rail system. Routing involves determining the appropriate way to move a shipment from its origin to its destination, while scheduling involves determining when the shipment should move along each link on the route. The system uses a heuristic called *simulated annealing* to determine a good route and schedule given a set of demands. The system receives demands and costs as inputs, generates schedules and routes, and displays the schedules and routes graphically along with tables and reports that illustrate the cost and performance of the routes. In this case, management uses this DSS as a strategic tool. Possible strategic decisions such as the purchase or rental of new railcars, the use of trains with different potential speeds, and the increase in the throughput rate at railyards can be considered. For each of these cases, historical demand data are entered into the system, the system calculates realistic schedules and routes and compares various reports.

The effectiveness of CARS as a tactical/operational tool was also explored. It was found that CARS schedules and routes were similar to those currently generated manually, although they did not take all of the parameters and constraints of the system into account. However, the routes were clearly sufficient for strategic analysis.

Lead time quotation. In many manufacturing operations, sales representatives commonly take orders over the phone and thus are able to immediately quote delivery lead times. In the past, sales reps often quoted long lead times to ensure that these lead times could be met. Lead time quotation DSSs allow the quotation of shorter lead times by determining exactly how long a particular order will take to deliver. This is done by taking current production schedules, manufacturing times, and delivery times into account. Typically, the sales rep still needs to use his or her judgment about the importance of an order. If a customer is not regarded as significant as certain others customers, it might be worthwhile for the sales rep to quote a later due date than the DSS suggests. This allows leeway to quote shorter lead times for future orders.

Production scheduling. Given a series of products to make, information about their production processes, and due dates for the product, production scheduling DSSs propose manufacturing sequences and schedules. A production scheduling DSS can use artificial intelligence and mathematical and simulation techniques to develop schedules. Artificial intelligence-based production schedules typically involve rules that were previously used by the

FIGURE 11.3

A typical production scheduling interface

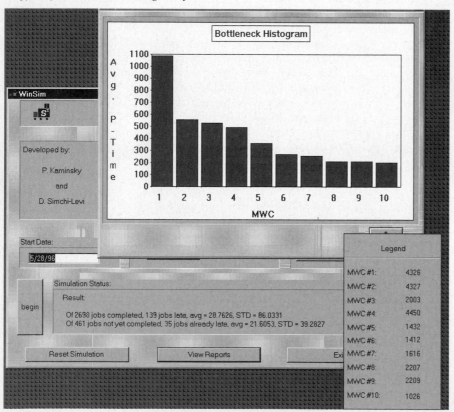

human schedulers who scheduled the particular processes in question. Optimization-based scheduling systems use algorithms to develop schedules that maximize or minimize some set of objectives. Finally, simulation-based scheduling systems typically allow the user to select a simple set of scheduling rules and "test" them in the simulation system. For example, the user might decide to test the impact of scheduling all jobs in the order of their due dates. The system would simulate the production process using this rule, and the decision maker could view the outcome. For example, the system can predict the number of late jobs or the average time late jobs are delivered after their due date. Figure 11.3 illustrates a typical production scheduling interface.

Workforce scheduling. Similarly, given a production (or service) schedule, information on labor costs, and a set of work rules (e.g., maximum working hours), a workforce scheduling DSS proposes a number of possible employee schedules to ensure that the necessary labor is available at all times and at the lowest possible cost. Often these systems have to take complicated union rules into account. The following example illustrates the use of a DSS for solving scheduling and resource allocation issues.

Example 11.3.7	Federal Express, see [19], has detailed manual processes for producing bid lines or packages of individual flights that pilots and crews bid on each month. These processes take federal flight and labor regulations and work rules, and individual preferences, into account in determining legal and desirable bid lines. In 1993 FedEx pilots were represented by a union for the first time, and this led to contract negotiations. However, FedEx needed analytical tools to determine the impact of alternative work rules that were suggested during the negotiation. To assist with this negotiation, FedEx developed an automatic bid-line generator. This decision-support system developed bid lines that met all of the work rules and enabled FedEx to perform what-if analysis to determine the impact of new work rules. The system took all of the work rules and required flights as input and, using simulated annealing, developed a set of bid lines that could be analyzed. The tool was successfully used during the initial contract negotiation and continues to be a valuable analytical tool.

For each of the systems described above, it is easy to see how several different output presentations would be appropriate. In many cases, a geographic display or chart looks good, but neither provides sufficient information. In these situations, other reports will be required to help the decision maker.

11.4 Selecting a Supply Chain DSS

For each of the supply chain problems and issues listed above, decision-support systems are available in many configurations, platforms, and price ranges. DSS platforms have evolved in the last 15 years from relatively inflexible mainframe systems, to isolated PC tools, to client/server processes; lately, there is a new breed of high-performance and extensible enterprise decision-support applications. These systems come in a wide range of pricing from PC systems costing several thousand dollars to company-wide installations costing a few million dollars, see [28].

When evaluating a particular DSS, the following issues need to be considered:

- The scope of the problem addressed by the decision maker, including the planning horizon.
- The data required by the decision-support system.
- User interface capabilities.
- Analysis requirements, including accuracy of the model, ability to quantify performance measures, desired analytical tools—that is, optimization, heuristics, simulation, financial calculations requirements, and computational speed needed.
- The system's ability to generate a variety of solutions so that the user can select the most appropriate one, typically based on issues that cannot be quantified.
- The presentation requirements, including issues such as user-friendliness, graphic interface, geographic abilities, tables, reports, and so on.
- Compatibility and integration with existing systems. This includes the ability of the database interface to accept and produce standard PC file formats such as Excel, dBase, Access, and FoxPro.
- Hardware and software system requirements, including platform requirements, flexibility to changes, user interfaces, and technical support available.
- The overall price, including the basic model, customization, and long-term upgrades. Note that support and customization are often far more expensive than the initial investment.
- Finally, consider complementary systems. Does the vendor have suites of products that make it easier to purchase from one source? For example, in some cases a routing DSS also includes load planning.

| **Example 11.4.1** | A small steel manufacturer in the Chicago area needs to review the location of its distribution centers (DCs). Some customers in the South are not receiving next-day |

service and there are extensive transportation costs. Management has asked the logistics team to come up with an analysis and plan of where to open new DCs and to close down some existing facilities.

This is a strategic issue that is required for long-term planning. The logistics team has decided to review the software packages on the market and purchase or lease the appropriate tool to assist in the analysis. One M.B.A. on the team tried to model the problem as a *linear-programming model*, but there were many factors that could not be taken into account.

The team quickly realized that annual data would be required in this analysis and, because the manufacturer has many clients, aggregating data is essential. They would prefer a stand-alone PC tool that could be operated from their desktops. They did not care about integration with other systems but wanted the database interface to accept standard PC file formats (e.g., Excel and dBase) and to provide the resulting output in standard formats.

Using various logistics magazines and the Internet, the logistics team found five or six vendors who provide these types of systems. Unfortunately, no comparison was available for the different systems—at most some anecdotal evidence from customers.

The team proceeded to collect literature and demos, and came up with the following list of items for the vendors' response.

- Database requirements.
- Geographic information system (GIS) capabilities.
- Transportation modeling requirements.
- Distribution center cost structures.
- Model assumptions and flexibility.
- Manufacturing cost structures.
- Optimization methods used.
- Reporting capabilities.
- Customization options.
- Pricing, leasing, and purchasing costs.
- Support and training.
- Company experience and references.

Finally, they reviewed and rated the different systems and decided on the vendor that seemed to have the system most appropriate for their requirements. They decided to lease the product with an option to purchase.

There is a confusing array of supply chain DSS or APS, as they are sometimes called, in the market. The terminology can vary from one supplier to another as well as the scope, quality, and price of the solution offered. Of course, it is important for users to understand their requirements as well as the value of the systems to their organization. They should also understand their internal capabilities so that they can decide whether they want to take responsibility for integrating the DSS into their information systems or purchasing supply chain DSS capabilities with their ERP system.

SUMMARY

Decision-support systems for supply chain management are a fast-growing sector of the logistics software industry. DSSs will continue evolving and adopting standard features and interfaces in order to adapt to the competitive environment and provide the flexible solutions required in today's markets, see [28]. Since the basic data that are required to make decisions are being collected, there is a strong drive to utilize this information in sophisticated ways to gain competitive advantage by improving service and cutting supply chain costs. The following are the major trends in DSS and especially supply chain DSS and advanced planning systems.

- **Integration with ERP systems.** DSS will be easier to integrate with ERP systems through standard interfaces, and in many cases there will be embedded DSS logic in ERP systems. The first example is the SAP Advanced Planner and Optimizer (APO), which is part of the Supply Chain Optimization, Planning and Execution (SCOPE) initiative. Other ERP vendors, such as PeopleSoft, are also adding DSS functionality to their systems.

- **Improved optimization.** Many DSS lack a true optimization capability, i.e., these systems either use heuristics to generate feasible strategies, not necessarily the best one, or the systems are typically limited to optimizing fairly small problems. For instance, most existing DRP and MRP systems do not optimize at all and in many cases do not take capacities into account.

- **Standards.** As we noted in Chapter 10, development of standards is an important prerequisite to reducing the complexity and cost of systems. The current market includes many DSS that are not compatible and difficult to integrate. In addition, strategic partnering forces the various partners to define standards so that they can efficiently integrate processes. For instance, CPFR is a web-based tool that allows different supply chain parties to collaborate on forecasting and planning.

APPENDIX A

Computerized Beer Game

A.1 Introduction

If you've taken an operations management course in the last 20 years, you are no doubt familiar with the Beer Game. This role-playing simulation of a simple production and distribution system has been used in countless undergraduate, graduate, and executive education courses since it was first developed at MIT in the 1960s.

The Computerized Beer Game, included with this text, is similar in many respects to the traditional Beer Game. As you will learn in the following pages, however, it has many options and features which enable you to explore a variety of simple and advanced supply chain management concepts that cannot be easily taught using the traditional game.

Windows 95, 98, or *NT* is required to operate the game. To install the software, place the included CD in your CD-ROM drive. If the installation program doesn't run automatically, select run from the **Start** menu, and then type g:\setup.exe and follow the directions on the screen (Replace g:\ with the appropriate driver letter if necessary.)

A.2 The Traditional Beer Game

For comparative purposes, we will briefly review the traditional manual Beer Game, which is typically played on a large board. Locations on the board represent four components, or stages, of the beer supply chain: the factory, the distributor, the wholesaler, and the retailer. Orders placed by each of the component managers, as well as inventory in transit and at each of the locations, are represented by markers and pennies that are placed at the appropriate locations on the board. External demand is represented by a stack of cards.

One player manages each of the supply chain components. Each week, the retail manger observes external demand (by drawing the next "demand card"), fills as much of this demand as possible, records back orders to be filled, and places an order with the wholesaler. In turn, the manager of the wholesaler observes demand from the retailer, fills as much of this demand as possible, records back orders, and places an order with the distributor. The distributor manager repeats this process, ordering from the factory. Finally, the factory manager, after observing and filling demand and back orders, begins production. Order processing and filling delays are incorporated into the game to represent order processing, transportation, and manufacturing lead times. The rules of the game require all back orders to be filled as soon as possible. At each stage of the supply chain, the manager at that stage has only local information; only the retail manager knows customer demand. The goal of the game is to minimize the total holding and back-order cost at the stage you are managing. Each week a cost of $0.50 for each unit in inventory and $1.00 for each unit of back order is accrued.

A typical game is played 25 to 50 "weeks." During the game, communication between players is limited. Inventory and back-order levels usually vary dramatically from week to week. At the end of the game, the players are asked to estimate customer demand. Except for the retail manager, who knows the demand, players often estimate wildly varying demand. After being informed that demand was constant at four units per week for the first four weeks, and then eight units per week for the remaining weeks, players are often surprised. Instinctively, they blame the other players for following inappropriate strategies.

A.2.1   The Difficulties with the Traditional Beer Game

When the Beer Game was first introduced in the 1960s, the concept of *integrated supply chain management*—as well as advanced information systems that support this concept—was not yet developed. In many cases, the supply chain was managed by different managers at each stage based on their individual intuition, experience, and objectives. Since then, however, both the theory and the practice of supply chain management have improved significantly. Unfortunately, as traditionally played the Beer Game does not necessarily reflect current supply chain practices. Perhaps more importantly, the Beer Game does not necessarily provide students with insight on how to *better manage the supply chain*.

These weaknesses of the traditional Beer Game can be attributed to several of its characteristics. Our experience with the game suggests that the students typically are so occupied with the mechanics of the game, making sure that they correctly follow the rules of the game, that they have no time to develop an effective strategy. Even if a participant uses a sophisticated strategy, he or she may tend to attribute inventory and back-order problems, as well as higher-than-expected cost, to the other participants' strategies, rather than to search for potential flaws in his or her own strategic decisions.

In addition, the demand pattern exhibited in the Beer Game does not reflect a realistic supply chain scenario. In the traditional game, demand unexpectedly doubles in the fifth week of play and remains at that level until the end of the game. In real life, it is unrealistic to expect that managers of each of the supply chain facilities would not be informed of such a huge change in demand patterns.

Finally, the traditional Beer Game doesn't demonstrate several other important supply chain management issues. For example, in many real-world supply chains, several (or all) of the stages have a single owner. Thus, the real objective is to minimize the total system cost, not individual performance. Unfortunately, in the traditional Beer Game there is no way to judge how much is lost by managing stages individually.

Many of the difficulties in managing the supply chain that are highlighted by the Beer Game can be addressed by shortening cycle times and centralizing information and decision making. Unfortunately, these approaches to solving many supply chain management problems cannot be demonstrated in the traditional Beer Game—students can learn about them only in the lecture following game play.

The Computerized Beer Game was developed precisely to address the difficulties inherent in the traditional Beer Game. In the following sections, we describe the scenario, the commands and options available, and, finally, several supply chain management concepts that we have taught successfully using the Computerized Beer Game.

A.3   The Scenario

The Beer Game (computerized and traditional) models the following scenarios. First, consider a simplified beer supply chain, consisting of a single retailer, a single wholesaler that supplies this retailer, a single distributor that supplies the wholesaler, and a single factory with unlimited raw materials that brews the beer and supplies the distributor. Each component in the supply chain has unlimited storage capacity, and there is a fixed supply lead time and order delay time between each component.

Every week, each component in the supply chain tries to meet the demand of the downstream component. Any orders that cannot be met are recorded as back orders and met as soon as possible. No orders will be ignored, and all orders must eventually be met. At each week, each component in the supply chain is charged a $1.00 shortage cost per back-ordered item. Also at each week, each component owns the inventory at that facility. In addition, the wholesaler owns inventory in transit to the retailer, the distributor owns inventory in transit to the wholesaler, and the factory owns both items being manufactured and items in transit to the distributor. Each location is charged $0.50 inventory holding cost per inventory item that it owns. Also, each supply chain member orders some amount from its upstream supplier. It takes one week for this order to arrive at the supplier. Once the order arrives, the supplier attempts to fill it with available inventory, and there is an additional two-week transportation delay before the material shipped by the supplier arrives at the customer who placed the order. Each supply chain member has no knowledge of the external demand (except, of course, the retailer), or the orders and inventory of the other members. The goal of the retailer, wholesaler, distributor, and factory, is to minimize total cost, either individually or for the system.

The Computerized Beer Game has other options which model various situations. These differing options enable the instructor to illustrate and compare concepts such as lead time reduction, global information sharing, and centralized management. For instance, consider a scenario exactly as described above, except that each supply chain member has full knowledge of the external demand, orders, and inventories of all other supply chain members. In another possible scenario, lead times are reduced from the two weeks described above to only one week.

Finally, in a centralized scenario, the game is changed as follows: The manager of the factory controls the entire supply chain and has information about all of the inventory levels throughout the supply chain, as well as the external demand. Because the system is centralized, stages other than the factory do not place orders; all inventory is moved through the system as quickly as possible. In addition, because there can be no back order at any stage except the first one, the retailer pays a $4.00 shortage cost for each back-ordered item. This enables a fair comparison between the decentralized scenario described above and the centralized scenario. Because three sets of orders are eliminated, the product moves through this supply chain three weeks faster than in the supply chain described above. These are the main scenarios modeled by the Computerized Beer Game. In the following sections, we describe specifically how to use the software to model these situations.

A.4 Playing a Round

In this section, we describe how to play a round of the Computerized Beer Game, using the default settings, to model the first scenario described above. In the next section, we describe each of the menu commands in detail, so that a variety of scenarios can also be modeled.

A.4.1   Introducing the Game

When the Computerized Beer Game software is started, the following screen appears:

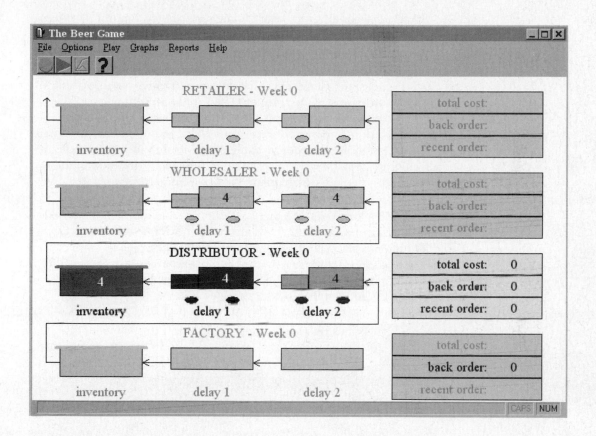

In this simulation, the player takes the role of manager of one of the components of the beer supply chain, either the retailer, the supplier, the distributor, or the factory. This will be called the *interactive* role. The computer takes the remaining roles. On the game display, the interactive role is displayed in color, and the remaining roles are displayed in gray. The information for the interactive roles is also displayed, but the information for other roles is hidden (with the exception of back orders at the supply chain member immediately upstream from the interactive supply chain member, and the two outgoing trucks). In the example screen displayed above, the distributor is the interactive role. *Downstream* means the direction of the supply chain leading to the external demand while *upstream* means the direction of the factory. In addition, we refer to components of the supply chain as *facilities*.

Order of Events. The simulation is run as a series of weeks. Within each week, first the retailer, then the wholesaler, then the distributor, and finally the factory, executes the following series of events, as the simulation proceeds upstream. For each facility:

Step 1. The contents of *Delay 2* is moved to *Delay 1*, and the contents of *Delay 1* is moved to inventory. *Delay 2* is 0 at this point.

Step 2. Orders from the immediate downstream facility (in the case of the retailer, external customers) are filled to the extent possible. Remember that an order consists of the current order and all accumulated back orders. Remaining orders (equal to current inventory minus the sum of the current orders and back orders) are backlogged, to be met as soon as possible. Except for retailers, which ship orders outside the system, the orders are filled to the *Delay 2* location of the immediate downstream facility. This is the start of the two-week delay.

Step 3. Back-order and inventory costs are calculated and added to accumulated total costs from previous periods. This incremental cost is calculated as follows: The total inventory at the facility and in transit to the next downstream facility is multiplied by the holding cost, $0.50, while the total back order is multiplied by shortage cost, $1.00.

Step 4. Orders are placed. If this is the interactive role, the user indicates the desired order amount. If this is one of the automatic roles, the computer places an order using one of several typical inventory control schemes. The schemes can be controlled by the instructor, as we will explain in the next section.

Delays and Order Filling. This sequence of events implies several things. First, once an upstream facility fills an order, there is a two-week delay before this material can be used to fill a downstream order. *Also, there is a one-week order delay. This means that if, for example, the retailer places an order for 5 units in this period, the wholesaler does not even attempt to fill the order until the next period. This period, the wholesaler attempts to fill the order from the previous period.* This can be considered a one-period order processing lag. Thus, there is a total of three weeks of delays between the time a facility places an order and when the results of that order arrive in inventory.

Recall also that there is no guarantee that an order will be met, even with that three-week lag. An upstream supplier can fill an order only if it has the necessary inventory. Otherwise it will backlog that order and attempt to fill it as soon as possible. *The exception to this is the factory. There is no limit to production capacity, so the factory's order will always be filled in its entirety after the appropriate delay.*

A.4.2   Understanding the Screen

Each facility in the supply chain is represented on the display. As an example, the *Distributor* is displayed below:

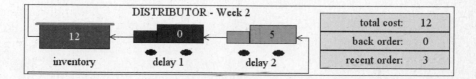

On the left of the screen, the number of items in inventory is displayed. The next two elements (from left to right) represent items in transit to inventory; that is, the numbers in the box labeled *Delay 1* represent the number of items that will arrive in inventory in one week, and similarly for *Delay 2*. The box on the right lists (1) the total inventory and shortage cost up to the current time; (2) the back order; that is, the demands which have been received at this facility, but have not been filled yet due to lack of inventory; and (3) the most recent order placed by this facility, in this example the *Distributor*, to its upstream facility, the *Factory*. Note that in this case, back order refers to orders received by the *Distributor*, but not yet met from inventory. To find out the orders placed by the *Distributor* that have been backlogged—that is, not yet met by the factory—check the back order at the *Factory*. Also, the recent order number displayed in the box represents the most recent order sent by the *Distributor* to the *Factory*. There is a one-week lag before this order arrives at the upstream supplier.

A.4.3   Playing the Game

To start the game, select **Start** from the **Play** menu, or push the start button on the toolbar. The computer will automatically play the first round for the automatic facilities downstream from the interactive facility. For example, if the *Distributor* is the interactive facility, the computer will play for the *Retailer* and the *Wholesaler*, in that order.

Once this is completed, the first round for the interactive facility is played. Steps 1 and 2 (advance inventories and fill orders, described in the section labeled "Order of Events" are completed. At this point, inventory numbers are updated on the screen, and the Order Entry dialog box appears. The screen looks as follows:

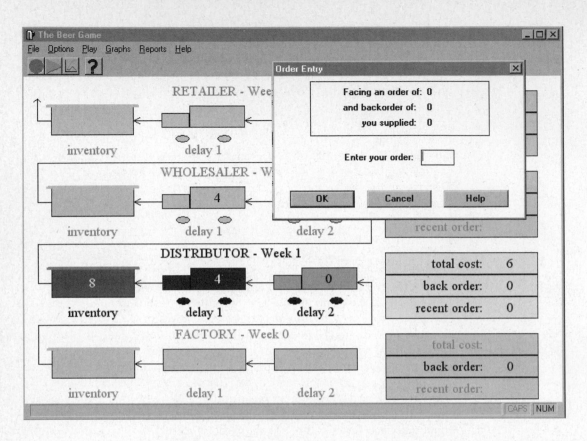

Examine this screen in detail. Recall (you can see this from the previous screen shown on page 279) that the initial inventory was 4, and both *Delay 1* and *Delay 2* contained 4 units. This holds true for each of the supply chain facilities. Now, steps 1 and 2 have been completed. As you can see from the Order Entry dialog box, there is initially no back order and no order from the *Wholesaler*. Since the starting inventory was 8 (the initial 4 plus 4 from *Delay 1*), 8 remain in inventory. *Delay 2* is now empty. In *Delay 1* at the *Wholesaler*, there are 4 units, for which the *Distributor* will pay holding costs for this period. This is the first round, so there are no previous orders from the *Distributor* to the *Factory*. Thus, the *recent order* box reads 0. However, if this was a later round and an order was placed by the *Distributor* to the *Factory* during the previous round, it would appear in the *recent order* box.

The Order Entry dialog box indicates how much total back order and order was faced by the interactive player in this round, (again, in our example, the *Distributor*), and how much of it was successfully filled. Note that the back-order box on the right side of the screen indicates the current level of back order, while the dialog box shows the level of back order at the beginning of this round, before the player (in this case, the *Distributor*) attempted to fill downstream orders (in this case, from the *Wholesaler*).

At this point, enter a demand amount. This can be zero or any other integer. Remember that you are trying to balance inventory holding costs and shortage costs. Also, by looking at the back-order box at your supplier (in this example, the *Factory*), you can see how much back order your upstream supplier already has to fill; that is, how many items you have ordered in prior rounds but have not yet received. Once an amount has been entered, the remaining upstream supply chain members play automatically, and the screen is updated. If you enter an order of 3 for the *Distributor*, the remainder of Week 1 play is carried out, and the *Distributor* portion of the screen looks like:

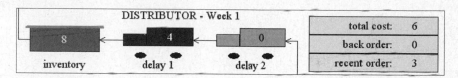

The order of 3 is reflected in the recent order box, and the total cost box reflects holding cost charged due to the 8 units in inventory and the 4 units in *Delay 1* at the *Wholesaler*.

To play the next round, select **Next round** from the **Play** menu, or push the *next round button* on the toolbar. The computer again automatically plays the next round for the automatic facility downstream from the interactive facility. Once again, the order entry dialog appears. At this point, both *Delay 1* and *Delay 2* show an inventory of 0, since the inventory was advanced and *Delay 2* was initially 0. Recall that after you input an order, the upstream supplier (in this case the *Factory*) will try to meet last period's order of 3. If you order 6 this period and the remaining upstream supply chain members play automatically, the distributor portion of the screen at the end of Week 2 will look like:

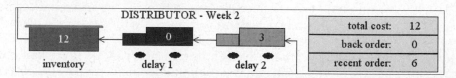

Continue play by selecting **Next round** from the **Play** menu, or pushing the *next round button* at the beginning of each round. At any time, you can view a graph of your performance to date by selecting **Player** from the **Graphs** menu, or pushing the *player graph button*. This graph will display orders, back order, inventory, and total cost over time. A sample graph follows:

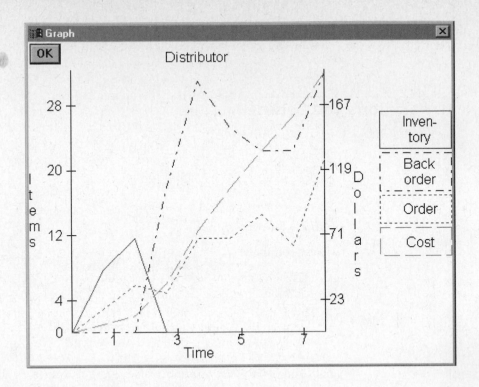

You can also view a list of your orders to date by selecting **Player** from the **Reports** menu.

A.4.4 *Other Features*

In addition to playing the Computerized Beer Game as we have just described it, it is possible to play the game in three other modes: The *Global Information Mode*, in which inventory levels and orders at all facilities and external demand, is available to the interactive player; the *Short Lead Time Mode*, in which lead time through the system is reduced by eliminating *Delay 2* at each of the facilities; and the *Centralized Mode*, in which all information is available to the interactive player, and orders are placed at the *Factory* and sent through the system to the *Retailer* as soon as possible. These options will be described in the next section.

The software also has additional functions. Most of these selections are made from the **Options** menu and control game setup options. For example, they allow the selection of inventory policies used by the computer for the automatic players and selection of the interactive player. In addition, graphs and reports of the performance of each of the supply chain members and of the system as a whole can be viewed. These options will also be described in more detail in the next section.

A.5 Options and Settings

This section follows the menu in the Computerized Beer Game, and describes the function of each of the parameters and options that the user can set. In the following subsections, the convention **menu—menu** item is used to describe menu selections.

A.5.1   File Commands

These commands are used to stop and reset play, and exit the system:

File—Reset. This command resets the game. All data from the previous game are lost.

File—Exit. This command exits the Computerized Beer Game and returns you to the Windows environment.

A.5.2   Options Commands

These commands allow the game options to be set, so that different scenarios can be modeled.

Options—Player. This command displays the following Player Dialog in order to select the *interactive player*. This is the role that the player will take. The computer takes the other three roles.

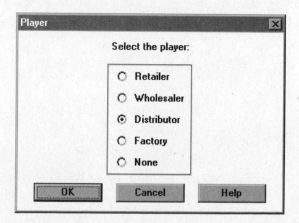

Click on the player button or name to select a player, and then select OK. To cancel the command, select Cancel. Note that if None is selected, the computer will take all of the roles, so that the results can be observed.

Options—Policy. This command displays the following Policy Dialog so that policies for each of the automatic players can be selected.

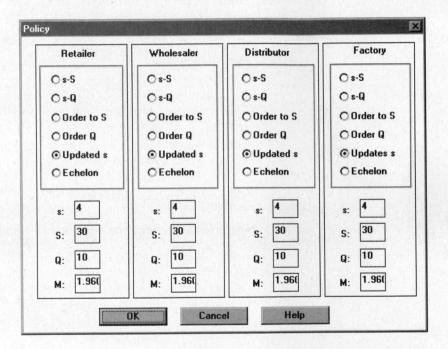

These policies and parameters apply only to computer-controlled players. Different policies can be selected for each of the automatic players. Six policies are available. (Note that by inventory position in the following, we mean the sum of inventory at a location, back order owed to that location, items being transported to that location, and back order owed by that location.):

> **s-S.** When inventory falls below *s*, the system places an order to bring inventory to *S*. In this example, *s* is set to 4, and *S* is set to 30.

s-Q. When inventory falls below *s*, the system places an order for *Q*.

Order to S. Each week, the system places an order to bring inventory to *S*.

Order Q. The system orders *Q* each week.

Updated s. The order-up-to-level *s* is continuously updated to the following value: the moving average of demand received by that player over the past 10 weeks (or fewer if 10 periods have not yet been played) times the lead time for an order placed by that player, plus *M* times an estimate the standard deviation during the lead time (based on the same 10-week period). When the inventory level falls below *s*, the system orders up to *s*. However, the maximum possible order size is *S*. Also, the ordering for the first four weeks is adjusted to account for start-up by not ordering (or including in the moving average) demand during the first week at the wholesaler, the first two weeks at the distributor, and the first three weeks at the factory.

Echelon. This is a modified version of the standard echelon inventory policy. The value of *s* for each of the players is determined as follows. Let $AVG(D)$ be the 10-week moving average of external customer demand, let $STD(D)$ be the standard deviation of that external demand, and let *L* equal 3 in the regular game, and 2 in the short lead time game (described below). Then, at each period at each stage, *s* is determined as follows:

$$\text{retailer:} \quad s = L * AVG(D) + M * STD(D) * (L)^{.5}$$

$$\text{wholesaler:} \quad s = (L - 1 + L) * AVG(D) + M * STD(D) * (L - 1 + L)^{.5}$$

$$\text{distributor:} \quad s = (2 * (L - 1) + L) * AVG(D) + M * STD(D) * (2 * (L - 1) + L)^{.5}$$

$$\text{factory:} \quad s = (3 * (L - 1) + L) * AVG(D) + M * STD(D) * (3 * (L - 1) + L)^{.5}$$

When the inventory position falls below *s*, the system orders up to *s*. However, the maximum possible order size is *S*.

Options—Short Lead Time. This command shortens system lead times by eliminating *Delay 2* from the system. Each lead time is thus shortened by one week, and the system displayed is changed as follows:

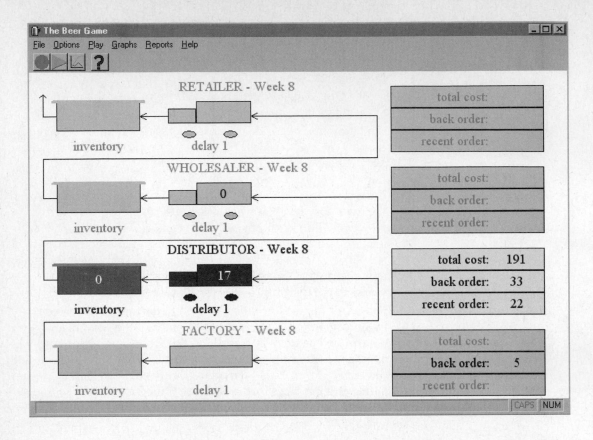

Options—Centralized. This command toggles between standard play and centralized play. In centralized play, the interactive player manages the factory. External demand can be observed and the factory manager can react to it. In addition, when inventory reaches a stage, it is immediately sent forward to the next stage so that inventory is only held by the *Retailer*. This implies that more information is available to the player and that lead time is shortened, since there is no order delay at any stage except the *Factory*.

Options—Demand. This command displays the demand dialog in order to set the external customer demand.

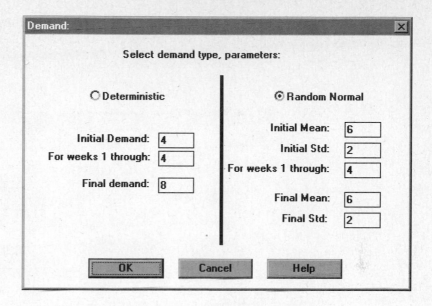

Using this dialog, play can be switched between random normal and deterministic demand. For the deterministic demand, a different constant demand can be selected for a number of initial weeks and the remainder of play. Similarly, for random normal demand, a different mean and standard deviation can be selected for the initial weeks and the remainder of play.

Options—Global Information. This command displays inventory and cost information at all of the stages, not just the interactive stage. External demand is also displayed. This is the default setting for centralized play.

A.5.3   The Play Commands

These commands enable the start and continuation of play.

Play—Start. This command starts play. It can also be called by using the *play toolbar button*.

Play—Next Round. Once play has started, this command continues play. Each week, this command must be selected for play to continue. It can also be called using the *next round toolbar button*.

A.5.4   The Graphs Commands

These commands present status information graphically.

Graphs—Player. This command displays a graph of orders, back order, inventory, and cost for the current interactive player. This command can also be called using the *graphs toolbar button.* An example follows:

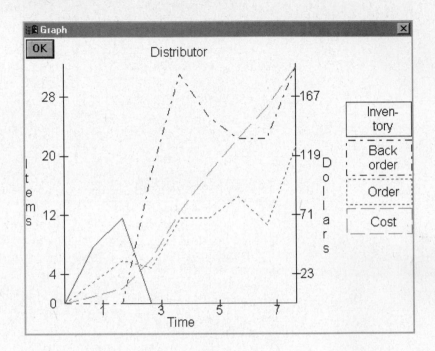

Graphs—Others. When this command is selected, you are first asked to select a player on the following dialog:

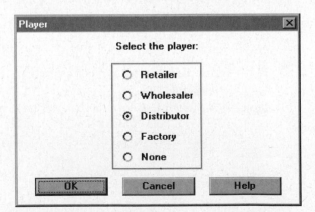

A graph of orders, back order, inventory, and cost for the selected player is then displayed. This differs from the preceding Graphs—Player command which only displays a graph for the current interactive player.

Graphs—System. This command displays a graph of orders for each stage.

A.5.5   *The Reports Commands*

These commands display a series of reports on the status of the system when the command is selected.

Reports—Player. This command displays the Status Report for the current interactive player. A sample report follows:

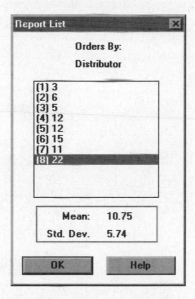

This report lists all orders placed by the player listed at the top of the dialog, as well as the mean and standard deviation of these orders.

Reports—Other. When this command is selected, you are first asked to select a player on the following dialog:

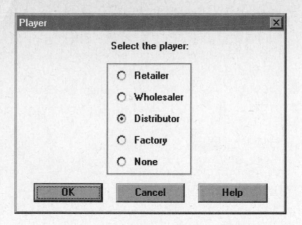

A status report for the selected player is then displayed. This differs from the preceding Reports—Player command which only displays a status report for the current interactive player.

Reports—System. This command displays the System Summary Report:

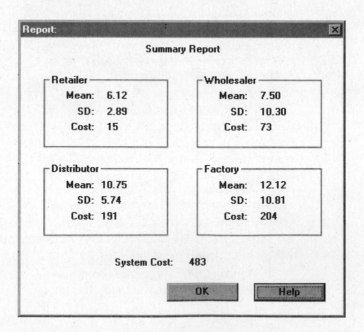

This report summarizes the mean and standard deviation of orders placed by each player up to this point, the total cost experienced by each player, and the total system cost (at the bottom of the dialog).

APPENDIX
B

The Risk Pool Game

B.1 Introduction

One of the most important concepts in supply chain management is "risk pooling." Recall that risk pooling involves the use of centralized inventory to take advantage of the fact that if demand is higher than average at some retailers, it is likely to be lower than average at others. Thus, if each retailer maintains separate inventory and safety stock, a higher level of inventory has to be maintained than if the inventory and safety stock is pooled. Therefore, the system with risk pooling has less overall inventory and is thus cheaper to operate with the same service level.

We developed the Risk Pool Game, included with this text, to illustrate risk pooling concepts. In the game, you simultaneously manage both a system with risk pooling (we also call this a centralized system) and a system without risk pooling (a decentralized system). The system records the profits of both systems, so you can compare performance.

Windows 95, 98, or *NT* is required to operate the game. To install the software, place the included CD in your CD-ROM drive. If the installation program doesn't run automatically, select run from the **Start** menu, and then type g:\setup.exe and follow the directions on the screen. (Replace g:\ with the appropriate driver letter if necessary.)

B.2 The Scenario

The Risk Pool Game models the following scenarios. The top half of the screen, the centralized game, consists of the following supply chain: A supplier serves a warehouse, which in turn serves three retailers. It takes two time periods for material to arrive from the supplier at the warehouse.

This material can be shipped out during the same period or held in inventory. Once shipped, it takes an additional two periods for material to arrive at the retailers. The retailers then fill all the demand that they can. If demand cannot be met at the time it arrives, it is lost.

The bottom half of the screen represents the decentralized system. Three retailers order separately from the supplier, and the supplier ships material directly to each retailer. This takes four periods from the time the order is placed, the same length of time as the minimum total lead time in the centralized system. As in the centralized system, the retailers fill as much demand as possible—demand which if not met is lost. In each system, total holding cost, materials costs, and revenue are tracked. The goal in both systems is to maximize profit.

B.3   Playing Several Rounds

In this section, we describe how to play several rounds of the Risk Pool Game using the default settings. In the next section, we describe each of the menu settings and options so that you can customize the game play.

B.3.1   Introducing the Game

When the Risk Pool Game software is started, the following screen appears:

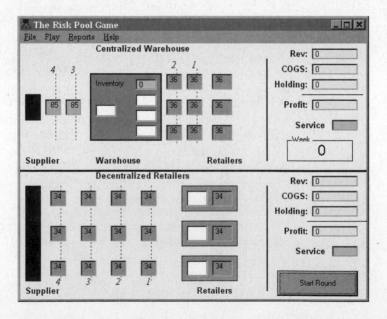

Order of events.   During each period or round of the game, several events occur.

Step 1. *To start this step, press the* **Start Round** *button*. The inventory is advanced. In the centralized game, this means that inventory four periods away moves to three periods away, inventory three periods away is added to the warehouse inventory, inventory two periods away is moved to one period away, and inventory one period away is added to retailer inventory. In the decentralized game, inventory four, three, and two periods away is moved, respectively, three, two, and one period away. Inventory one period away is added to retailer inventory.

Step 2. *This step starts automatically.* Demand is met. Each retailer experiences demand, and fills as much as possible. Note that the top retailer in both the centralized and decentralized systems faces the same demand; the same is true for the middle and bottom retailers. Also, demand is not back ordered. Demand that cannot be met immediately is lost.

Step 3. *Place orders.* In the centralized system, enter an order for the supplier in the box closest to the supplier. Allocate the warehouse inventory to the three retailers in the three boxes closest to the retailers. Note that the allocation amount must be less than or equal to the total warehouse inventory. In the decentralized system, enter an order for each retailer. The system will present a default selection for each entry. You can keep the default or type in new values. As we describe in the next section, you have control over how the system selects default values. When entries are completed (or the decision has been made to keep the default values), *press the* **Place Orders** *button*.

Step 4. *This step starts automatically.* Orders are filled. The amount ordered is moved into the inventory slots four weeks away. In the centralized system, the amount allocated to each retailer is moved into the inventory slots two weeks away.

Step 5. *This step starts automatically.* Cost, revenue, and service level. A holding cost is charged for each unit in inventory, revenue is realized for each unit sold, and the cost of each item sold is subtracted from revenue. Service level is calculated as the fraction of demand met over total demand. For that reason, we refer to service level in the game as the *fill rate*.

Lead times.   Note that in both systems, it takes a minimum of four periods for material that has been ordered to reach the retailer. In the centralized system, it can take longer if inventory is held in the warehouse.

B.3.2   *Understanding the Screen*

At the start of each round, the screen looks like this:

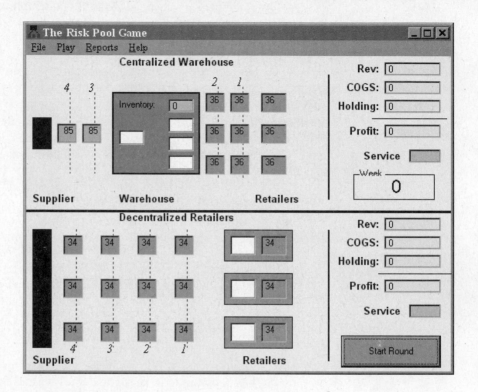

On the top half of the screen, the supplier is represented by the box at the left. The two vertical dotted lines labeled 4 and 3 have boxes on them representing inventory at least four or three periods away from the retailers, respectively. The large middle box represents the warehouse. The top line in the warehouse indicates the inventory contained there; the other boxes are used to enter an order from the supplier and allocation to the warehouse when appropriate. Note that the button in the lower right-hand corner of the screen initially says *Start Round*. This indicates that it is not the appropriate time to enter the orders and allocation. The two vertical dotted lines to the right of the warehouse are labeled 2 and 1, indicating inventory two and one period from the retailers, respectively. Note that unlike the 3 and 4 lines to the left of the warehouse, lines 1 and 2 can have up to three inventory boxes, representing inventory going to each of the three retailers. To the right of these lines are the three boxes representing the retailers—the numbers in these boxes represent retailer inventory. The right-hand side of the screen contains cost and profit data.

Holding costs and cost of goods sold (COGS) are subtracted from revenue to get profit. Service level and period number are also indicated.

The bottom half of the screen is similar to the top half, except that there is no warehouse. Also, when appropriate, orders are entered directly at the retailers.

The button in the lower right-hand corner initially reads *Start Round*. After the round has started, it looks like this:

Place Orders

B.3.3   Playing the Game

The game follows the order of events listed above. To start each round, press the *Start Round* button. Inventory is advanced, and then as much demand as possible is met. At this point, the button in the lower right-hand corner of the screen will change to read *Place Orders*. Do so either by accepting the default choices that are displayed or by typing in new ones. Recall that in the centralized game, you can allocate up to the total amount of inventory in the warehouse to the retailers. Once orders are placed, press the *Place Orders* button. Orders are filled, and cost, revenue, and service level are calculated. You can continue playing for any number of rounds.

B.3.4   Other Features

The game has several other features, which we discuss in detail in the next section. The **Play** menu has options that allow you to set various game parameters. The **Reports** menu allows you to display lists of demands and orders for all of the periods up to the current one.

B.4   Options and Settings

This section follows the menu in the Risk Pool Game, and describes the function of each of the parameters and options that can be set by the user or instructor. In the following subsections, the convention **menu—menu** item is used to describe menu selections.

B.4.1   File Commands

These commands are used to stop and reset play, and exit the system.

File—Reset. This command resets the game. All data from the previous game is lost.

File—Exit. This command exits the game.

B.4.2   *Play Commands*

These commands control game play and allow various parameters to be set.

Play—Start Round. This command duplicates the *Start Round* button on the lower right-hand corner of the screen. Selecting it starts each round.

Play—Place Orders. This command duplicates the **Place Orders** button on the lower right-hand corner of the screen. Select it after entering orders and allocations.

Play—Options. This command displays a submenu with the following choices:

Initial Conditions. This command displays the following dialog box:

This enables you to select starting inventories throughout both systems. Note that in the centralized system, each retailer must have the same initial inventory level, and the inventory in transit from the warehouse to the retailer must be the same level for each of the retailers, and for both periods. Similar restrictions exist for the decentralized system. After making changes, enter **OK** to accept the changes or **Cancel** to keep the current levels. Note that this option can only be used before the first round is played.

Demand. This command displays the following dialog box:

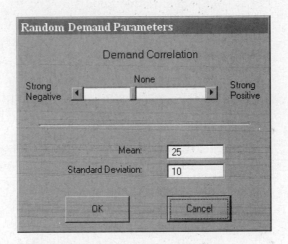

This enables you to control the demand faced by each of the retailers. The demand is normally distributed, with the mean and standard deviation that can be entered on the dialog box. The slider control at the top of the box enables you to control the correlation of the demand at the retailers. If the slider is in the center of its range, demand will be independent. At the right, demand is strongly positively correlated while at the left, demand is strongly negatively correlated. Intermediate positions allow correlation between these extremes.[1] After making changes, select **OK** to accept the changes or **Cancel** to keep the current levels. Note that this option can only be used before the first round is played.

Inventory Policy. This command displays the following dialog box:

---

[1]If demand is positively correlated, it is likely that if one retailer has high demand, all of them will; if one retailer has low demand, all of them will. If demand is negatively correlated, it is likely that if one retailer has high demand, at least one other will have low demand.

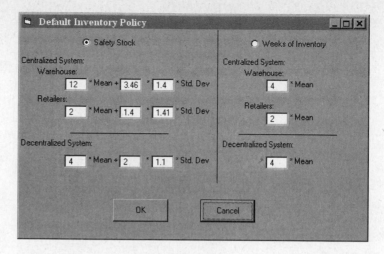

This enables you to control the inventory policy which displays the default order and allocation quantities. Note that you can always override the default suggestions when you are playing, but having good defaults speeds up game play. There are two types of default policies, the *Safety Stock* policy and the *Weeks of Inventory* policy. Select between them using the radio buttons at the top of the dialog box. The Safety Stock policy allows you to select order-up-to-levels for the warehouse and retailers in the centralized system and the retailers in the decentralized system as a function of demand mean and standard deviation. There are three input boxes for each level: the first box is the mean multiplier, and the second and third are multiplied by the standard deviation. These quantities are then summed to get the final order-up-to-level.

When the Weeks of Inventory policy is used, a single value multiplied by the mean demand is used to determine order-up-to-level.

To determine default orders, the system does the following: For the centralized system, warehouse echelon inventory (i.e., inventory in transit to the warehouse, inventory at the warehouse, inventory in transit to the retailers, and inventory at the retailers) is subtracted from the order-up-to-levels to determine order quantity. Inventory at the retailers and in transit from the warehouse to the retailers is subtracted from retailer order-up-to-level to determine allocations. If insufficient inventory is available at the warehouse, the available inventory is allocated so that the same fraction of desired level is sent to each retailer. For the decentralized system, inventory at each retailer plus inventory in transit to the retailer is raised to the order up-to-level.

After making changes, select **OK** to accept the changes or **Cancel** to keep the current levels. Note that this option can be used at the start of any round.

Costs. This command displays the following dialog:

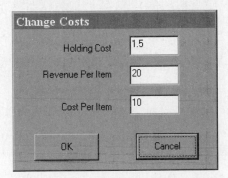

You can adjust costs using this dialog. Holding cost is per item per period; cost and revenue are per item. After making changes, select **OK** to accept the changes or **Cancel** to keep the current levels. Note that this option can only be used before the first round is played.

B.4.3   The Reports Commands

These commands display game-related information.

Reports—Orders. This command displays the following report, which lists orders placed by the warehouse in the centralized game and retailers in the decentralized game:

Order Report

Week	Decentralized Retailer 1	Decentralized Retailer 2	Decentralized Retailer 3	Centralized Warehouse
1	0	0	0	0
2	11	10	9	28
3	23	29	2	54
4	6	25	43	74
5	37	25	36	88
6	27	8	15	50
7	26	24	23	73

Select **Done** to hide the report.

Reports—Demands. This command displays the following report, which lists demand faced by the retailers since the start of the game:

Demand History			
Week	Retailer 1	Retailer 2	Retailer
1	31	30	29
2	28	28	28
3	23	29	2
4	6	25	43
5	37	25	36
6	27	8	15
7	26	24	23
8	24	27	17

Done

Select **Done** to hide the report.

Bibliography

[1] Andel, T. "There's Power In Numbers." *Transportation & Distribution* 36 (1995), pp. 67–72.

[2] Andel, T. "Manage Inventory, Own Information." *Transportation & Distribution* 37 (1996), p. 54.

[3] Andreoli, T. "VMI Confab Examines Value-Added Services." *Discount Store News* 34 (1995), pp. 4–61.

[4] Anonymous. "Divorce: Third-Party Style." *Distribution* 94 (1995), pp. 46–51.

[5] Anonymous. "Choosing Service Providers." *Transportation & Distribution* 36 (1995), pp. 74–76.

[6] Artman, L. B. "The Paradigm Shift from 'Push' to 'Pull' Logistics—What's the Impact on Manufacturing?" Northwestern University, Manufacturing Management Symposium, Evanston, IL, May 1995.

[7] Ballou, R. H. *Business Logistics Management*. 3rd ed. Englewood Cliffs, NJ: Prentice Hall, 1992.

[8] Bausch, D. O.; G. G. Brown; and D. Ronen. "Consolidating and Dispatching Truck Shipments of Mobil Heavy Petroleum Products." *Interfaces* 25 (1995), pp. 1–17.

[9] Signorelli, S., and J. Heskett. "Benetton (A)." Harvard University Business School Case (1984).

[10] Blumenfeld, D. E.; L. D. Burns; C. F. Daganzo; M. C. Frick; and R. W. Hall. "Reducing Logistics Costs at General Motors." *Interfaces* 17 (1987), pp. 26–47.

[11] Bovet, D., and Y. Sheffi. "The Brave New World of Supply Chain Management." *Supply Chain Management Review*, Spring 1998, pp. 14–22.

[12] Bowers, M. R., and A. Agarwal. "Lower In-Process Inventories and Better On-Time Performance at Tanner Companies, Inc." *Interfaces* 25 (1995), pp. 30-43.

[13] Bowman, R. "A High Wire Act." *Distribution* 94 (1995), pp. 36–39.

[14] Bramel, J., and D. Simchi-Levi. *The Logic of Logistics: Theory, Algorithms and Applications for Logistics Management*. New York: Springer, 1997.

[15] Buzzell, R. D., and G. Ortmeyer. "Channel Partnerships Streamline Distribution." *Sloan Management Review* 36 (1995), p. 85.

[16] Byrne, P., and W. Markham. "Global Logistics: Only 10 Percent of Companies Satisfy Customers." *Transportation and Distribution* 34 (1993), pp. 41–45.

[17] Caldwell B. "Wal-Mart Ups the Pace." *http://*www.informationweek.com, December 9, 1996.

[18] Caldwell, B.; T. Stein; and M. K. McGee. "Uncertainty: A Thing of the Past?" *http://*www.informationweek.com, December 9, 1996.

[19] Cambell, K. W.; R. B. Durfee; and G. S. Hines. "FedEx Generates Bid Lines Using Simulated Annealing." *Interfaces* 27 (1997), pp. 1–16.

[20] Camm, J. D.; T. E. Chorman; F. A. Dill; J. R. Evans; D. J. Sweeney; and G. W. Wegryn. "Blending OR/MS, Judgement, and GIS: Restructuring P&G's Supply Chain." *Interfaces* 27 (1997), pp. 128–42.

[21] Chesbrough, H., and D. Teece. "When Is Virtual Virtuous: Organizing for Innovation." *Harvard Business Review* 74, no. 1 (1996), pp. 65–74.

[22] Chen, F. Y.; J. K. Ryan; and D. Simchi-Levi. "The Impact of Exponential Smoothing Forecasts on the Bullwhip Effect." Working paper, Northwestern University, 1997.

[23] Chen, F. Y.; Z. Drezner; J. K. Ryan; and D. Simchi-Levi. "The Bullwhip Effect: Managerial Insights on the Impact of Forecasting and Information on Variability in the Supply Chain." In *Quantitative Models for Supply Chain Management.* S. Tayur; R. Ganeshan; and M. Magazine, eds. Norwell, MA: Kluwer Academic Publishing, 1998, Chap. 14.

[24] Clemmet, A. "Demanding Supply." *Work Study* 44 (1995), pp. 23–24.

[25] Davis, D., and T. Foster. "Bulk Squeezes Shipping Bosts." *Distribution Worldwide* 78, no. 8 (1979), pp. 25–30.

[26] Davis, D. "State of a New Art." *Manufacturing Systems* 13 (1995), pp. 2–10.

[27] ———. "Third Parties Deliver." *Manufacturing Systems* 13 (1995), pp. 66–68.

[28] Deutsch, C. H. "New Software Manages Supply to Match Demand." *New York Times*, December 16, 1996.

[29] Dornier, P.; R. Ernst; M. Fender; and P. Kouvelis. *Global Operations and Logistics: Text and Cases.* New York: John Wiley, 1998.

[30] Drezner, Z.; J. K. Ryan; and D. Simchi-Levi. "Quantifying the Bullwhip Effect: The Impact of Forecasting, Leadtime and Information." Working paper, Northwestern University, 1996, To appear in *Management Science.*

[31] Eid, M. K.; D. J. Seith; and M. A. Tomazic. "Developing a Truly Effective Way to Manage Inventory," Council of Logistics Management conference, October 5–8, 1997.

[32] Feitzinger, E., and H. Lee. "Mass Customization at Hewlett-Packard: The Power of Postponement." *Harvard Business Review* 75, no. 1 (1977), pp. 116–21.

[33] Fernie, J. "International Comparisons of Supply Chain Management in Grocery Retailing." *Service Industries Journal* 15 (1995), pp. 134–47.

[34] Fisher, M. L. "National Bicycle Industrial Co.: A Case Study." The Wharton School, University of Pennsylvania, 1993.

[35] Fisher, M. L.; J. Hammond; W. Obermeyer; and A. Raman. "Making Supply Meet Demand in an Uncertain World." *Harvard Business Review,* May–June 1994, pp. 83–93.

[36] Fisher, M. L. "What Is the Right Supply Chain for Your Product?" *Harvard Business Review,* March–April 1997, pp. 105–17.

[37] Fites, D. "Make Your Dealers Your Partners." *Harvard Business Review,* March–April 1996, pp. 84–95.

[38] Flickinger, B. H., and T. E. Baker. "Supply Chain Management in the 1990's." *http://www.chesapeake.com/supchain.html.*

[39] Fox, M. S.; J. F. Chionglo; and M. Barbuceanu. "The Integrated Supply Chain Management System." Working paper, University of Toronto, 1993.

[40] Gamble, R. "Financially Efficient Partnerships." *Corporate Cashflow* 15 (1994), pp. 29–34.

[41] Geoffrion, A., and T. J. Van Roy. "Caution: Common Sense Planning Methods Can Be Hazardous to Your Corporate Health." *Sloan Management Review* 20 (1979), pp. 30–42.

[42] Guengerich, S., and V. G. Green. *Introduction to Client/Server Computing.* SME Blue Book Series, 1996.

[43] Handfield, R., and B. Withers. "A Comparison of Logistics Management in Hungary, China, Korea, and Japan." *Journal of Business Logistics* 14 (1993), pp. 81–109.

[44] Henkoff, R. "Delivering the Goods." *Fortune,* November 28, 1994, pp. 64–78.

[45] Harrington, L. "Logistics Assets: Should You Own or Manage?" *Transportation & Distribution* 37 (1996), pp. 51–54.

[46] Hax, A. C., and D. Candea. *Production and Inventory Management.* Englewood Cliffs, NJ: Prentice Hall, 1984.

[47] Hopp, W., and M. Spearman. *Factory Physics.* Burr Ridge, IL: Richard D. Irwin, 1996.

[48] Hornback, R. "An EDI Costs/Benefits Framework." *EDI World Institute,* January 27, 1997.

[49] House, R. G., and K. D. Jamie. "Measuring the Impact of Alternative Market Classification Systems in Distribution Planning." *Journal of Business Logistics* 2 (1981), pp. 1–31.

[50] Huang, Y.; A. Federgruen; O. Bakkalbasi; R. Desiraju; and R. Kranski. "Vendor-Managed-Replenishment in an Agile Manufacturing Environment." Working paper, Philips Research.

[51] Huntley, C. L.; D. E. Brown; D. E. Sappington; and B. P. Markowicz. "Freight Routing and Scheduling at CSX Transportation." *Interfaces* 25 (1995), pp. 58–71.

[52] Jacobs, D. A.; M. N. Silan; and B. A. Clemson. "An Analysis of Alternative Locations and Service Areas of American Red Cross Blood Facilities." *Interfaces* 26 (1996), pp. 40–50.

[53] Johnson, J. C., and D. F. Wood. *Contemporary Physical Distribution and Logistics.* 3rd ed. New York: Macmillan, 1986.

[54] Jones, H. "Ikea's Global Strategy Is a Winning Formula." *Marketing Week* 18, no. 50 (1996), p. 22.

[55] King, J. "The Service Advantage." *Computerworld,* October 28, 1998.

[56] Kogut, B. "Designing Global Strategies: Profiting from Operational Flexibility." *Sloan Management Review* 27 (1985), pp. 27–38.

[57] Koloszyc, G. "Retailers, Suppliers Push Joint Sales Forecasting." *Stores*, June 1998.

[58] Lawrence, J. A., and B. A. Pasternack. *Applied Management Science: A Computer Integrated Approach for Decision Making.* New York: John Wiley, 1998.

[59] Leahy, S.; P. Murphy; and R. Poist. "Determinants of Successful Logistical Relationships: A Third Party Provider Perspective." *Transportation Journal* 35 (1995), pp. 5–13.

[60] Lee, H. L., and C. Billington. "Managing Supply Chain Inventory: Pitfalls and Opportunities." *Sloan Management Review*, Spring 1992, pp. 65–73.

[61] Lee, H.; P. Padmanabhan; and S. Whang. "The Paralyzing Curse of the Bullwhip Effect in a Supply Chain." *Sloan Management Review*, Spring 1997, pp. 93–102.

[62] ———. "Information Distortion in a Supply Chain: The Bullwhip Effect." *Management Science* 43 (1996), pp. 546–58.

[63] Lee H. "Design for Supply Chain Management: Concepts and Examples." Working paper. Department of Industrial Engineering and Engineering Management, Stanford University, 1992.

[64] Lessard, D., and J. Lightstone. "Volatile Exchange Rates Put Operations at Risk." *Harvard Business Review* 64 (1986), pp. 107–14.

[65] Levitt, T. "The Globalization of Markets." *Harvard Business Review* 61 (1983), pp. 92–102.

[66] Lewis, J. *Partnerships for Profit.* New York: Free Press, 1990.

[67] Lindsey. *A Communication to the AGIS-L List Server.*

[68] *Logistics Technology News*, May 23, 1997.

[69] Magretta, J. "The Power of Virtual Integration: An Interview with Dell Computer's Michael Dell." *Harvard Business Review*, March–April 1998, pp. 72–84.

[70] Maltz, A. "Why You Outsource Dictates How." *Transportation & Distribution* 36 (1995), pp. 73–80.

[71] "Management Brief: Furnishing the World." *The Economist*, November 19, 1994, pp. 79–80.

[72] Manrodt, K. B.; M. C. Holcomb; and R. H. Thompson. "What's Missing in Supply Chain Management? *Supply Chain Management Review*, Fall 1997, pp. 80–86.

[73] Manugistics Supply Chain Compass, 1997.

[74] Markides, C., and N. Berg. "Manufacturing Offshore Is Bad Business." *Harvard Business Review* 66 (1988), pp. 113–20.

[75] Martin, J. *Cybercorp: The New Business Revolution.* New York: American Management Association, 1996.

[76] Mathews, R. "Spartan Pulls the Plug on VMI." *Progressive Grocer* 74 (1995), pp. 64–65.

[77] McGrath, M., and R. Hoole. "Manufacturing's New Economies of Scale." *Harvard Business Review* 70 (1992), pp. 94–102.

[78] McKay, J. "The SCOR Model." Presented in *Designing and Managing the Supply Chain*, an Executive Program at Northwestern University, James L. Allen Center, 1998.

[79] McWilliams, G. "Whirlwind on the Web." *Business Week*, April 7, 1997, pp. 132–36.

[80] Microsoft. "VCI." Presented at the 1997 Council of Logistics Management Conference, October 1997.

[81] Mische, M. "EDI in the EC: Easier Said Than Done." *Journal of European Business* 4 (1992), pp. 19–22.

[82] Monczka, R.; G. Ragatz; R. Handfield; R. Trent; and D. Frayer. "Executive Summary: Supplier Integration into New Product Development: A Strategy for Competitive Advantage." *The Global Procurement and Supply Chain Benchmarking Initiative*, Michigan State University, The Eli Broad Graduate School of Management, 1997.

[83] Mottley, R. "Dead in Nine Months." *American Shipper*, December 1998, pp. 30–33.

[84] Narus, J., and J. Anderson. "Turn Your Industrial Distributors into Partners." *Harvard Business Review*, March–April 1986, pp. 66–71.

[85] ———. "Rethinking Distribution: Adaptive Channels." *Harvard Business Review*, July–August 1986, pp. 112–20.

[86] Nussbaum, B. "Designs for Living." *Business Week*, June 2, 1997, p. 99.

[87] Ohmae, K. "Managing in a Borderless World." *Harvard Business Review* 67 (1989), pp. 152–61.

[88] Patton, E. P. "Carrier Rates and Tariffs." In *The Distribution Management Handbook*. J. A. Tompkins and D. Harmelink, eds. New York: McGraw-Hill, 1994, chap. 12.

[89] Peppers, D., and M. Rogers. *Enterprise One to One*. New York: Doubleday, 1997.

[90] Pike, H. "IKEA Still Committed to U.S., Despite Uncertain Economy." *Discount Store News* 33, no. 8 (1994), pp. 17–19.

[91] Pine, J. B. II, and J. Gilmore. "Welcome to the Experience Economy." *Harvard Business Review*, July–August 1998, pp. 97–108.

[92] Pine, J. B. II; D. Peppers; and M. Rogers. "Do You Want to Keep Your Customers Forever?" *Harvard Business Review*, March–April 1995, pp. 103–15.

[93] Pine, J. B. II. *Mass Customization*. Boston: Harvard University Business School Press, 1993.

[94] Pine, J. B. II, and A. Boynton. "Making Mass Customization Work." *Harvard Business Review* 71, no. 5 (1993), pp. 108–19.

[95] Pollack, E. "Partnership: Buzzword or Best Practice?" *Chain Store Age Executive* 71 (1995), pp. 11A–12A.

[96] Rayport, J. F., and J. J. Sviokla. "Exploiting the Virtual Value Chain." *Harvard Business Review*, November–December 1995, pp. 75–85.

[97] Reichheld, F. F. "Learning from Customer Defections." *Harvard Business Review*, March–April 1996, pp. 57–69.

[98] Ries, A., and L. Ries. *The 22 Immutable Laws of Branding*. New York: HarperBusiness, 1998.

[99] Rifkin, G. "Technology Brings the Music Giant a Whole New Spin." *Forbes ASAP*, February 27, 1995, p. 32.

[100] Robeson, J. F., and W. C. Copacino, eds. *The Logistics Handbook.* New York: Free Press, 1994.

[101] Robins, G. "Pushing the Limits of VMI." *Stores* 77 (1995), pp. 42–44.

[102] Ross, D. F. *Competing through Supply Chain Management.* New York: Chapman & Hall, 1998.

[103] Schoneberger, R. J. "Strategic Collaboration: Breaching the Castle Walls." *Business Horizons* 39 (1996), p. 20.

[104] Schwind, G. "A Systems Approach to Docks and Cross-Docking." *Material Handling Engineering* 51, no. 2 (1996), pp. 59–62.

[105] Shenk, D. *Data Smog: Surviving the Information Glut.* New York: HarperCollins, 1997.

[106] Stalk, G.; P. Evans; and L. E. Shulman. "Competing on Capabilities: The New Rule of Corporate Strategy." *Harvard Business Review*, March–April 1992, pp. 57–69.

[107] The Supply Chain Council. "SCOR Introduction," release 2.0, August 1, 1997.

[108] Troyer, T., and D. Denny. "Quick Response Evolution." *Discount Merchandiser* 32 (1992), pp. 104–7.

[109] Troyer, C., and R. Cooper. "Smart Moves in Supply Chain Integration." *Transportation & Distribution* 36 (1995), pp. 55–62.

[110] Trunnick, P.; H. Richardson; and L. Harrington. "CLM: Breakthroughs of Champions." *Transportation & Distribution* 35 (1994), pp. 41–50.

[111] Verity, J. "Clearing the Cobwebs from the Stockroom." *Business Week*, October 21, 1996.

[112] Wood, D.; A. Barone; P. Murphy; and D. Wardlow. *International Logistics.* New York: Chapman & Hall, 1995.

[113] Zweben, M. "Delivering on Every Promise." *APICS*, March 1996, p. 50.

[114] *Journal of Business Strategy*, October–November 1997.

[115] *The Wall Street Journal*, October 23, 1997.

[116] *U.S. Surgical Quarterly Report*, July 15, 1993.

[117] *The Wall Street Journal*, October 7, 1994.

[118] *The Wall Street Journal*, August, 1993.
      *(Dell Computer ref.)

[119] *The Wall Street Journal*, July 15, 1993.
      *(Liz Claiborne ref.)

[120] *The Wall Street Journal*, October 7, 1994.
      *(IBM ThinkPad ref.)

*Brief topical reference

Index